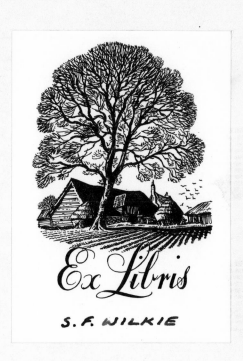

Also by 'Adam Smith'

The Money Game

SUPERMONEY

$UPER

MONEY

'ADAM
SMITH'

MICHAEL JOSEPH
LONDON

First published in Great Britain by
Michael Joseph Ltd
52 Bedford Square
London, W.C.1
1973

Acknowledgment is made to McGraw-Hill Book
Company for permission to quote from
Security Analysis by Benjamin Graham,
© 1962 by McGraw-Hill Inc.

7181 1128 1

Printed in Great Britain by
Hollen Street Press Limited at Slough
on paper supplied by
P. F. Bingham Limited and bound by
James Burn at Esher, Surrey

For Mark O. Park
and
Susannah B. Fish

CONTENTS

[ix]

Contents

I:

Supermoney

1: METAPHYSICAL DOUBTS, VERY SHORT

NOT even a decade ago, everybody believed.

Events did seem under control. Inflation would creep, not gallop; the New Economics would fine-tune the economy; productivity would increase; wars would be fought, but not by us—we were the mediators, understanding but tough; problems would be articulated, and that articulation was half the solution; we would begin upon the solutions. Kennedy rhetoric: let us begin; let the word go forth; let us never negotiate from fear, nor fear to negotiate; let anybody call upon us. Confident, ambitious, optimistic, even naïve— the very best of the American tradition. Hail Columbia, happy land.

Then, one thing and another, the John Philip Sousa music faded a bit. Could rational men make events behave rationally? Maybe they couldn't. (Nobody then asked for a definition of "rational.") Maybe the falcons could not hear the falconers. They were still wheeling around up there; would they listen?

2: LIQUIDITY: MR. ODD-LOT ROBERT IS ASKED HOW HE FEELS

WE have a capital market that is a great national asset, like the wheat fields of Kansas and the Grand Canyon. Some of the Yankee monopoly in technology and management techniques has been broken, gone to Wolfsburg and Milan and Toyota City. But Tokyo and Amsterdam and Frankfurt and Buenos Aires do not have that great, deep capital market, ready to handle the world's investable funds, so everybody still has to come to New York, and when they come, they bring money not only for what they buy but also for commissions, tips and shoeshines. Everybody came because the great capital market was so liquid and honest and continuous; today's price related to yesterday's price, and you could buy and sell in almost any size.

But there were some nagging doubts. We had a market slide, the biggest since 1929, and some crises. Market slides frighten the Public, and 1969–1970 was no exception. What would the Public do?

I think it was Gertrude Stein's cousin, according to Miss Stein, who said that money is always there, but the pockets change; it is not in the same pockets after a change, and that is all there is to say about money. Well, maybe.

From all accounts, we are now in a marvelous economy, moving forward to Normal—Normal being July 4, 1955, during the Eisenhower Regency: peace, prosperity and harmony. Did the Public get a little frightened there for a year or two? They are coming back; the brokers all sit like hunters in a blind, with the first honks already coming over the horizon. Did the Big Bear leave some scars? Welcome to the club: Justice Holmes said that a man has to be part of the actions and passions of the times.

Only two years ago, you could fire off a cannon in a downtown restaurant like Oscar's and not hit anybody, because the price of Beef Wellington had been moving up with the prime rate, and many citizens in the financial community had switched to tuna on white toast. Now the corks are popping again; wonderful, the cyclicality of life.

What happened to the money community has some relevance to the larger drifts of our society, for that community is in charge of much of the liquid wealth of the country. The money community's health affects our savings and investments, the assets of university endowments and foundations, the cost of government, and whether the pension money will be there when the employees are ready to retire.

In turn, some of the changing attitudes about work and play and people and the uses of the present are going to affect the money community and what it shepherds.

A while back, there were some metaphysical doubts and some specific doubts. The metaphysical doubts were perhaps common to the country as a whole, and concerned the assumption that rational men could make events behave rationally. Maybe the falcons could not hear the falconers.

The jury has to be counted as still out on whether the falcons are within earshot. On the bread-and-butter level, the specific doubts concerned liquidity, which can mean a number of things but in this context meant the ability of buyers to buy and sellers to sell. We have that capital market that brings in the people from everywhere.

Liquidity seemed to be disappearing. The Public was beginning to cash in its mutual funds, and the minus signs were getting fatter on line 30 of the Federal Reserve's computer print-out labeled *Flow of Funds, The Sector Statements of Saving and Investment: Households, Personal Trusts, and Nonprofit Organizations*. William McChesney Martin, Jr., was upset. Mr. Martin—a former president of the New York Stock Exchange and a former chairman of the Board of Governors of the Federal Reserve —is to the money business what de Gaulle was to France, which is to say he was there when times were bad and he was the only man everybody could agree on when they got bad again. "I'm very concerned about the liquidity of the stock market," Mr. Martin said, "and I've talked to corporation heads who are worried to death about it." (When asked why individuals were leaving, Mr. Martin said he thought the lack of integrity in the marketplace was a reason, and when asked where the individuals were putting their money, Mr. Martin said some of those he talked to were putting the money into lotteries. But there is no line on the Fed's *Flow of Funds* for lotteries.) Institutions— mutual funds, insurance companies, pension funds and so on—were coming to dominate the marketplace, and that was thought to be troubling for liquidity. Edgar Bunce runs the $3.5 billion of Prudential's stock portfolio, and *The Wall Street Journal* quoted him thus: "If everybody buys at the same time, who will we sell to?"

There were those who were prepared to write off the thirty-one million shareholders as far as liquidity was concerned. Liquidity means not only the smoothness of the market but the depth of the market. This point of view maintained that you heard only of panic-stricken institutions suddenly dumping thousands of shares, creating 10- and 20-point air pockets in stocks. You never heard of the quiet, orderly, day-by-day functions that went on without comment. Anyway, it was said, the public dealt mostly through half a dozen brokerage firms, and a buy or sell recommendation from one of those could move a whole battalion of individuals, with the same net effect as an institution.

In order to get a better perspective on what had gone on, I had lunch with my friend Odd-Lot Robert. A little micro look at the macro scene, as the learned economists would say. An odd-lotter, you will recall, is one who buys or sells less than a hundred shares. There are theories around that the way to make money is to do the opposite of what the odd-lotters do, and there are services that keep track of this. I asked Robert how he had done in the past couple of years.

"Not very well," he said. "But better than my friends. Of course, you have to remember that we are not exactly little old ladies. We do not just buy Telephone and sit with it. A good thing, too, because Telephone has gone from seventy to forty, and over the last six years you could have lost damn near half your money in good old Ma Bell and not even have had any fun. But my friends and I— frankly, we're prepared to speculate."

I asked Robert how his friends had done.

"Terrible," he said. "At least the market hasn't changed my life. But take my dentist's wife. During the early sixties, she got very interested in the market, she studied very hard, she worked the thing like mad, and I must say, she hit it like a fixed slot machine. I mean, she must have made a couple hundred grand. I think she even got out pretty well in 68, but she couldn't stay away."

"She gave it back?"

"She gave most of it back, she went into a deep depression, and now she's in group therapy. The other members of the group say she thinks she was the stocks, and when they melted away, so did she, like the Wicked Witch of the West in the *Wizard of Oz*. Or was it the North? The one who just faded out from under her hat. Then I have another friend who also made a lot of money. He was in his early fifties and he was going to retire. He hated his job, and he was going to leave it, finally, and then he lost a hell of a lot of money and he's still at the job and he's out of the market."

"But it didn't change your life?"

"No, I never made that much in the first place. I don't mind telling you, I've taken some very healthy losses. My Brian Lloyd went from six to one."

"You're still active, though?"

"I'm not as active as I used to be. There was one period when I almost didn't do anything at all. This friend of my sister's had an account with a firm, and the firm got in a lot of trouble, and she couldn't get her stocks back, and there was stuff in the paper every day about brokers going busted, so I got scared. Firms closing every day, so I asked for the papers."

"What papers?"

"You know, the papers, the ones the stocks are printed on."

"The stock certificates."

"Right. Of course, I didn't want to tell my broker why I was asking—that I was afraid he might go *broke*. Or that maybe he didn't have the stocks at all. Or that he was really screwed up somewhere. So I said I was making a will.

I said my lawyer wanted me to have my stocks so I could make a will. My broker bought the story completely. It took a while, but he sent me the stocks."

"And then?"

"Well, first I put them in the drawer of this table in the living room where we keep the bills we haven't paid yet. Then somebody spilled coffee on the table and some of it dribbled into the drawer, I'm not quite sure how. None of the coffee actually got onto the stocks, it just got onto the bills, but I had to move them. I mean, a stock with coffee on it is still probably legal, but what if I wanted to sell it— and you know, some stores won't take a torn five-dollar bill —and what if I sold a stock and the buyer said, 'Hey, wait a minute, this one has *coffee* on it.' So I moved the stocks to my dresser drawer."

"In your bedroom."

"Yeah, under my socks. But every time I got a pair of socks out, I would see some of those turkeys, it would make my stomach turn sour. Also, if I sold one, I had to take it out of the dresser drawer and mail it back, and that was a drag, and then if I bought something they had to mail me the new one, and it was always late and I was wondering if they'd screwed up somewhere. Finally I got tired of all the mailing, and I didn't hear so much about the problems any more, so I mailed the stocks back to the broker. I told him the will was all made and the lawyer was through, and he bought that story completely."

"You didn't sell when the market went down?"

"No, my stuff went down too fast, and then I didn't want to take the loss. Actually, when the market was going down, I wanted to sell short. I wanted to be going in the same direction as the market, for once. But my broker wouldn't let me. And then, when things were *really* going down, I had a funny feeling. I wanted everything to collapse. I mean really collapse."

"So you could buy at the bottom, like 1932?"

"Well, yes, if I had any money, but that wasn't my main thought. When things were *really* going down, I figured if the market really collapsed, that would be the end of our government, and we'd have socialism or something. I thought, What the hell, let's have socialism."

"You still feel that way?"

"No, I hollered at my broker a lot and got it out of my system. The most depressing thing of all is when they don't list your stocks in the paper any more. I really like looking up my stocks in the paper, and when they're not there, it really hurts. I look at the odd-lot figures, too. The odd-lotters were selling, all the way down. That's one of the reasons I didn't sell. I didn't want to be an odd-lotter."

I wanted to pursue the question of liquidity, so I told Robert there was controversy over the specialists on the floor, and over contentions that the liquidity, the orderly market, was disappearing. The structure of the market was changing, and maybe stocks were more volatile. Robert could buy a stock at 20, and find it at 16 twenty minutes later because an institutional seller has appeared. He wasn't greatly disturbed.

"Twenty to sixteen, a few points more or less, what the hell, it might work the other way too. Maybe I'd buy it at twenty and that big mother would move it to twenty-four. You can't quibble over a few points. I want a stock to have a move I can really see."

Then I said there was controversy about accounting procedures and about what earnings really are. Some maintain that the small investor couldn't hope to sort those things out. Could he?

"I pay attention to the earnings, but I pay more attention to the mathematics of the whole thing."

"The mathematics?"

"Yeah, like when my broker says, 'I think this one has

ten points in it,' then I watch to see if it makes the ten points. Hell, all I want is a break. If I have a stock that's thirty, and it goes to forty, and then it goes to nine, I had my chance, I could have sold it at forty. It's my own fault. But I do need a break like that, say, ten points."

"You had a stock like that?"

"My Hy-Grade Foods went from thirty to eighty and then to nine. But we hung on, and it finally made it back to thirty, and I got out with a two-hundred-dollar profit."

Still another controversy, I said, continuing to probe, was the institutional investor and the information they seemed to get before the small investor.

"Oh, hell, everybody knows that, and the funds have computers and research and all that. I think the strategy for the small investor is to jump aboard once he sees that the big boys are moving the market. My broker knows some of them, so we get some inside information once in a while. I got some myself. It was a stock related to those gambling casinos in the Bahamas. The stock was down from twenty to eight because it was thought there might be some trouble with the Bahamas government. Then I heard from some guys I was working with that a report was coming out that would be very good for the casinos. So I bought some."

"What happened?"

"The stock went to seven, and now it's four. It's very cheap on earnings. You ought to buy some."

I asked Robert how he felt in general now.

"When the market was going down, I asked my broker why it was going down. He said 'Nixon. The market has no confidence in Nixon.' Then it went up again and I asked him if it had confidence in Nixon now. He said it wasn't Nixon, it was the funds buying, and foreigners. I don't see how it can have been Nixon on the way down and not on the way up, but my broker is brighter than most of them, so he must know."

If Robert had done so badly, why did he think his broker was better than most?

"For one thing, he's still in business. That's no joke. I got into a cab at La Guardia a couple of months ago and I got to talking to the cabdriver, and this cabdriver had been a broker with one of the houses that went busted. I asked him if still followed the market and he said not so much any more.

"Look, I know some things aren't fair. Take the commissions. I was watching a stock called Data Lease Financial. It used to sell at twenty-nine, so when it got to two, I figured, How low can it go, and I bought two hundred shares. They charged me a twenty-one-dollar commission for the two hundred, a four-hundred-dollar order. And I guess another twenty-one dollars to sell. That's more than ten percent in commissions. What the hell, the track is only seventeen percent and that at least goes to the government, the track is gambling, sort of socially disapproved, and the market is getting up near the track. Except for the big boys. The big boys don't pay any commissions at all.

"But what am I going to do, write my congressman? It's the only wheel in town. Listen, I have friends who had accounts, they're small investors just like me, and they can't even get a broker. Nobody wants them. You're lucky to have a *broker* these days; first your broker has to survive, then he has to keep you, they keep trying to shove you into some mutual fund where you wouldn't be able to watch the stocks. I have a good relationship with my broker, so I don't think he would drop me, but when I holler I don't holler too much, even about a ten percent commission.

"My wife wants me to get out of the market. She says the market makes her feel insecure, and she wants to buy a piece of land or put another room on the house or something, if we have any money left."

"Are you going to do that?"

"I suppose it makes more sense, my house has gone up more than any of my stocks—and so have the taxes on it, I might add. But I can't give it up now. I might be quitting just at the bottom. And if I couldn't look my stocks up in the paper, I'd really miss it. Part of my life that I enjoy would be gone."

Are Odd-Lot Robert and his cousins in or out of the market? With all the quantification going on of security prices, volume and movements, and all the computer memories chock-full, still no one knows whether the Public is in or out of the market, or even more important, how their individual portfolios have done. We have the most elaborate machinery possible for tracking *prices*, but that is like bending over the buffalo tracks and saying, "Yes, many buffalo go this way." Very good if there are a lot of buffalo all going in the same direction. The Investment Company Institute can tell us whether, on balance, mutual funds are being bought or sold; the Federal Reserve can tell us whether there are minus signs on lines 30 and 31 of its *Flow of Funds* computer print-out (mutual funds and "other corp. shares"), and even where some of the money might be going, perhaps bonds (line 27), savings accounts at commercial banks (line 22), or savings and loans (line 23). (For your very own *Flow of Funds* print-out, a little more up-to-date, you can ask the same people I do, the Board of Governors of the Federal Reserve System of the United States, Constitution Ave. and 20th St. N.W., Washington, D.C. 20551.) Pollster Albert Sindlinger says the number of individual accounts has dropped 10 percent; yet at the same time margin debits can quadruple and volume can increase, which traditionally mean the Public is increasing its participation.

I used to think that somewhere there was somebody who knew where the Public was and what its behavior meant, and that if I tried long enough and hard enough we could find that corner of the library or the agency or the computer room. But knowledge is still spotty. Further, virtually no one has paid much attention to *people*. The assumption is that price behavior and volume behavior equal people behavior. *The Money Game* attempted to sketch some of the irrational forms of people behavior, and to suggest that emotions had as much influence as buffalo tracks. I once commissioned a psychologist to write a paper on anxiety as a market force, and until I got together with Dave Campbell, a psychologist from the University of Minnesota, nobody had even made an elementary sketch of professional money managers as people.

As in the old maps of Africa, the outlines are all there, but the interiors are all blank. The rivers are marked, but there are big gaps where we might as well have pictures of elephants and the word "unexplored."

Be all that as it may, the New York Stock Exchange says there are 31 million shareholders, and that there will be 40 million in 1975 and 50 million in 1980, plus all those indirect shareholders in pension funds, insurance policies and mutual funds. They must be looking for something. Maybe they realize that the green stuff in their wallets is not the real money.

3:   SUPERMONEY, WHERE IT IS: THE SUPERCURRENCY

THERE is a certain amount of mileage, politicians discover periodically, in griping about our tax system. It is discovered that last year three hundred people had incomes of $200,000 and paid no taxes, and let's get the bastids. Or the Atlantic Richfield Company, a major oil producer, paid no taxes on $454 million. Jean Paul Getty has an income of $300,000 a day and pays no taxes. And so on. Then there is some thrashing around, and some pulling at the drawstrings of the loopholes. You have only to turn to the classifieds in *The Wall Street Journal* and read the bold letters TAX SHELTER to realize that a large group of our citizens minimize their taxes. Sheltering *income* does not produce Supercurrency—Supercurrency being a term I made up to describe the real money of the country. Supercurrency is capitalized income, not sheltered income, and in a moment this chapter will explain it. Instinctively people know that they are not going to get rich working for a salary; part of the reason they drift toward the securities markets is that they know that is where the Supercurrency lives. But since much of the publicity is about reducing taxes on *income,* let us get that out of the way first.

People send the congressmen to the U.S. Congress, and Congress writes the tax laws. When the Congress wants to encourage something, it writes a favorable tax law. Cynics and Mr. Dooley could say that Congress responds to lobbies because it wants to encourage its own reelection. Congress wants to encourage the search for energy, so it writes the oil laws the way it does. As a social objective, Congress wants everybody to own his own home, so it triple-subsidizes personal housing, which incidentally makes a house one of the best investments you can make. (Do not write and say that you made your investment and then they raised the taxes and then the roof fell down and then the freeway came through.) Congress subsidizes personal housing by creating agencies to provide mortgages, by making the interest on those mortgages and the taxes on the property deductible, and by deferring the taxes when the house is sold if another one is bought within a year.

If I were making up a list of readings for a sociology course about American life, I would put *The United States Master Tax Guide* at the top of the list. That marvelous book will show you that Congress values *things;* the *people* may be born, get married and die, but the *things* live on. For a work to be of superior worth in the eyes of the *Master Tax Guide,* it must be a *thing.* If you write a poem, whatever you sell it for will always be income, taxed at the highest earned rate. That is because you created the poem. The tax law very specifically (and anti-intellectually) says that creations, particularly copyrightable ones, are always income. If you sell me your poem for $10, it then becomes a property, a thing; when I resell it for $1,000, I pay a capital-gains rate, because exchanges of things are more socially desirable than the creation of them. The anomaly develops because the privileges granted to one group can be bought by another, at a premium.

If, for example, you write a poem or sing a song or discover a cure for the common cold in your basement lab, and you are successful, your wise tax counselor might tell you to quick, go drill an oil well. But if you drill a successful oil well, no one is going to tell you to quick, go write a poem or sing a song. If one man sits alone in a room with some paper and an idea, and the ideas become words on paper, and then actors act them or singers sing them—straight income, call the driller. If one man sits in a room with some paper and an idea, and the ideas become diagrams, and the diagrams are machined into metal—you have made a *thing*; you can capitalize it, borrow on it, build a company with pensions, stock options, floating yachts, a little private jet, and a capital gain at the end.

The dentist who has a good year and adds up his potential tax bill may decide to drill oil, not teeth, or to go into real estate or to try some other venture. Wall Street is gearing up more and more to the selling of these packages; it can make more on them than from the commissions on stocks. The tax shelter will take the income tax from dentistry, run it through an approved *thing,* and produce an eventual capital gain taxed at rates lower than the dentist's earned income rate, though if the dentist would calculate the discounted present value of the deferral, he would see that unless he is very lucky, the fees he pays to the brokers and lawyers and accountants and drillers and ranchers will probably make up the difference in the rates.

I have done this myself sometimes just to defer income from one year to another and have more time to think about it, because part of my family is in the cattle business. To defer income, you call my brother-in-law Bill and buy a lot of feed. All the feed is deductible. Then you borrow on the feed to buy the steers—the interest is deductible—and while the steers chomp away at the feed, getting fatter, you cross January 1 and into another year, when the sold steers return as income. There is, of course, a problem in addition to the income returning: the grain is real and the steers are real and they do not always get fat on schedule, and the prices at whimh they are sold go up and down.

I may have gotten too close to the business. In a borrowed cowboy hat, I was once sitting on a rail fence with Bill when a steer with a very ugly red eye walked by.

"That's one of yours," Bill said.

If there were turkey vultures circling high in the Arizona sky, Bill would say, "Must be some of yours over there," and if the vet was heading for a particular pen with a foot-long needle, I knew whose steers *those* were. One year —obviously a long time ago—I watched steer prices go from 19¢ a pound to 27¢ a pound, and I thought we were in fat city, but the profit for the year came in at $57.32. "Some of yours died," Bill said. I do have to say that Bill is very fair and dispenses justice with a tempered hand. The next year prices went down, and my loss was only $57.32, for which I was grateful. "The other fella's died," Bill said. "See, it all evens out."

Everybody knows that for rich people, taxpaying is a game of hare and hounds, the revenuers against high-priced accountants, in which you never have to settle for 100 percent of the assessment anyway. But rich people are not those who have deferred their taxes, though rich people may do that because they have smart lawyers. Your income is still your income even if the taxes are a bit lower. The real money comes from Supercurrency. The most pure forms of Supercurrency are the great companies with broad markets selling at high multiples of earnings. Granddad and Uncle Harry had a partnership. They took the money home. Uncle Harry turned it into a company, and it was then worth whatever a private buyer might pay for it. But Uncle Harry sold it to Eli Lilly or IBM or Xerox or Coca-Cola, and now Uncle Harry's side of the family is *rich* and peels off the Supercurrency—shares of IBM or Coca-Cola—whenever it wants a new boat.

There are some profound social implications here, because it is not lost on the smaller proprietors of American business that the way to cash in is to turn the family business into Supercurrency, whether by selling to the public or to IBM, or hopefully first to one and then to the other. For in addition to those impulses to concentration that come from economies of scale and the aggregation of capital, there are the impulses of the owners to cash in their business for a superior currency. Further, the multiplier on the Supercurrency increases the distance between wage earners and capital owners.

The tax reforms we hear about concern the various subsidies of some taxpayers by other taxpayers. In a recent study, The Brookings Institution said that these subsidies, or benefits, or loopholes, come to $77 billion annually, so presumably the elimination of the privileges for the subsidized taxpayers would drop the rates for all the others.

But Supercurrency is beyond tax reform; it is, as any currency is, the fiber of the society. Only on the periphery, where there are stock options and other devices to let the latecomers in, is there some talk of how to get in. To reform Supercurrency would be to change the whole notion of wealth in America, to change trusts and multiple trusts, and estates and inheritance laws, and the nature of the corporate animal itself. So Supercurrency will be around for a while.

It used to be, in the imperfectly developed securities markets of days of yore, that if the company had some assets, you could sell stock to the public. The common stock then had some claim on these assets, after the bonds and the preferred. But that style has changed and the love of assets has been left far behind; it now is the income stream—and the market's readiness to capitalize it—that matters. Uncle Harry's company will "go public," and in fact, its goal is not just to take care of Uncle Harry and Aunt Edna and that worthless hippie Cousin Eugene, but to make it to the public marketplace; the company will merge, borrow and doll itself up to that end objective. If the company is marginal, there are years when it may have to wait, but the commissions are fat on underwriting original issues and generally there is always a hungry underwriter.

Let us make up a capricious example. There are two Park Avenue doctors swabbing children's throats. They are doing a land-office business. Together they make $100,000 a year. (They could make even more, but taxes are high, they like to ski, and they do not like children.) With their $100,000, they pay taxes and grocery bills, and maybe put something in the savings bank.

They form Pediatricians, Inc., meet the hungry underwriter, and sell the stock to the public at thirty times earnings. Their after-tax net is $50,000, so their stock is worth $1,500,000. Now when they want to pay grocery bills, they peel off some of the $1,500,000, as much as the market can stand. They have moved into the Supercurrency class. If their auditors had made a statement of their net worth before, it would have consisted of stethoscopes, fluoroscopes and a jar of lollipops. Now their net worth is $1,500,000—partly in cash, which they sold to the public, and the rest in their stock. Their old net worth—the sum of stethoscopes, fluoroscopes and lollipops—came, let us say, to $10,000. Their new net worth is $1,500,000. The difference of $1,490,000 is new money to the economy, just as if the

Fed had printed it, and should be included in all the calculations of the money supply.

You have to have a good market to sell Pediatricians, Inc., but perhaps the example is not so capricious. Advertising agencies consisting of three hot talents, two typewriters, four crayons, a telephone and a line on some zippy accounts have made it into the Supercurrency class, thereby turning the $60,000 made by the participants into a multiple thereof.

In 1972 we had a good example of Supercurrency. The Levitz brothers—Ralph, Gary, Leon and Phillip—of Pottstown, Pennsylvania, were furniture retailers whose company netted $60,000 or so a year. Then the company noticed that sales were terrific when they ran the year-end clearance sale from the warehouse: furniture right in the carton, cash on the barrelhead, 20 percent off. The idea was very successful, they added more warehouses, and the company went public—in fact, superpublic. At one point, it was selling for seventeen times its book value, one hundred times its earnings, and Ralph, Gary, Leon and Phillip had banked $33 million of public money for their stock, and they still held $300 million worth. (History will tell, of course, whether selling furniture from warehouses is really worth 100 times earnings, but the $33 million is safely in the bank.)

Paul Newman is going public, along with Shirley MacLaine and Sidney Poitier. That is not the end of the line by any means.

I have an ambivalent attitude toward this. On the one hand, there is no question that hungry underwriters have sold lots of junk to the public. Should they be policed in some way? We get then to the other hand. In almost no other country do small enterprises have such easy access to capital, and easy access to the public markets is part of this, a great national asset. Caveat emptor: the odds are better than at the track. Small enterprises provide ferment, keep the Establishment on its toes, and sometimes even grow into great enterprises.

Does Mrs. Rudkin bake good bread at her home in Fairfield, Connecticut? She does indeed. But after her business expands into a bakery called Pepperidge Farm, the Rudkins want to trade it in for the real money. (Supercurrency brings more than cash almost every time), so they trade the bakery for $28 million of Campbell's Soup, very good Supercurrency. With the broad stock exchange listing of Campbell's Soup, they can peel off some, turn it into cash, diversify, and start behaving like rich people. In fact, you can go through the Supercurrency-history exercise right in the kitchen: you can see the food families' trading right up there on the label, because usually the family name was well enough known that the Supercurrency company kept its own identity to a quiet little line somewhere. Is there some Hellmann's mayonnaise? Obviously there once were some Hellmanns in the mayonnaise business: that is not a name an ad agency would think up. The Supercurrency ultimately turned up as CPS, formerly Corn Products, via Best Foods. Dannon is not a family name, but Isaac Carasso, a Spanish businessman, named his product after his son Daniel—hence Danone, later Anglicized to Dannon. At some point Dannon was traded in for Beatrice Foods, billion-dollar dairy Supercurrency. Is there some Breakstone cottage cheese? The Supercurrency is Kraft.

Finally, all of the following were good businesses on their own, and they all have something in common: Avis Rent a Car, Cannon Electric, Federal Electric, Sheraton Hotels, Howard W. Sams (a publisher), Continental Baking, Grinnell Corporation (pipes and pipe fittings), Hartford Fire Insurance Company (a major insurer), Rayonier, Pennsylvania Glass Sand, Southern Wood Preserving Company, and Levitt and Sons, the famous builders of Levittowns. What do all of these thriving enterprises have in common? Their owners all traded up for the *same* Supercurrency, ITT, formerly International Telephone and Telegraph, which has been the prime example of how a Supercurrency company uses its premium currency to buy what it stalks.

The capricious examples have a lot of "good will" in the Supercurrency (for "good will" some skeptics sometimes read "air"), but all capitalized earnings count as Supercurrency, especially the legitimate and broadly traded ones. The people in the big house on the hill have Supercurrency because Granddad bought the Tabulator company that turned into IBM, and IBM is regal Supercurrency.

Make no mistake about it, this is real money. The psychiatrists and social scientists have other definitions, but economists start with a basic definition: money is M_1, all the coins and currency in circulation outside the banks, plus demand deposits (i.e., checking accounts) in the banks. To this, most economists add M_2, which includes savings accounts and time deposits in banks. This can be spent almost as easily as M_1. Everyone does not cash in his savings account on the same day, but all you have to do is transfer your savings account to your checking account to get M_2 to M_1, and that's pretty easy. Some economists add short-term government bills to this, since they are also practically cash.

To this I suggest we add M_3, Supercurrency. Supercurrency is the before-and-after of a stock going public, in at book and out at market. That act of going public creates additional currency, just as switching a savings account to a checking account moves M_2 to M_1. To get M_3 to M_1, you buy at book, sell at market, peel off some stock, move it to your checking account and presto! M_1, you are rich.

A while ago, there was a debate among economists on

what really moved the economy, and the monetarists said, being monetarists, that it was the money supply which was most important. But in calculating the money supply, few economists paid much attention to Supercurrency, yet there it was. (All I wanted for my own efforts was a little footnote, just to the left of Say's Law and the Hicks-Hansen Synthesis, called Smith's Increment. A former member of the Council of Economic Advisers asked, "Are you willing to do some serious work on this?" That shut me up. I knew that meant writing up Supercurrency in Boolean algebra in *Kyklos*, or maybe *Econometrica,* presenting a paper full of Σs and Δs and little numbers lying on their sides, writing "The Social Implications of Supercurrency" for *The Public Interest* or maybe even the *New York Review,* and finally souping it all up for *The New York Times Magazine.* Unfortunately, even with my new electronic calculator I am lousy at multiple regressions, stochastic series and such. It might be more respectable to write up Supercurrency in algebra, but I have to do it in English. So, in English.

Everything in Smith's Increment is Supercurrency, but only that Supercurrency which has just changed from stethoscopes and lollipops to a *multiple* of net counts as Smith's Increment. At some point, all Supercurrency went through that process, but we count it only the first time it happens.

So we have a somewhat skewed income pattern in the society. There are people below or outside the level of M_1. They have problems earning any money at all, because they are badly educated or not motivated or they can't get to where they have to go. They have no money to speak of, whether currency, coins, or checking accounts, and many of them are on welfare. Then we have the vast majority of people, earners of M_1. They go to work; their employers pay them; they spend the money at the grocery store, mail checks to the druggist, pay their taxes, stash a little into M_2, and struggle on. And finally we have the Supercurrency holders, the serene owners of the M_3.

The poor innocents among us do not realize the impact of a superior currency around. They still think the green stuff in their wallets is money. We can all huff and puff and work overtime, but there is no way we can catch up, because there is nothing to capitalize our earnings. And Supercurrency compounds beautifully, given a bit of time. The Rockefellers may be smart, but the gap between our smartness and theirs is not equal to the difference between our currency and theirs, by several light-years.

A friend of mine bought himself a twenty-eight-acre *palazzo* in Greenwich and fixed it up handsomely before the bear market. He said he could always get a million for it. I asked him who would have a million to spend on a house in spare times, and he said, "There will always be somebody whose company has gone public and gotten listed who can peel off some of the stuff and spread it around. There will be more of those guys than there will be houses with twenty-eight acres in Greenwich."

Corporations sell stock to retire debt, to build new plants or what have you. That is not Supercurrency because on the books of the company the money received turns into the new plant. But when the Selling Stockholders dispense of their equity, they move into the Supercurrency class, at capital-gains rates.

There are other ways of compounding wealth, usually involving borrowing on the asset—the real property or the oil in the ground—and buying some more. But the most easily accessible form is Supercurrency, obtained as close to the source as possible. That is your number, M_3, and if riches gleam in your eye, at least you know where they are.

While there are other forms of wealth, Supercurrency is the superior currency of the country, because if they make a profit, even the oil deals and the real estate deals and the farm deals and the equipment-leasing deals will be brought to market and sold at a multiple of their earnings so that their participants can get the real stuff, traded paper.

Obviously, the laws and mechanisms of the country are built around the protection not just of currency but also of Supercurrency. It would not be the same society—whichever way you like it—without the structure and mechanisms that support the currencies, both Super and regular. Yet a very short time ago, the structure and mechanism went through some perilous times.

What happened in 1970 helps to explain why so many investors have recent scars. The shaking of the structure was a much nearer thing than anyone realizes—that is, anyone except those who were in at the countdown—and there are some lessons to be learned.

It is not easy to have a story about something that did not quite happen, and it is particularly not easy to have that story revolve around abstractions, concepts that may be unfamiliar, and statistics. To avoid footnotes, the statistics have been chucked into the back of the book. Most of the numbers are from the Board of Governors of the Federal Reserve, or the Federal Reserve Banks of New York and St. Louis, whose help is hereby acknowledged, or from equally public sources. It is more important for a general reader to get the *feel* of what happened than to walk through the mechanics, so if it gets a bit abstract, just keep going.

Given what happened, there was no way for the market to stay up. Though a repetition of these events is not likely, at least for a while, there is nothing to say that they could not happen again.

The first of the two moments when the structure swayed perilously is the weekend the United States almost ran out of money. That is more metaphoric than precise, but it does serve to introduce the first of the great near misses.

Most investors turn only to the stock-market page, but the stock market does not exist all by itself. There are also bond markets, commercial-paper markets, commodity markets, a banking system and so on. None of these is self-contained: money does flow and the markets are interdependent. Any disaster or near disaster brings a search for villains, who fleeced the lambs, and so on. In the Crunch, the villains were very widely dispersed; in fact, the crisis point came from a rather broad sweep of history.

II:

The Day
the Music
Almost Died

THE DAY THE MUSIC
ALMOST DIED

1:

THE BANKS
JUNE 1970

IN a Crunch, the country runs very dry of money. It is hard to understand that a country can run out of money because, after all, countries by definition can print money. But they can also be overtaken by events, after which the printing power does not alleviate the pain.

Everybody could tell, that June weekend in 1970, that a Crunch was on: it was difficult for small borrowers to breathe, and their ribs hurt. If you wanted to buy a $40,000 house, five years previous you might have put up $6,000 in cash and paid 5½ percent for twenty-five years. Now, in the late spring of 1970, the savings and loan wanted $15,000 down and 8½ percent, if it would make the loan at all, and some did not. Some smaller businesses were even worse off. They had been, let us say, used to taking out a bank loan for taxes, and then repaying that loan over a year. Now they were told the loan would be cut down or out, and if they went to other banks, the other banks said they weren't taking any new clients. That meant the small borrower was out on the street, hustling for money wherever he could find it.

Interest rates were at their highest levels in a *hundred years*. The prime lending rate at banks had been as high as 8½ percent, and some said there was no reason it could not go to 10 or 12 or 15 percent. If the prime rate is at 15 percent, that is such a new ball game that the Dow Jones averages could fairly surely be predicted to sell at 002.

There are bankers around who say there was no crisis in 1970; you could always get money if you wanted it—you might have to pay 20 percent interest for it, that's all. Or maybe take it in blocked dinars. Even the use of the word "crisis" is controversial—it always is—but the Federal Reserve Bank of New York used it in a retrospective. As that June weekend begins to fade, the crisis seems less acute. By the time of the annual report of the Fed's Board of Governors, the language applied to the events was "serious uncertainties."

The liquidity crisis of that time didn't have much to do with the inability of buyers and sellers of stock to find each other and touch fingertips. Liquidity in this case meant usable funds, borrowable funds for American business. A decade ago nobody could imagine that money in the United States was finite. It was like all the rest of our natural resources: there was plenty for everybody, you could get what you needed, and you certainly didn't have to worry about running out. The discovery that the supply of money was limited seems to have had a profound social effect as well, for, as with middle age, it does mean that you may be able to think of what you would like to do, but that does not mean you get to do it.

There were two popular off-the-top-of-the-head rationales for the Crunch, and both of them were true. One was that nobody had bothered to finance the Vietnam war. There were no major increased taxes to pay for Vietnam, for reasons well spelled out by political commentators. It was not supposed to last that long, and increased taxes would endanger the Great Society program. The second reason was "inflation psychology," which meant that you had better buy it today, because tomorrow it, whatever it might be, would cost more. Right after the summer the money almost ran out, I had a long talk with the treasurer of the telephone company in one of our major industrial states. The telephone company has excellent credit, and even in a Crunch it can borrow. This particular treasurer—and his appropriate committee—committed his company to pay more than 9 percent for twenty years. If he had waited through the crisis, it might have cost his company only 8 percent or even less. One percent on many millions of dollars can buy a lot of telephones. I wanted to know if he felt dumb, though I didn't put the question quite so baldly. He said he didn't, and he had worked out a nice rationale. He had had a leeway of only six or eight months, he said, in which to borrow the money.

"The rates were eight percent, so I decided to wait a bit," he said. "Then they went to eight and a half. That is historically very high, so I wanted to wait until the rate came back to eight. Then the rates were nine—more than nine—and there was talk that they might go to ten or twelve. We needed the money, and I had run out of time. So I had to do it."

I pressed him a bit.

"Listen," he said, "we borrow money all the time, and if the rates stay down I'll borrow some more and then the average won't look so bad. Anyway, I'm retiring in four years."

It still sounded dumb to me, but then I have never had

to borrow money for the telephone company, and quarter-backing is easier from the grandstand, especially after the game is over. Even Presidents know that.

Once again, the story of what happened can be seen from the tables of the Federal Reserve, this one called *Funds Raised, Nonfinancial Sectors.* Vietnam and inflation were indeed the causes of the Crunch, but from the Fed's figures we can see that the stage was well set, for the demand for credit had increased by more than twice the savings that could supply it.

In the early sixties, the demands for money were more or less consistent with the growth of personal and corporate savings. But by 1964 the demands for credit by business and by state and local governments had begun to increase. After a period of fairly slow economic growth, business began to spend for new capacity and new technology. By 1965 corporations had more than doubled their 1960 borrowing, from $14 billion to $29.6 billion. State and local governments increased their borrowing 40 percent. And in consumer credit and mortgage, individuals and households increased their borrowing 72 percent.

All this was against an increase in the gross national product of 36 percent and in personal savings of 40 percent. Against that 40 percent, the total of credit demands by all borrowers moved up *ninety* percent. So that even before the escalation in the Vietnam war, much of the flexibility in the credit system had been lost. The demand for funds was already pushing the available supply.

Then between 1965 and 1968 the Federal Government increased its expenditures by *$60 billion*—about half of it related to defense—without raising the taxes to cover this burst of spending. In 1966 the Federal Reserve made one stab at an anti-inflationary policy by restricting the money supply; then, its fingertips burned by the brief "crunch" of that year, during the two years following, it let loose a

$24 billion addition to the money supply. In mid-1968 Congress passed a 10 percent income tax surcharge, which was supposed to take the steam out of the economy that had been supplied by all that new money.

By that time the momentum of inflation had really taken hold. Much of the borrowing was short-term, because the borrower didn't want to commit himself to a lifetime of high interest rates. It was a dumb corporate treasurer who had not borrowed at 4½ percent back in 1964. Besides, borrowing was a way to boost the earnings per share of the stock, and that was what the stock market wanted—increasing earnings per share. So off to the market they went, better late than never. And individuals did not cut back on spending as much as all the econometric models suggested they would, because they had no choice. Their spending was more for the essentials of life than for the so-called discretionary items. The cost of those essentials increased faster than personal income. If you wanted a house, the mortgage cost that much more—if indeed you could get a mortgage—and if you needed a doctor or a hospital, that cost a lot more. The state and local governments had to meet increases in teachers' salaries, in paving contracts, and so on.

American business, impressed with the ugliness of cash as an asset, increased its borrowing to $47.9 billion in 1969, almost three and a half times the 1960 total. The banks had about loaned out the amounts they were permitted to by the Fed; they went to Europe and borrowed Eurodollars—dollars that had been generated abroad or taken abroad—and then reloaned them here.

The Federal Reserve figured inflation could be cut back if borrowing could be cut back, and it began to restrict the borrowing of its associate banks. It even moved to cut off the borrowing of Eurodollars. But the lead time of the corporations did not permit them to turn around so quickly. The money was committed to be spent. So the corporations, in aggregate, borrowed up full at the banks, edged out of the long-term debt market, and began to sign IOU's: short-term commercial paper.

Some say the Federal Reserve indirectly encouraged the growth of this paper by forbidding banks to pay the going interest rate on large time deposits. Some say the banks steered their clients into paper because they couldn't accommodate them; certainly the dealers in that paper sold their product aggressively. Commercial paper is just that: an IOU. It says that Sears Roebuck or Chrysler or what-have-you promises to pay you, in thirty or sixty or ninety days, the face amount. Most commercial paper does not have a maturity of more than ninety days, and much of it matures in under thirty days. The buyers of commercial paper are big buyers: the smallest customary denomination is $25,000, and some pieces run $1 million. Some pension funds and banks buy commercial paper, but most often the buyers are corporate treasurers who want to put money to work for just a few days at a higher rate than Treasury bills and similar instruments will yield.

A company treasurer or a country bank buying commercial paper expects to get its money back in a few days, plus interest. If the U.S. Treasury will pay him 7 percent for those days, he may get 8½ percent from commercial paper. Obviously he believes the commercial paper is a good risk, or he could not take a chance with all that money for only a few days' worth of extra interest. Traditionally, a company is supposed to have bank credit equal to its outstanding commercial paper. After the debacle, or near debacle, questions were asked and lawsuits filed: how come the credit behind the paper hadn't been thoroughly analyzed? The answer will not be found here; the question is part of the feeling of the time. But obviously the buyers once thought all the paper was good; they were wrong about a small part of it; then for a time, they thought no paper was good.

With the banks tight and their ability to sell bonds limited, American corporations sold IOU's, commercial paper. From 1966 to 1970, the amount of outstanding commercial paper more than quadrupled, from $9 billion to nearly $40 billion. For the twelve months up to the June Crunch weekend, it had doubled.

The lack of liquidity in the economy had its roots half a decade back. Much of the borrowing done by business had been under at least some assumptions that sales would be good, but they were disappointing. The flow of cash in corporations was 10 to 30 percent below expectations, and that in itself built up the necessity to borrow.

By June of 1970 the sixth largest enterprise in the United States and the largest railroad in the country, the Penn Central, was busted, busted enough to be very slow to pay the conductors on its trains. It was having trouble renewing, or rolling over, its maturing commercial paper, and it had $200 million outstanding. For weeks, the Penn Central's bankers had worked night and day on an emergency loan to be guaranteed by the U.S. Government. The Administration lobbied in Congress for the loan. On Friday, June 19, the bankers were so confident that they gathered in the Northwest Conference Room on the tenth floor of the Federal Reserve Bank of New York to sign the papers as soon as word came from Washington that the government guarantee would be in effect. But the word did not come.

Congressional disapproval had been hardening. The $200-million loan, said Wright Patman, chairman of the House Banking Committee, would be "only the beginning of the welfare program for this giant corporation." It would risk "hundreds of millions of the taxpayers' money in a highly questionable scheme." (Later, Patman told Congress that the Administration had asked the Federal Reserve Bank of New York to check out the loan; the Bank replied that the loan "would provide no significant relief to the Company," that it "could not recommend approval of the proposed loan on the basis of factors normally considered in appraising credit risks," and that it did not see how the taxpayers would ever get their money back. But the Administration, said Patman, did not bother to give Congress that report when it was lobbying. All this is in the *Congressional Record*.)

Shortly before 5 P.M., a government official, the intended guarantor of the loan, told the assembled bankers in New York that there would be no approval.

"The bankers who had been working on the project so intensely," said the notes of a later Federal Reserve meeting, "were shell-shocked but not resentful. They left our building and went to the uptown office of the First National City Bank, where they tried to figure out how they could protect themselves."

In Philadelphia, the Penn Central's lawyers began to draw up the bankruptcy papers; they would rather, they reasoned, march in orderly under a white flag than have some creditor put them into bankruptcy. The Penn Central's chairman, Paul Gorman, and three of his directors went to Washington to see Patman on Saturday. Patman had not changed his mind. The directors went back to Philadelphia. The Penn Central's board met again in Philadelphia on Sunday and threw in the towel; one of the lawyers drove to the suburban home of U.S. District Judge C. William Kraft, Jr., with the papers. Sunday is always a good day to go busted.

Once the Penn Central had handed over the papers, it did not have to pay its debts, except under reorganization.

Most important for this story, it would not pay the holders of its IOU's, its commercial paper. They could paper their bathrooms with all $200 million. The corporate treasurers who had thought they would put money out at a better rate than Treasury bills would get back neither interest nor principal, at least not without lengthy lawsuits. They would lose *all* the money they had put up. The Walt Disney Corporation lost $1.5 million that way, American Express $4.8 million, Homestake Mining $1 million, and so on. (The paper holders eventually sued everybody in sight, and some settled for a fractional reimbursement from the dealers.)

There were some other very large American corporations also in a state of gasping illiquidity. It is not polite to name names, but you could start with Lockheed, Chrysler, TWA, Pan American, and LTV. In particular, two finance companies, Chrysler Financial and Commercial Credit, had commercial paper out far in excess of their approved credit at banks.

The worriers began to see the following script: the holders of the Penn Central's commercial paper would be busy papering the bathroom and calling their lawyers. Like Mark Twain's cat, who sat on a hot stove, and then would not sit on any kind of stove, hot or cold, investors would not exactly be reaching for more commercial paper. The commercial paper from other companies had short maturity: some would come up Monday, some Tuesday, and so on.

There was $40 billion of commercial paper outstanding, and if nobody was to sit on that particular stove again, where would $40 billion come from as the notes matured, day by day? Not from the stock market: the stock market was flat on its back, and anyway, it takes time to register to sell stock. Not from the bond market: the bond market was in disarray, and the bond dealers were still working off inventories from weeks previous. Not from the banks: the banks were all loaned out.

"I was on a summer weekend in Cape Cod," says the economist of a major New York bank. "I went to town to get the paper, and I just stood there reading it in the grocery store. I could see the U.S. banking system might have to pick up an extra fifteen billion dollars, and it just didn't have it to give. I remember thinking to myself, *This could be another Credit Anstalt.*"

The Credit Anstalt was the Austrian bank that failed in 1931, and turned out to be the first domino to fall; it triggered a whole series of bank failures and helped to bring on the world-wide depression.

Wasn't that a bit extreme? I asked the senior economist.

"The sixth biggest enterprise in the United States goes broke," he said, "but it's a railroad. There are special provisions for railroads, left from the 1930's; they keep operating. But you let half a dozen major U.S. companies default on their short-term debts, their creditors throw them into the courts, their suppliers and contractors are afraid they won't get paid and *they* rush for the courts, and meanwhile everybody tightens up and cuts operations and starts laying off people. You could have a real panic that would snowball, a panic that would feed on itself. It's happened in this country before."

But, I said, in this day and age, that wasn't likely.

"You've never lived through a panic," he said.

But there is a lender of last resort; that is why we have a Federal Reserve system. Congress, by the Constitution, can create money, and Congress gave that money-printing function to the Federal Reserve in 1913, when that agency was created. The Fed reports to Congress once a year; it is an independent agency; its seven governors are appointed by the President for terms of fourteen years apiece. This is

not the place for the college-freshman-economics-course
explanation for the mechanics of the working of the Fed.
Suffice it to say it can turn money on and off. By the way
it turns the faucet, the Fed hopes to speed up the economy
when it slows down, and slow down the economy when it
gets overheated. It used to believe that if the cost of money
went up, buyers would drop away. At this point, however,
the Fed was working more with monetary aggregates, which
one Fed official described as "roller-skating on three wheels
—it will work, but you need new body movements."

There is a philosophy that the way to cure inflation is
to get everybody to stop reaching out. You want them to
curl up in a fetal position and stop breathing for a while;
that cures enthusiasm. Then things cool off. The Fed had
had the money valve largely off, because inflation was certainly roaring. The Fed itself had been criticized: for cut-
ting off money too abruptly in 1966, for increasing it too
fast in 1967 and early 1968.

Fed meetings are not public, but the two possible positions were fairly clear. The first position said thus: only.*we*
can print money. Once we print it, we can't control how it is
used. Printing money has to be part of an overall plan,
involving foreign balances, taxes and so on. Our Official
Policy is one of restraint, and if we depart from it, not
only are we not able to control where the money goes, but
the news of a sudden change might have a reverse effect and
scare everybody to death.

The second possible position for a Fed governor was to
worry about Monday morning, and to treat the weekend
as something special in history. The issuers of commercial
paper would not be able to sell any more; they would go
to their banks; the banks would say, sorry; the issuers
would be brought into the courts by the people to whom
they owed money; the issuers would start to lay off people
and cut back operations; everybody could stake out a

corner for an apple stand, if the corner wasn't already occupied by a fried-chicken stand. The notes of a Fed official to a Fed meeting later that summer uses this language: "inability of the issuers to pay their paper at maturity would have dire consequences for the issuers, the commercial paper market, other financial markets, and the banking system." *Dire consequences* is a phrase not used lightly.

The Monday morning worriers won.

Alfred Hayes, the president of the Federal Reserve Bank of New York, was in London; acting for him was a sixty-three-year-old former Wall Street lawyer, William Treiber, now the executive vice-president of the New York Fed. Treiber is a pleasant, white-haired type, given to conservative three-piece suits, just as you would expect from a Columbia College, Columbia Law, Sullivan and Cromwell executive vice-president of a Federal Reserve bank. Treiber left the massive Federal Reserve building, modeled after the Strozzi Palace in Florence, at the same time the shell-shocked bankers went up to the First National City's offices. Treiber drove to his weekend home, a two-hundred-year-old farmhouse in East Winchester, Connecticut. He called the First National City Bank; at 10:30 P.M., he reported later, the bankers were all still there and still in a state of shock. Treiber got on the phone. Over the weekend, that was all he did. He moved a card table with a phone on it into the dining room of his farmhouse. He talked to Arthur Burns, chairman of the Board of Governors and captain of the Monday-morning worriers. He called the head of every major bank in New York at home, or the next in command if the chief executive couldn't be found. (David Rockefeller of the Chase Manhattan was on his boat, off Bar Harbor, Maine.) Treiber couldn't leave his card table, except briefly, because the farmhouse only had one line, and frequently he had to leave word. His daughter took a picture of "Daddy's weekend office." In the dry language in which these things are reported, it was said the bankers were told that "the use of the discount window would be appropriate," which does not mean everyone got a cut rate.

Sunday night Treiber flew to Washington; the Fed's Board of Governors met Monday at 9 A.M. By Monday night, phone calls had gone out through the twelve Federal Reserve banks to every bank in the system—not just to big city banks, but to small-town banks all over the country. The Fed's index finger was beginning to bleed from all the dialing. The message was the same: if anybody comes into your bank and wants a loan, *give it to him.* Then if you're all loaned out, come to us and we'll see that you have the money.

I began to speculate: What would have happened if teenagers tied up the home phones? Or if the Fed's own Paul Revere were unable to get through? The Penn Central's lawyers are driving through suburban Philadelphia looking for the judge's house, nervously thumbing the paper, and the line is busy.

I could see the following scene. After all, school was out.

"Hello, Mr. _____, please."

"This is Timmy."

"Hello, Timmy, can I speak to your father."

"No."

"Please, Timmy, it's important."

"No."

"Why can't I speak to your father?"

"He's not here."

"Where is he?"

"He's outside practicing his golf swing."

"Could you go get him?"

"No."

"Why can't you go get him?"

"I'm not allowed to leave the kitchen until I finish my lunch."

"This time it's all right. I'll fix it for you, I promise."

"I have to finish my lunch."

"How long will it take to finish your lunch?"

"I don't know. I don't like carrots. But I have to eat them."

"Could you call him from where you are?"

"No."

"Is anybody else home?"

"Yes."

"Who? Let me talk to them."

"Arthur can't talk."

"Who can't talk? Why can't they talk?"

"He a dog."

"Timmy, listen closely. I want you to *put the carrots in Arthur's dish,* and then go get your father."

"They'll find out. Arthur doesn't eat carrots."

"Just do it. Listen, Timmy, would you like a new football helmet? Would you like an autographed picture of Arthur Burns. *In uniform?*"

"Yes."

"Good boy. Just do what I say."

After an appropriate interval, the banker makes it to the phone.

"Hello."

"Rodney, this is the Federal Reserve calling. I'm sure you know why."

"Uh, I think my kid got the message garbled, he said you said to put the carrots in the dog's dish."

The Fed official says, sorry to call him at home, but that if anybody wanders into his bank, dispense money. Rodney thanks him and reminds him: "Don't forget the autographed picture of Arthur Burns."

On Monday, June 22, Arthur Burns, the Fed's pipe-smoking chairman, pressed not only for the additional reserves but to do away with Regulation Q, which would permit the banks to take in large short-term time deposits. The Fed had taken those large time deposits away from the banks as an anti-inflation move. Now it decided to worry about inflation some other time, and gave them back. After an all-day debate, Burns won his point.

From that point on, events followed the script. The Penn Central went broke, but no one else did. Six billion dollars fell away from the commercial paper market, as buyers recoiled in horror. The companies that were going to sell the commercial paper and were unable to do so went to their banks and begged for money. The banks went to the Fed, the Fed loaned them the money, and the banks reloaned the money to the would-be insurers of IOU's. In one July week alone, the banks lined up for $1,700,000,000 at the Fed window. More than $2,000,000,000 in bank money went to companies whose commercial paper was coming due. Not only that, with Regulation Q wafted away, the banks took in $10,000,000,000—ten billion dollars—in time deposits, just in case anybody needed more money. Some of the bankers who had stayed awake that summer, fretting that if anybody added up the losses in their bond portfolios they might think the bank was busted, were stunned to find that they were having a very good year.

The Fed was pleased. Not only had there not been a crisis, but the money had been recycled. It had been there as debts before and it was still there; now, however, it was owed to banks, not to individual borrowers, and with the banks, the borrowers could have some breathing room to sit down and work repayments out in an orderly way. And there was no great inflationary addition to the supply of money.

Gradually, there began to be faint, faint cheers for the Fed's actions from all of the seventeen people who understood them. A New York banker said the Fed had done "a classic job." *Business Week* said "a wrong move by the Fed could have allowed Penn Central's financial distress to infect the nation's financial system . . . touching off a chain reaction of corporate failures."

As the Crunch abated, the bankers and the Fed performed the equivalent of the pro football touchdown ritual: lots of fanny-patting, jumping up and down, and hugging the ball-carrier. I can see it all in a ghostly, silent instant replay, except that the stadium is empty. It is empty because nobody knows it happened—not only Mr. and Mrs. America, who think that the Fed is the FBI, but all the readers of those papers that carry financial pages. It is all too abstract, and too hard to explain. A 105-yard razzle-dazzle touchdown in absolute stony silence.

William Treiber's September 10 report to New York Fed directors contained some sense of satisfaction. "The commercial paper market was in a near crisis situation," he said. "The banks stepped into the breach promptly to provide credit . . . aided, of course, by . . . the expressed desire of the Federal Reserve to assist the banks in avoiding a crisis. The commercial paper market is now calm."

Treiber had to add a final sentence. "It was an interesting," he said, "at times, a highly *exciting* experience."

I have to figure the crisis of June 19–23, 1970, as a very near miss, because the normal language of banks—and especially of the Fed, is dry, abstract, full of passive tenses, and unemotional. Things are not supposed to be "interesting" in the banking business, and when they become highly exciting for the participants, I begin to hold my breath. When it was over, the Fed returned to its nice, dry language. Here is some of its description of the events transpired, from the *Monthly Review* (August 1970) of the

Federal Reserve Bank of New York. Never mind the phrases that are strange; keep going, and get the feel:

> Fears of a general liquidity crisis rose to a peak late in the second quarter after the Penn Central Company filed a petition for reorganization on Sunday, June 21. These worries were exaggerated . . . nevertheless, concern during the second quarter over the possible widening of liquidity problems aggravated the uneasy atmosphere in the money and bond markets . . . these pressures were most evident in the commercial paper market, where participants became apprehensive that some borrowers would be unable to refinance a large volume of existing debt, some of which was of very short maturity. The Federal Reserve System acted to facilitate refinancing of these debts by the banking system, by suspending Regulation Q ceilings on large short-term time deposits, and by using the discount window and open market operations to guard against liquidity pressures. These actions had a salutary effect on most financial markets, tensions subsided . . .

and everybody lived happily ever after. Just that easy.

Yet something bothered me. It was in the phrase, "the lender of last resort." Why was everybody cheering the Fed? Did not some people say that the Fed's stop-go policies had helped *cause* the Crunch? Was it not their job to do just what they did? I asked the Fed.

"It seems to me," I said, "that the Fed did just what it should. That is why we have a Fed, so we do not have the panics that we had in 1873 and 1893 and 1907, with banks failing and markets collapsing and everybody out of work. It's like having a fire. You call the fire department."

The Fed officer leapt at the metaphor. I guess Fed officers are so used to saying, "The discount window might be appropriate," that a metaphor has seductive charm for them.

"Exactly!" said the Fed officer. "Exactly! The fire department! *This never happened before!* And it worked! The engines, and the hoses, and the water pressure, and the foam—it works! It all works!"

In time, as nobody else went busted, some confidence crept back into the commercial paper market. The demand for funds abated. The banks reduced their prime rate to 8 percent, then to 7½, then to 7 percent, and they built up their own liquidity. What could have been a crisis was over.

And why is this drama relevant to understanding what went wrong in the stock market?

Any investor has a choice: he can buy a stock or he can buy a bond. If bonds are yielding 2 percent, he may well figure he can do better in the stock market. If bonds are yielding 10 percent, he may just settle for that. If you are running a pension fund, and all you need to supply the the pensions is a return of 4½ percent, and you can buy a telephone bond at 9 percent, you buy the telephone bond and play golf until you retire, for your job is over. When there isn't enough credit, people will bid up the price of money, and telephone bonds will sell at 9 percent.

Then the money that could go into stocks will go into bonds instead. Or stockholders—professional and individual—will sell their stocks and buy bonds. And that means that everybody who bought an 8 percent telephone bond at 100 finds it marked down to 97 when there is a new telephone bond at 100 that yields 9 percent. When there is a 9 percent telephone bond, everybody that owns an *old* bond, even a week old, has a loss.

That is a description of an uneasy bond market, and why it is bad for the stock market. If you add to that a real Crunch, with the possibility of major companies not paying their bills and their payrolls, nobody will buy stocks. Maybe some other time, maybe they will be cheaper later: maybe we will get a chance to buy Chrysler at the 1933 prices, if there still is a Chrysler. If you add to that just a few rumors of a bank holiday—well, it does something to the atmosphere. A bank holiday is a misnomer. Everybody else gets the holiday; the bankers have to stay till midnight figuring out which companies to save and how to keep the bank going.

By historical standards, American business is still not enormously liquid, but the summer of the Crunch created a great thirst. The first order of business was to get a cushion back into the balance sheet. According to Tilford Gaines, senior economist of the Manufacturers Hanover, business needed more than $50 billion—over and beyond any needs for new money—just to get back to the relative stability of the early 1960's. Within a year, that was down to $35 billion, and it is still going. Secondary borrowers have a much harder time than the big boys, but once more there is money for everybody. The prime rate for bank lending has come down three percentage points, which doesn't sound dramatic enough, so they say "three hundred basis points," which is dizzying.

In the days since the Great Crunch, there have been other threats to peace, serenity, and the stock market, notably in the balance-of-payments crisis and the devaluation of the dollar. Government intervention in the economy increased in the forms of various controls and Phases. While it would be possible to tell some near-miss stories of these events, they occurred after the market had passed its points of greatest vulnerability, both in terms of prices and of structure.

All the banks have been reminded of the name, address and telephone number of the lender of last resort, and all the bankers' children know that if the phone rings on Sunday and it is a man from the Fed sounding breathless, it is perfectly okay to go outside and get Daddy without finishing your lunch.

THE DAY THE MUSIC
ALMOST DIED

2:

THE BROKERS
SEPTEMBER 1970

I F there was a lesson learned from the Crunch, it was that illiquidity snuffs out a stock market. People who need money bid the price up, and then bond yields go up, and then other people take their money out of the market and buy bonds, and the market goes down. Nice and simple. So you have to look one page past where your stocks are listed, to the bond page. If well-rated bonds are yielding 7½ percent, that is an amber light. If they are at 8 or 8½ percent, you can start to get nervous. By the time they get to 9 percent, it is probably too late.

There were people, respectable people, who thought the bear market was going to last for five years or ten years or maybe forever. That was how long it was going to take to get liquidity restored. Corporations needed $50 billion, and states and cities and the Federal Government—well, they would never be through with the money demands at all. But once the cycle was cracked, the treasurers—both public and corporate—who once had hurried to market because next week the rate would be higher, held off. Now if they simply waited a month or two, they were rewarded with lower rates, and that brought back the more normal supply-and-demand flow.

But the liquidity crunch was not the only near miss in the Big Bear. Wall Street itself almost collapsed from its own mismanagement. We need not go into too much detail, because this story has been told elsewhere, and there are few lessons to be learned by individuals not involved in the business. But it is possible to write a near-miss, equally hair-raising script about the last day of American capitalism, and focus it on good old Wall Street, which itself had been so used to judging the rest of corporate life.

The middle sixties were a euphoric period for the broker types. It should be said right away that some people kept their houses in order and did not get their names into the paper, and both of them are still happy. One hundred and twenty firms went out of business.

The center of this drama is a piece of paper, the stock certificate. In the old days, under the buttonwood tree, one Knickerbocker would hand over the coins and the other would hold forth the piece of paper. That was in a time when all the trading was over by morning-coffee time. A century and a half later, the mechanism was still the same.

The people who got into trouble were the so-called retail brokerage houses. They dealt with the public, and the public was in the market. The name of the game was "production," which meant "writing tickets." To do that you opened a new branch office, hired some new salesmen— bored housewives, failed accountants, dropout aluminum-pan salesmen—and told them to call everybody they knew with the hot new stock ideas. The ex-aluminum-pan-salesman's Aunt Mary and his lodge brothers opened accounts, the production went up, and the tickets went up. That was

c

where the trouble started. For Wall Street, by and large, was like a beautiful, fan-tailed, Detroit Belchfire Eight with leather seats, remote-control windows, color TV in the back seat, and under the hood—six perspiring squirrels running on a treadmill. The branch offices were equipped with beautiful quote machines, that great promotional device, the "tape"—now probably in orange symbols electronically flashing on a black background—and a Dow Jones ticker so demure it went *clack muffle muffle clack* instead of *tocketa tocketa*.

When the lodge brother bought a stock, the transaction would be recorded in the back room by a gentleman wearing gym shoes and a jacket indicating the freshman basketball team of Cardinal Hayes High School, who would lick his pencil as he recorded the trade. With such personnel it was not uncommon to have mistakes. The securities, if they could be found, would be delivered to the brokerage firm by another gentleman in a Salvation Army overcoat, a nine-day growth of beard, and a certain air of muscatel, California 1973. Sometimes he would get where he was going, and sometimes he would not. Sometimes his parcel would get there with him, and sometimes it would not.

Business was very good. You could walk into a teller's cage and walk out with securities. They were lying on the floor, on the tables, all over the place. Did not bad people then take the securities away, and never bring them back? Yes, they did. In 1971 they took $500 million worth. Sometimes good people did too. It was commonly assumed that The Mob was responsible for all the missing securities. It was very easy to put in your very own man. You could dress him in a Salvation Army overcoat if you wanted to get the securities that way, and you could dress him in acne and a Cardinal Hayes letter sweater if you wanted them that way. If you wanted to move him up one step in sophistication, you put a man in the clerical department as the bank transfer agent, or in some other record-keeping capacity, and then nobody could figure out the records. One step up from that, you took the securities to a country bank in Limburger, Ohio, put them up as collateral, took out a loan, and then simply left them there forever—why not? Not your stocks. One operator, known as The Paper Hanger, told Congress just how to do it.

I was having a drink one evening with a governor of the stock exchange who had worked very long and hard hours on the problems.

"The Mafia couldn't possibly have stolen that much money," he said. "Good people had to steal too. The temptation was too great."

The FBI—the other Fed—apprehended some bad people and located some missing securities, to wit, some 3,400 shares of IBM belonging to a well-known brokerage firm. Plucky public servants that they are, they called up the firm and told them to be happy, their IBM was found.

"We're not missing any IBM," they were told. (Months later, when the records were a bit more straight, the firm sheepishly asked the FBI if it could have the IBM back. The FBI said yes. It is not recorded what else they said.)

Not all the securities, of course, were stolen. Many were not there in the first place; they were clerical errors. In fact, most of the discrepancies probably belong in the bookkeeping category. Firms lost physical control of the pieces of paper. But if you think I am kidding, I recommend to you two splendid documents. One is the *Review of SEC Records of the Demise of Selected Broker-Dealers,* the report of the Securities Subcommittee of the House Committee on Interstate and Foreign Commerce. The other is *The Study of Unsafe and Unsound Practices,* done by the Securities and Exchange Commission in conjunction with Section 11(h) of the Securities Investor Protection Act of 1970. I particularly recommend the transmittal letter of the chairman of the Securities and Exchange Commission to the President of the Senate and the Speaker of the House, dated December 28, 1971. Here is one pithy summary:

> This statute was enacted against a backdrop of the most prolonged and severe crisis in the securities industry in forty years. Widespread failures of broker-dealer firms and concern for the funds of their customers had followed a prolonged period of easy business. Rising brokerage income and rising security prices had produced a general euphoria. In this mood, expansion of sales effort and overhead had not been properly supported by more capital and stronger back-office effort. A veritable explosion in trading volume clogged an inadequate machinery for the control and delivery of securities. Failures to deliver securities and to make payment ricocheted through the industry and firms lost control of their records and of the securities in their possession or charged to them. Operation conditions deteriorated so severely that securities markets were required to cease trading one day each week at one point, and later to limit daily trading hours.

The chairman of the SEC had a very strong sentence to conclude that paragraph. "Those conditions," he wrote, "should not be allowed to recur."

Why was the record-keeping so fouled up? Among other reasons, there is a simple sociological one. In times of prosperity, stockbroking is a prestige profession. You get to talk on the phone, sound important, know what's going on, and play with expensive electronic gadgets. Underwriting companies is even more prestigious. Being a partner of a firm is best of all. You get to order a splendid new office with books by the yard and a special shower off the men's room, or, if it is an older firm, an appropriate antique rolltop desk. From there you talk to the giants of capitalism.

It is not very prestigious to keep records, match up certificates, or in general do the dreary housekeeping known as "back office." So nobody wanted to be the partner in charge of dishwashing. And in many cases, nobody was.

Once the troubles started, all the business-school-type partners knew exactly what to do. They tell you that at business school. If you have a problem, you call in an outside consultant—Arthur D. Little or McKinsey or Booz, Allen, Hamilton, or one of the computer software people. The consultant says it is lucky you called. Your communication techniques are obsolete, your record-keeping is archaic. How can you expect to conduct a twentieth-century business with eighteenth-century record-keeping? What you need is an IBM 360-20 computer system—at $5,000 a month—and some staff to go with it.

You are relieved. You have made the right executive decision. At business school they told you you would have to use a computer.

That is when your firm goes busted. The computer fouls up.

I refer you to SEC Chairman Casey's points eight and nine in the transmittal letter referred to above:

8. New and expensive technologies were hastily brought to bear on the paperwork problem without adequate preparation, analysis of cost or mastery of technical requirements;
9. Records were put on computers without maintaining the old records for safety until the computer operation proved itself.

Of course you threw the old records away! The computer people told you everything was fine now, didn't they?

A sociologist came downtown and found that the computer people wouldn't talk to the securities people. The securities people wore wide ties and the computer people wore narrow ties. The securities people lived in Manhattan or commuted from the suburbs, and the computer people lived in Brooklyn and took the subway. If Jonathan Swift had written a story about a war between the people who thought you should tap the little end of the egg first and those who thought the big end should be first, everybody would think it was a fable by some crackpot who had a strange attitude toward Irish children anyway.

At the peak of the troubles, "fails to deliver" totaled $4 *billion*. Nobody could find four *billion* dollars' worth of stocks.

The New York Stock Exchange has certain requirements. A firm is supposed to have a certain amount of capital in relation to its obligations. Never mind that the obligations were getting out of hand. There was trouble on the capital end, too. If you had put capital into a Wall Street firm, you could take it out—sometimes in ninety days, sometimes in a year. Few other businesses have such an ease of exit. Some of the capitalists took their capital out. And the remaining capital—well, that was frequently in the stock market, and many of those stocks were melting away in market value.

Back to the near miss.

As firms began to fall grossly behind in their capital requirements, they would be suspended from dealings by the New York Stock Exchange. Except for very big firms. There was indeed a prejudice in favor of size. Said Robert Haack, president of the exchange, "We simply can't afford to have a major firm fail." Much later, the stock exchange gave three justifications for its prejudice in choosing to try to save the major firms, while letting lesser firms fail. The great number of customer accounts, they said, would not have allowed an orderly liquidation. Suspension of the firms would have lost them their technical clerical staffs at a time of intense competition for such people. And the announcement of a suspension of a major firm might cause a run on all brokers, even ones in good shape, by worried customers.

The stock exchange had established a trust fund early in the sixties, at the time of the salad-oil scandal which put Ira Haupt & Company out of business. Those funds were to provide an orderly liquidation for a failed firm so that the customers would not lose their money and maybe spread the word that you could lose all your money without even making a mistake in the market. That leads to the calling up of congressmen. As the major firms began to teeter, the exchange would authorize its members to increase the trust fund: the amounts increased from $10 million in 1965 (with an additional $15 million in stand-by credit), to a maximum of $55 million in 1970, to $75 million in January 1971, and finally to $110 million, with $30 million set aside in a customer-assistance program for Merrill Lynch's obligations in its Goodbody rescue. At each increase, some of the surviving members would ask, "Why don't we just let the bastards go down the tube?" And Felix Rohatyn, a soft-spoken governor of the exchange, a merger specialist from Lazard Freres (who had bought a number of companies for ITT), would say, "That is not an acceptable risk."

At 8:30 A.M. on September 11, 1970, Hayden, Stone was out of business. It had followed the classic pattern: increased production, disorganized record-keeping facilities, its capital impaired by being invested in falling securities, and a large number of fails. (At one time, it had been said that Hayden, Stone was so disorganized that "you could peel the wallpaper off the wall, deliver it to Hayden, and get paid.") Rohatyn and Bernard Lasker, chairman of the governors of the stock exchange, had applied all their merger-making talents to finding a firm that would take over the lagging giant. The problem was a group of Hayden, Stone's noteholders, who were reluctant to go along with the marriage arranged, by shotgun and persuasion, with Cogan, Berlind, Weill & Levitt.

"If the Hayden merger didn't go through," said an exchange governor, "that could have been the ball game."

The end of the ball game might have had the following script:

The opening bell rings. Hayden, Stone is declared in liquidation. A minimum of $25 million from the trust fund would have been needed to pay the overhead and clear up the records while the firm's affairs were straightened out. The firm's overhead had been running at $5 million a month; even reduced to $2.5 million, the costs of liquidating it would more likely have been $40 million to $70 million over eighteen months, perhaps as high as $100 million. Hayden, Stone's 90,000 customers would have been frozen in place, unable to buy or sell for many months. The cash and securities owed by Hayden, Stone to other firms would have forced those firms under; perhaps another fifty firms could have gone out of business. As those firms sold securities to raise cash, the Dow Jones average need not have stopped at 630, or indeed anywhere short of 400 or so, and broader market averages would have suffered equally.

But worse: the confidence of millions of investors, already impaired by the bear market, would be dealt a final blow by the sight of Hayden's immobilized and screaming customers. They would all race to their brokers and demand their cash and their securities. Wall Street had for years used its customers' cash, and many of the securities were very likely nowhere to be found. There would be a classic run—not on the bank, but on the brokers.

And beyond *that* loomed a specter so frightening nobody

wanted to think about it. There was $50 billion out there in mutual funds. A mutual fund can be redeemed in one day; you simply bring the papers in and say, Sidney, I want the money. The mutual funds had had a cushion: every year their salesmen sold more fund shares than fundholders redeemed. So they had to sell stocks only as a market strategy: if they thought the market was going down, they might want 10 percent in cash; if they thought it was going up, they might want to be fully invested. (Statistics show, parenthetically, that that is what they did when they thought those thoughts, but the market generally went the other way, rather perversely.) They did not sell stocks to give cash back to worried redeemers.

What if the holders of mutual funds got scared and started to cash in? Already fifty brokers were going out of business, hundreds of thousands of accounts were tied up, a run on the brokers was going on, brokers were selling stocks to beef up their capital accounts—and now, what if the mutual funds were *forced* into sales to raise cash to pay off nervous redeemers of their shares? To whom would they sell their stocks?

"I thought about that a lot," said my friend who was the exchange governor. "We would have had to close the exchange."

"Close the New York Stock Exchange?" I said. "What happens then?"

"I don't know, because it's never happened like that," he said. "But certainly you would have the government step in, and when the exchange finally reopened, things would be very, very different."

"Maybe like the Yugoslavia Stock Exchange," I suggested.

"Maybe," he said.

At 8:30 A.M. on September 11, 1970, the script was ninety minutes away from the bomb in the suitcase. To get

Hayden, Stone merged safely away took the approval of 108 noteholders of the company. Not only did the Hayden, Stone officials scramble to get the signatures; so did Robert Haack, the president of the New York Stock Exchange, and the ubiquitous and worrying governors, Messrs. Rohatyn and Lasker. By Friday, September 4, when the deal was supposed to have been set, all but a few of the noteholders had said they would go along. The merger was supposed to be delivered to the exchange's board of governors on Thursday, September 10, but one of the noteholders still had not signed. By the exchange's own rules, Hayden, Stone should have been suspended some time before; now the board of governors voted a reprieve of a few hours. The holdout was an Oklahoma City businessman named Jack Golsen, who had put $1.5 million into the firm only the previous March, believing, he said, that the firm's statements were up-to-date and that the New York Stock Exchange would not have allowed him to invest in a firm that was about to go busted. Golsen said he'd rather go into liquidation; maybe the tax consequences were better, and anyway, he was tired of being pushed around.

Having been given a few hours' reprieve, the Cogan, Berlind people, who were to take over the merged firm, raced for the Teterboro Airport, chartered a Lear jet, flew to Oklahoma City, and sat up all night with Golsen. At dawn Golsen was still shaking his head. At 8 A.M. Rohatyn and Bunny Lasker got on the phone in a conference call. "They hit me with a whole trainload of social responsibility," Golsen said. The government, said others, was aware of the situation. Golsen capitulated. At 9:55 A.M., five minutes before the liquidation would have been announced, the Dow Jones ticker flashed the news of the merger.

But the duties of Rohatyn, Lasker and the other worriers were far from over. Two other great firms were taking on water fast: Francis I. du Pont, with 275,000 accounts, the third largest brokerage house in the United States, and Goodbody & Company, 225,000 accounts, also one of the largest in the country. It did not take an adding machine to figure that if they both went down, the exchange's trust fund would be out of money and then some, and the whole run-on-the-bank script would be back in operation. Both of these accounts have been rendered elsewhere in the press. You could make a book out of all those adventures alone, or better yet, a successor to *Mission: Impossible,* with a cliff-hanger each week ending at the last commercial.

It was not easy to get people to take over Wall Street firms that were losing millions of dollars a month. Remember the alternate uses of money: you could get 9.35 percent a year, every year, in that good old telephone bond, and never worry about another thing. But in a takeover you had to put up more than money. You had to have the expertise to take over and, if necessary, shut down branch offices; you had to take over and straighten out the tangled records and finances; in short, you had to take over and run a large and failing business. Who needed that? Obviously, only a major financial institution could do it. There had been pressure from mutual funds and insurance companies to join the exchange, but that pressure had been resisted by the existing members, the brokers, for fear it would hurt their own businesses. So the exchange had no institutional members. Only two or three brokers could take over someone as big as Goodbody. It was decided that Merrill Lynch—by far the biggest broker—should have the new acquisition. Merrill drove a hard-nosed bargain: the exchange community was to put up $30 million against losses incurred in straightening Goodbody out, and absolutely no other firm should fail or the deal was off.

That left du Pont, and the du Ponts of Wilmington, Delaware, were in no mood to help. The candidate on the white horse was clear: it was a Texas billionaire called Ross Perot. Perot was not at all the traditional loud, cigar-chomping, super right-wing, cartoon Texas oilman. His money was all in shares of Electronic Data Systems, or EDS, a computer software company. Perot was so straight and H. Alger-like that even stricken Wall Streeters could not believe it. As a boy, he had gotten up at 3:30 A.M. and ridden twenty miles on horseback to deliver the *Texarkana Gazette* to poor neighborhoods that no one else wanted to service. He was an honors graduate of the Naval Academy. His billion came from the high price at which EDS shares sold, but he said often that the day he became an Eagle Scout was more significant than the day he became a billionaire, and he gave several million to the Boy and Girl Scouts. He had joined IBM as a salesman and had met his yearly quota by the third week in January. He started EDS with $1,000, and was turned down eighty times before he made his first sale. Perot is five feet six, has a crew cut and wears straight ties. His night life is playing basketball with his wife and five children, or taking everybody out for a hamburger.

Perot first came into the news because of his efforts to take Christmas packages to prisoners in North Vietnam; his chartered planes had gotten as far as Laos.

The Nixon Administration knew both Wall Street and Perot. Attorney General John Mitchell was a partner in a law firm specializing in municipal bonds; Richard Nixon himself had been a senior partner of that firm. Peter Flanagan, a special assistant to the President, had been a partner in Dillon, Read. Mitchell had managed the 1968 campaign, to which Perot had been a contributor. Furthermore, Perot certainly knew Francis I. du Pont and Company, even if he did not know Wall Street; EDS had been hired to do the computer work for the firm, and in fact the firm accounted for 15 percent of EDS's revenues.

"John Mitchell was very helpful in getting Perot involved," said an exchange governor. That whole story need not be recounted here. The cynics said that if EDS revenues were $50 million, and 15 percent of that came from the du Pont contract, then it should have been worth a $100 million to keep that business alive, and anyway, maybe Perot wanted EDS to take over all the computer work for the stock exchange and a lot of other firms. The believers say Perot wanted to save Wall Street and the system that had been so nice to him. One friend of mine who knows him well says that Perot is "half Boy Scout and half horse trader, totally sincere at both, and very good at both."

Perot took over du Pont. First he put in $10 million; then he put in another $30 million; so far, he has had to put up about $50 million, but the place is still in business.

Taking over Hayden, Stone had involved teams of people; taking over Goodbody had enlisted the biggest firm in Wall Street; the final role—and it is so extremely rare that this falls to one man—had fallen to a single individual, who said that if Wall Street had been impaired, "even temporarily, the consequences would have been dire, not only for industries, but for the cities, counties and school systems of the country."

It would be easy, said the current chairman of the Securities and Exchange Commission, to point out errors, omissions and failures in the last five years. "Firms and self-regulatory authorities were thrashing about," wrote Mr. Casey, in his transmittal letter to Congress, "in all directions, fighting to avoid catastrophe. Time and time again they had to select the lesser evil. Decisions had to be made in a rapidly changing situation."

Maybe Congress could understand if it read *War and Peace,* said Mr. Casey, in what surely must be the only time the SEC has ever reported to Congress by quoting Tolstoy.

There was Kutuzov, facing Napoleon before Moscow. And, said Casey, said Tolstoy:

> The commander-in-chief is always in the midst of a series of shifting events and so he never can at any moment consider the whole import of an event that is occurring. Moment by moment the event is imperceptibly shaping itself, and at every moment of this continuous, uninterrupted shaping of events, the commander-in-chief is in the midst of the most complex play of intrigues, worries, contingencies, authorities, projects, counsels, threats, and deceptions, and is continually obliged to reply to innumerable questions addressed to him, which constantly conflict with one another.
>
> An order (to retreat) must be given to (the adjutant) at once, that instant. And the order to retreat carries us past the turn to the Kaluga road. And after the adjutant comes the commissary-general asking where the stores are to be taken and the chief of the hospitals asks where the wounded are to go, and a courier from Petersburg brings a letter from the sovereign which does not admit of the possibility of abandoning Moscow, and the commander-in-chief's rival, the man who is undermining him (and there are always not merely one but several such) presents a new project diametrically opposed to that of turning to the Kaluga road.

Everybody knows what happened. Kutuzov survived. Wall Street survived. No other major firms went out of business. Congress, mindful of the 1,500 letters a month the SEC was getting, and of its own mail, passed the Securities Investor Protection Act of 1970, which created an agency that could borrow up to $1 billion from the U.S. Treasury, if necessary, to protect customers against losses if it became necessary to liquidate the firm in which their securities and cash balances were held. That took the pressure off the industry and off the New York Stock Exchange, and restored some public confidence.

Securities in the "fail to deliver" class dropped from $4.1 billion at the end of 1968 to $1 billion at the end of 1971. The narrow-tie computer people were given new prestige, more money, and some partnerships, or the equivalents in corporate form.

The piece of paper—the stock certificate—is still at the center of the transaction, and delivery is still made by gentlemen in Salvation Army overcoats. That is still troubling, but the mechanism of transaction, it is safe to say, has everyone's attention. And, said the chairman of the SEC, "looking down the road a little" (not the Kaluga road, a metaphoric road), "the time will come when the execution of a trade will be electronically conveyed to a point where securities are transferred by electronic record with paper print-out and payment is made by similar electronic means."

The future of the New York Stock Exchange is not totally clear, but what is clear is that it will not be moving to Dubrovnik. The structure of the securities industry is going to be quite different, but that concerns the people in it more than the multitude of investors. The involvement of Congress in passing the Securities Investor Protection Act means a continuing involvement of Congress; the government rarely leaves any endeavor where it has created an additional staff.

So. Bad things happened that need not and should not have happened; but catastrophic things did not happen—at least not catastrophic enough to send the whole business to Dubrovnik.

The individual investor, it seems fairly safe to say, slept unaware of the liquidity crunch, and read in the papers about the problems of brokerage firms. All he knew was that his stocks were going down. But what of They, the big boys, the professionals? They with the research and the computers and the experience—was the hand steady at the helm? The gaze steely and cool? There are answers to these questions, because this is an industry that keeps score daily, unlike almost any other in the world. But statistics provide rather bloodless answers.

Let us go back, just for a sense of atmosphere, to see how far we have come. For it was not so long ago that you could have panic in the Street—and that is a buying panic as well as a selling panic.

III:

The Pros

1:

NOSTALGIA TIME: THE GREAT BUYING PANIC

J UST one term ago the President then incumbent said he did not choose to run. The response of the marketplace was unmitigated enthusiasm. The previous volume records had occurred in the great selling convulsions of 1929 and 1962. The I-do-not-choose-to-run speech triggered off a buying panic, and now there were new volume records.

With all the brouhaha about Vietnam and the cities recently, a Wall Street panic seems like very small potatoes, almost irrelevant beside the cosmic problems. But panic there was, and very interesting to a handful of students of mass psychology. The panic is interesting because it is a reverse panic, therefore requiring a new line in the dictionary. The old line in the *Random House Dictionary* reads:

pan-ic (pan' ik) n., adj., v. . . . . 3. *Finance,* a sudden widespread fear concerning financial affairs leading to credit contraction and widespread sale of securities at depressed prices in an effort to acquire cash.

That is the dictionary definition. All the rest about panics you can ask Granddad about. The roar on the Floor increases. The phone lines jam. The volume of all the shares traded breaks new records.

Now you can see that we did indeed have a panic: sudden widespread fear and credit contraction. The difference in 1968 was that this time cash was sold at depressed prices to acquire stocks. The panic was so great that all the old 1929 volume records have gone out the window. The new 1968 records belong to the Great Buying Panic. It was, in general, a much happier panic, since it was only some of the professional money managers who bore the brunt of the malaise. Everybody else got to feel smart. The board-room watchers felt smart because the stocks they forgot to sell were going up. And downtown the brokers felt like absolute geniuses because they all met their 1975 profit projections eight years ahead of time, and any industry that far ahead of its projections must be populated by geniuses indeed. The President did not choose to run, and peace is bullish. Are the causal relationships that simple?

I happened to be having breakfast on April 1, the morning the panic began, with Poor Grenville. This epithet is at least partly ironic. Poor Grenville runs a swinging fund, and with his tall, blond, Establishment looks, Poor Grenville is a Hickey-Freeman model or an ad for the Racquet Club, not poor. One of Poor Grenville's great-grandmothers had a duck farm, and part of the duck farm is still kicking around in the family. There aren't very many live ducks on it any more, since the duck farm ran roughly from Madison Avenue east, bounded by, say, 59th Street and 80th Street, but then you never know how much the descendants get their fingers on, what with estate taxes and trusts and all. Poor Grenville was suddenly called poor because he had just gotten nicely into cash—$25 million of it—in 1966, when the market turned around and ran away. If you are a true performance-fund manager, you should be 100 percent invested when the market is moving up.

Now here it was only March of 1968, and Poor Grenville has just gotten himself back into cash—$42 million this time—and the President has just said he isn't going to run and peace is in the air. Poor Grenville was very fidgety at breakfast because last year he had had to come up fast on the outside to stay in the performance-fund derby at all. Win, place and show in the derby means the salesmen can sell that record into hundreds of millions.

"I think it's a whole new ball game," Poor Grenville said that morning. "I have to lose all my cash, right away."

So I stuck around after breakfast, just to see how Poor Grenville would spend $42 million. I asked Poor Grenville why he had sold so much in the preceding weeks.

"I wasn't that unhappy with some of the stocks," Poor Grenville said. "But I didn't like the international monetary situation. I thought Washington had lost control. I thought it would take high interest rates to get the balance of payments back in line. And Johnson—who could believe Johnson? Confidence is an important factor."

"And now the international monetary situation is okay, and you believe Johnson," I said. "All from that one sentence last night, 'I do not choose to run.' "

"I don't believe anything he says," Poor Grenville said. "It's probably some trick. The international money situation is still fouled up. So what, it's still a new ball game. It doesn't matter what's true; what matters is what everybody else thinks. Every fund you and I know is about to come piling in. Let's get on the phone."

So we got on the phone. Poor Grenville put in an order for 20,000 Burroughs at 170. That's $3.4 million. Burroughs had been in Poor Grenville's notebook to buy at 150, but this was a new ball game. Poor Grenville also tried for a block of Mohawk Data at 140, and bid for a block of Control Data. These were the stocks that helped Poor Grenville come up fast on the outside last year. The market opened and while we were waiting for the first $20 million to go to work we gossiped on the phone with some other managers around the country.

"Oh, we might nibble a little this morning," said one West Coast denizen coolly. He was so cool he had been in his office since 5 A.M. practicing his buying. "Actually, we bought a lot last week."

"I can see the history of this whole event shaping up," I told Poor Grenville. "If the market goes up this week, it's last week all the smart fellows will have bought."

"Nibble, hell," Poor Grenville said. "I hear he is loaded with cash. I bet he's in there bidding for my Burroughs."

Poor Grenville called the broker he had picked for the Burroughs. He was told Burroughs hadn't opened yet. Nor had Control Data. Nor had Mohawk. Heavy buyers on the floor. No sellers. Temporarily, the great auction market had come to a halt. Poor Grenville began to nibble at a fingernail. He called the broker back again and raised the bid to 172.

"That's an awful big order for the floor on a day like today," the broker said. "Have you tried the block houses?"

Block houses are Wall Street firms who arrange large trades, blocks, like Poor Grenville's 30,000 shares. We called two block houses. One of them thought he could get a nice block of 30,000 Burroughs for Grenville at 200. "Robbers, thieves," said Grenville. "That's one million dollars more than Friday. You think a million dollars grow on trees?"

The first figures on the market came in. The volume was setting new records. The market was up $17.

"Look at them all piling in, the greedy bastards," Poor Grenville said.

The Burroughs broker called back. Burroughs was trading at 184. It had opened on a large gap, which is to say it did not go up a neat point or two at a time, but simply started a whole fifteen points or so higher than it had last closed. "Idiots," Poor Grenville said. "Do they think peace comes overnight? Don't they know the Korean War went on for two years after the talks started? Okay, I'll take it at one eighty-four." The broker said he would call back, and in a few minutes he did.

"How much did I get at one eighty-four?" Poor Grenville wanted to know.

"You didn't get any," the broker said. "Burroughs is one eighty-nine."

"Madness," Poor Grenville said. "See if you can get it at one eighty-eight."

Poor Grenville had researched Burroughs, had worried over when the computer operation would become profitable, had even tried out one of the new electric accounting machines. He had carefully considered what he wanted to pay for it. Now, in two hours he had raised his bid on the Burroughs from 150 to 170 to 172 to 184 to 188, and he still didn't have any. He called the broker back.

"How much Burroughs do I have now?" he asked.

"You don't have any," the broker said. "Burroughs is one ninety-one."

It was lunchtime. We sent for sandwiches. The volume was setting records every minute. The lights on the phones flashed every thirty seconds. Poor Grenville's Mohawk and Control Data were way over his bids, too.

"My God," Poor Grenville said, "it's twelve thirty, and I still have forty-two million in cash." It was true; Poor

Grenville had been chasing his favorites, but they had outrun him. He had yet to buy a share.

"This market has come too far, too fast," Poor Grenville said. "We'll pick some things up on the reaction. There's bound to be some profit-taking."

There *was* a reaction, about half past one. It lasted about three minutes. Poor Grenville missed it because he was eating his bacon, lettuce and tomato, and anyway, a three-minute sinking spell doesn't do you much good when you have $42 million to spend. Now Poor Grenville was beginning to clutch.

"Every fund in the country is going to be up three percent today," he said. "They're going to be up eight percent for the week. Within two weeks they'll be up fifteen percent, and I'll still have this lousy damn forty-two million." Poor Grenville wrote $42 million on a notepad and stared at it, hating it. "I've got it," he said. "Let's buy what the hedge funds are short."

Hedge funds, as you may know, try both sides of the market. They increase their leverage by selling some stocks short while they buy others. In a big upswing, obviously they would have to buy back what they had sold. It took us about five phone calls to find out where there were some blocks short. Now we could make them suffer a bit by buying those stocks we knew they would have to be buying. We called up one hedge fund, just to chat.

The hedge fund was paranoid. It pulled up its drawbridge and poured boiling oil over the ramparts. It had troubles of its own. The volume was still setting new records.

"A friend of mine is buying a sheep farm," Poor Grenville sighed. "That would be a much more peaceful and productive way to make a living."

"With your timing," I said, "you would sell all the sheep just as everybody was about to go long lambchops."

"We have to buy *something*," Poor Grenville said. "I can't just sit here in cash. I'm going to look stupid. They'll throw me out of the performance-fund union. Get on the phone and collect some stories. We'll buy stories."

It doesn't take long to collect stories. A story goes, "I hear XYZ is going to earn four dollars, but the Street doesn't realize it yet." Never mind why. Tomorrow there will be no more stocks for sale.

So we bought, and we bought, and we bought. The phones rang and the hold buttons were pushed and there was general tumult. At the end of the day I was helping Poor Grenville go through some of the tickets in the snowstorm on the floor. There were tickets for stocks Poor Grenville had never thought of. The only ones missing were the ones he had been chasing, his friendly highfliers, Burroughs, Control Data and Mohawk.

"What the hell's *this*?" he said. "Union *Carbide*? An old granddaddy company? Are you out of your mind? A hundred thousand shares of Union Carbide?"

A hundred thousand shares of Union Carbide is a nice block, about $4 million.

"I didn't buy any Union Carbide," I said. "I put that guy on the hold button. I thought you talked to him. There were four phones ringing."

"I never bought any Carbide," Poor Grenville said. "I would never buy a tired old mother like Carbide."

"Well, I didn't buy it either," I said. We stared at each other, and then at a smudged, penciled slip.

"It followed us home," Poor Grenville said. "What the hell. Just go out and get it some warm milk and a blanket."

The next day a *New York Times* reporter called Poor Grenville to check on the block. Poor Grenville learns fast, and he was ready. "Our fund," he said, "did not follow the mass panic into such highfliers as Burroughs and Control Data. In these times of turmoil, we are seeking value. Union Carbide, for example, whose additions to net plant make it attractive. We believe, after exhaustive research, that the chemicals are ready to turn." Next thing you know, *Newsweek* was about to quote Poor Grenville on value in these troubled times. Four more funds bought Carbide. Grenville the Statesman.

The headlines make causal relationships: market spurred by peace hopes, market rises on booming economy. But the real impulse behind the buying panic was not in the head-lines. It was in a statistic. On March 22, eight days before the beginning of the Great Buying Panic, the mutual funds had Grenvilled themselves into $3.4 billion in cash, just because things looked so gloomy. That's $1 billion more than "normal," and the $3.4 billion didn't count all the pension funds and colleges and foundations that were beginning to play the aggressive performance game. The object of the aggressive performance game is to be first, to have the stocks that go up the most; to buy stocks at the bottom, you have to sell them first, so you have the cash when you want to buy. Naturally, not everybody gets to be first back in, and when you have dramatic moves in war and politics, the swings can be of panic proportions, either way. Only the triggers are missing.

"Performance" is a new word among the funds, but a taste for quick gains is not new. In 1935 Our Lord Keynes wrote:

> The social object of skilled investment should be to defeat the dark forces of time and ignorance which en-velop our future. The actual, private object of the most skilled investment today is 'to beat the gun,' as the Ameri-cans so well express it, to outwit the crowd, to pass the bad, or depreciating, half-crown to the other fellow.
>
> This battle of wits to anticipate the basis of conven-tional valuation a few months hence . . . does not even

require gulls amongst the public to feed the maws of the professional; it can be played by the professionals amongst themselves. Nor is it necessary that anyone should keep his simple faith in the conventional basis of valuation having any genuine long-term validity. For it is, so to speak, a game of Snap, of Old Maid, of Musical Chairs— a pastime in which he is victor who says Snap neither too soon nor too late, who passes the Old Maid to his neighbor before the game is over, who secures a chair for himself when the music stops. The game can be played with zest and enjoyment, though all the players know that it is the Old Maid which is circulating, or that when the music stops some of the players will find themselves unseated.

Sometimes I wonder whether those paragraphs from *The General Theory of Employment, Interest and Money* will ever lose their validity. The games were—and are—indeed played with zest and enjoyment; the swings get shorter and more violent. It is not news but atmosphere, climate and psychology that set this up. Some market Copernicus might say that the news does not change; it is our perception of it that moves.

2:

AN UNSUCCESSFUL GROUP THERAPY SESSION FOR FIFTEEN HUNDRED INVESTMENT PROFESSIONALS

STARRING THE AVENGING ANGEL

THE swings did get bigger, and the living was easy for seven or eight months after President Johnson's speech. Brokerage firms that dealt with the general public opened new branch offices and scoured the countryside for salesmen. All kinds of stocks went from five to fifty. Flocks of them had the word "computer" in the title, or had names that suggested data processing. Still others franchised some sort of fast food, hamburgers or chicken. There were chains of nursing homes, for we had suddenly discovered geriatrics as a boom industry. Sideburned young men in Meladandri shirts were running five thousand into half a million by talking to other sideburned young men. Age was a great handicap. No one over thirty could understand the market. And everyone knew it would come to an end.

A mass-circulation magazine asked me to explain to its readers what was going on. I had this Fellini scene:

We are all at a wonderful ball where the champagne sparkles in every glass and soft laughter falls upon the summer air. We know, by the rules, that at some moment the Black Horsemen will come shattering through the great terrace doors, wreaking vengeance and scattering the survivors. Those who leave early are saved, but the ball is so splendid no one wants to leave while there is still time, so that everyone keeps asking "What time is it? What time is it?" but none of the clocks have any hands.

The Black Horsemen did come, of course, and most of the guests were still at the ball. In the same article, I suggested that the market did not make any sense to anybody with a sense of history. The way to participate, therefore, was to hire A Kid. A Kid would buy these stocks going up tenfold, where anyone else would be scared to death, and A Kid could be rented for $1.50 an hour plus room and board, and would mow the lawns on weekends. The satire was ineffective, to say the least, and the price was far too low. Just after the 1968 buying panic, I made my annual visit to the investment course at the Harvard Business School. While there, I asked the class how many were going to Wall Street. There was a forest of hands; usually numbers of them wanted to go to Procter and Gamble or General Motors, but the action was no longer that way. None of them, however, had in mind working for $1.50 plus weekend lawnmowing. They thought maybe $20,000 a year to start would be fair; the more venturesome wanted to run a hedge fund and get 20 percent of the action. After all, they had been running paper portfolios in class all year, and they had done extremely well all term, and they had analyzed complicated prospectuses, and some of them had been in the market on their own for two or three years. By the third section of the class I got a bit testy, and it was clear that the curmudgeon was out of his time and a thorough has-been. Some of the students did work with hedge funds—that must have lasted about a year—and some got quite handsome starting salaries. That doesn't happen so much any more, but then the institutions were in an expansive and hiring mood.

At the institutions—the mutual funds, investment counselors and endowment funds—a new generation had taken over. The old generation had concentrated on the preservation of capital, and inflation had taken its toll. McGeorge Bundy at the Ford Foundation, the biggest of all the foundations, delivered himself of a memorable blast.

> We recognize the risks of unconventional investing, but the true test of performance in the handling of money is the record of achievement, not the opinion of the respectable. We have the preliminary impression that over the long run caution has cost our colleges and universities much more than imprudence or excessive risk-taking.

The Ford Foundation gives out a lot of money to colleges and universities, and the Bundy statement was read religiously. It was true that respectability rather than performance had been the goal of most endowments, but now the implications were clear. Nobody had better get caught with caution. So the colleges and universities sold some of their bonds and increased their positions in the equity markets. They told their investment counselors to hunt for small growth companies like the ones that had brought the University of Rochester from nowhere to the fifth richest in the land in the previous ten years. The mutual funds were out on their own derby, because the salesmen could sell only the previous year's record. The bank trust departments were a bit frustrated, because the trust laws did bid them be prudent, but the definition of prudence had loosened up, and some of them started special equity funds to seek out performance.

So it was not merely greedy individuals who fueled the boomlet, picking up tips on the train or at the barbershop or what have you. You can't have a market fever any more without some institutional help.

Just to take one example, National Student Marketing was bought by Bankers Trust and Morgan Guaranty, the General Electric pension fund, the Northern Trust Company, the endowment funds of the University of Chicago, Harvard and Cornell, and the Continental Illinois Bank. That is by no means a complete list. The original symbol of go-go performance, Gerry Tsai, held 122,000 shares in his Manhattan Fund. The stock was recommended by the old-line firms of Kidder, Peabody and Eastman, Dillon, as well as by Roberts, Scott & Company, W. C. Langley & Company, Loewi & Company, and others. W. Cortes Randell, the thirty-four-year-old mastermind who put National Student Marketing together, had a net worth in his own stock of $50 million, a six-passenger Lear jet, a fifty-five-foot yacht that slept twelve, an apartment at the Waldorf, three cars, a snowmobile, and the rapt attention of both security analysts and deal-makers. In the "story" market, Randell had a concept that eager analysts could chew on.

National Student Marketing signed up students on the campuses to take market surveys, hand out samples, and put up posters. This was to be the franchise to tap into the "youth market," forty million Americans between fourteen and twenty-five, who had $45 billion a year to spend. With Wall Street underwriters and "deal men" leading the scouting, National Student Marketing acquired twenty-three companies in fiscal 1968 and 1969, including a travel agency, a youth-oriented insurance company, a maker of college rings and a collegiate beer-mug manufacturer, using its own stock selling at 150 times earnings, true Supercurrency. Even at that price, brokers were recommending it as "an attractive long-term speculation":

> Dynamic changes have occurred in society, at least in part due to the growing force and influence of the current sophisticated campus groups . . . student economic power . . . overlooked by marketing experts. National Student Marketing is a pioneer in closing the generation gap between the corporate client with a product or service for sale and the youth market with its purchasing power.

Preaching his company's gospel around the country, Cortes Randell reported net earnings of $3.2 million, with higher to come.

Barron's skeptical columnist, Alan Abelson, did his usual perceptive job. National Student Marketing's fiscal 1969 profits included three companies with which deals had been made, but which actually hadn't been part of the operation during that year, and five companies that hadn't even agreed to merge yet. Abelson subtracted the new companies from the operating results, a simple enough operation, and came up with a loss of $600,000 instead of a profit of $3.2 million.

The stock kept right on going. At corporate headquarters there was a whole middle management—some sixty to seventy strong, flush with the power of a new idea and, apparently, with rather lavish expense accounts. Only out there on the broad green lawns of the academy, not all the campus representatives were putting up their posters as they promised. Some of them out there must have gone to the basketball game or taken up dealing in grass, not an approved NSM line. The whole operation became expensive to maintain. Some of the on-campus stuff flopped totally, and a direct mail campaign was a disaster. Instead of glorious profits, the company was into a million-and-a-half-dollar loss for the first quarter alone of fiscal 1970. National Student Marketing went from 36 to 11½.

I did not check to see what the Morgan Bank did with its stock, nor the Northern Trust, the Continental Illinois, the Bankers Trust, the Manhattan Fund, and the University of Chicago, Harvard and Cornell. No longer could the last three be accused by McGeorge Bundy and the Ford Foundation of excessive caution. Not to single out those three—virtually every investing institution had something like that; the University of Vermont and Syracuse University had Four Seasons Nursing Homes, which made it from 91 to busted in a remarkably short time. The market value of the equity portion of Oberlin's endowment dropped 25 percent in 1970; Temple University moved its equity portion of the portfolio from 35 to 85 percent in 1967–68, and when asked how that had fared, the investment adviser at the Girard Trust in Philadelphia said, "Horribly."

Euphoric at the ball, few of the professionals really left early. And, though it was not their money they had lost, they did not feel good. They are competitive fellows, most of them, and they like to do a good job. So I thought that at one of the industry meetings we could dwell on what went wrong.

One of my functions within the investment community, and one which I enjoy, has been to be a moderator at seminars and conventions. There is one in particular, an annual meeting that attracts the largest number of bank trust officers and mutual fund managers. We assemble the investment types with the best records, and they tell what insights led them to their triumphs, what stocks they have just bought and therefore would like the audience to buy, and what they see ahead. Of course, it is not always genius that earns an investment type a slot on this panel. He may

D

have taken undue risks; he may be down 90 percent in the next year; he may have done the equivalent of flipping heads fifty-one times in a row. No matter; the figures are in, and up to the dais he comes. I have never found one who was inarticulate, and in fact most are willing to comment on the investment significance of foreign policy, economic policy, sociological changes and other subjects usually reserved for Eric Sevareid. It has become a minor tradition that I needle the panelists gently, reminding them perhaps of a sour stock they had confided to me some other time—rather like the slave in the Roman chariot assigned to whisper into the garlanded conqueror's ear that glory is fleeting.

I thought it would be a nice psychological purge, after the worst year of the Big Bear, if some of the previous winners would get up and confess their sins. Every one of the professionals in the audience, after all, harbored some dark secret, his own block of National Student Marketing which he had dropped behind the paper-towel bin in the men's room, hoping no one would notice. There they were, these professionals, walking around harboring these unconfessed misdeeds. Who could tell the damage being done to the collective unconscious of the investment community?

So I think I had in mind a group therapy session for fifteen hundred investment professionals. Previous winners would get up, face the audience and say that not only had they bought National Student Marketing, they still owned it—in case anybody would like to buy it—and further-more they had put it into their children's accounts. In Alcoholics Anonymous, you are supposed to be on the road to cure if you can face your peers and say, "My name is John Jones and I am an alcoholic." Not only would my session benefit the confessors, but the audience would iden-tify and go through something of the same process. Some of them might feel the spirit and rise from their chairs, crying, "I bought Four Seasons Nursing Homes!" The audience would respond with the business school equivalent of "Glory!" Everybody would leave feeling cleansed and free.

For a while it worked. Two of the previous winners talked with good temper about what they had done and would not do again. They would no longer have such a limited view of history: the limited view of history said that you don't sell good stocks in a decline because they'll come right back. They would no longer go into illiquid situations, no matter how great the promise. They would no longer fall in love with stocks, forgiving the first lapse, and then the second lapse, and so on all the way down.

"We didn't pay attention," said one speaker, which was to say everybody had paid attention to ten or fifteen stocks but not to Vietnam and Cambodia and the Federal Reserve and Washington and the world at large. Another speaker was going to laugh if somebody said, "There is only a limited supply of stock." And still another speaker was going to disregard his clients, or potential clients, especially the ones who, when you were bearish, would say, "Call me when you're more optimistic."

Snug in its chairs, the audience was warm and responsive. It was all going along well. Then I tapped David Babson. I should have known better what was coming. Babson is a crusty, amiable New Englander who heads the sixth biggest investment-counseling firm in the country. He was then just turning sixty. For a couple of years he had been preaching and scolding. The stock market, he had said, was becoming "a national crap game." If the sinning didn't stop, he had told other groups, if the whole "gigantic pari-mutuel operation" didn't stop, there would be government intervention.

Babson had told me once that when he brought good

grades home from Harvard to the family farm in Gloucester, Massachusetts, his father was down in a vegetable garden. The Babsons are 1630 New Englanders, but Yankees, not Brahmins. In addition to running the farm, Babson's father was the local veterinarian. Babson walked the length of the field and told his father the news. "That's good," said his father, "but you been home ten minutes and you still don't have your overalls on."

Babson had not always been scolding; in fact, his weekly letters proved him to be a cheery optimist and a bull on America in the late forties, a time in which the surrounding opinion was quite gloomy. He had started the weekly letter because, when he began his counseling service in 1940, "there was no line outside the door." In Babson's view, the most prized virtues were hard work and common sense—not smartness or cleverness, but common sense—and these virtues would triumph in the long run. Babson read off a list of eleven villains, which I will come back to in a moment. I picked him up on a statement: Was this terrible market due to the professionals?

"Of course," he said. "Nobody else. The professionals, people who ought to know how to manage investments, got sucked into speculation."

"What do you think we ought to do about this?" I asked.

Babson looked over his glasses at the audience.

"Some of you should leave this business," he said.

There was nervous laughter. I asked him if he had anybody in mind.

"Some of them have offices near here," he said.

I said I didn't know anybody with an office near here.

"Some of them are sitting quite close," he said. "When a prospect for a new account asks how much growth he can expect, and we tell him ten percent, and he says somebody else has promised him twenty percent a year, we ask him which Fred promised him that."

By sheer coincidence, there were some very well-known aggressive portfolio managers named Fred. We had one, by another coincidence, sitting with us. (Later, each of the Freds was to express resentment at having been lumped in with the other Freds.)

"Too many Freds," I heard Babson mutter, and then he said, "Should a manager who put Parvin Dohrmann into a client's account be allowed to advise anyone again?" Parvin Dohrmann had gone from 142 to 14.

"I have a list here," Babson said. He pulled it out and began to read.

"Four Seasons Nursing Homes," he said. "The high was ninety-one and the low is bankrupt. Anybody that went to bed with Four Seasons—"

"David," I said gently into the microphone. The audience was beginning to rustle. You can tell something has happened to the good feelings when the water pitchers start to clink nervously against the water glasses in a rising cacophony.

"Commonwealth United," he said. "The high was twenty-five and the current price is one. Susquehanna, the high was eighty and the current price is seven. Unexcelled, the high was sixty-eight and the current price is four. All great institutional favorites."

"Don't read the list," I said.

The audience was beginning to scrape its chairs. My massive group therapy session had taken a sour turn. Nobody was going to confess if they were being accused.

"Computers," Babson said. "Management Assistance, forty-six to two. Levin-Townsend, sixty-eight to three."

"David," I said.

"Leasco Data Processing, fifty-seven to nine. Data Processing and Financial General, ninety-two to eight."

"David," I said, "you have passed the pain threshold of the audience."

He stopped. The audience was absolutely silent. Well, I remember thinking, maybe catharsis was the wrong idea anyway. Maybe Sinners in the Hands of an Angry God is more appropriate.

"Thank you, Jonathan Edwards," I said.

Babson did not get a standing ovation.

We had questions from the audience. There was one rather plaintive one for Babson, which showed that my original idea had at least taken hold.

"Isn't there just *one mistake* of yours that you could point to?" the questioner asked Babson.

That got the applause.

Babson said he could find a few if he dug hard, but no serious ones. Babson's own fund had taken seven years to double when others were doing that in months, but it had held its ground while the others melted away.

"My host asked me what my strategy is," he said. "It is the same this year as for any year. To try to use our common sense."

I asked all my other winners whether the game was coming back. They all said that sooner or later it was. Except Babson.

"No greater period of skulduggery in American financial history exists than 1967 to 1969," he said. "It has burned this generation like 1929 did another one, and it will be a long, long time before it happens again."

"The day I went to work in 1932," Babson said later, "steel mills were running at eight percent of capacity. I remember days when the trading was so slow people played ball on the floor of the exchange. The ticker didn't move at all, and then Armour crossed at $4 a share.

"After the war, I pushed growth stocks when today's performance managers were in their playpens. The Census Bureau predicted the U.S. population would be a hundred and sixty-five million—in 1990! I was a radical then, and maybe I'm a curmudgeon now—times change, the economy changes—but another group has to grow up out of the playpens and the scars have to heal before you do it all again."

I said that was pretty optimistic.

"Maybe so, but common sense will go a long way to help."

Here is Babson's list of villains:

1) The conglomerate movement, "with all its fancy rhetoric about synergism and leverage."
2) Accountants who played footsie with stock-promoting managements by certifying earnings that weren't earnings at all.
3) "Modern" corporate treasurers who looked upon their company pension funds as new-found profit centers and pressured their investment advisers into speculating with them.
4) Investment advisers who massacred clients' portfolios because they were trying to make good on the over-promises that they had made to attract the business.
5) The new breed of investment managers who bought and churned the worst collection of new issues and other junk in history, and the underwriters who made fortunes bringing them out.
6) Elements of the financial press which promoted into new investment geniuses a group of neophytes who didn't even have the first requisite for managing other people's money—namely, a sense of responsibility.
7) The securities salesmen who peddle the items with the best stories—or the biggest markups—even though such issues were totally unsuited to the customers' needs.
8) The sanctimonious partners of major investment

houses who wrung their hands over all these shame-
less happenings while they deployed an army of
untrained salesmen to forage among even less trained
investors.

9) Mutual fund managers who tried to become million-
aires overnight by using every gimmick imaginable to
manufacture their own paper performance.

10) Portfolio managers who collected bonanza incentives
of the "heads I win, tails you lose" kind, which made
them fortunes in the bull market but turned the portfolios they managed into disasters in the bear market.

11) Security analysts who forgot about their professional
ethics to become storytellers and let their institutions
be taken in by a whole parade of confidence men.

This was the "list of horrors that people in our field did
to set the stage for the greatest blood bath in forty years,"
Babson said. The doctor in Pocatello, Idaho, did not by
himself think up the idea of buying Liquidonics and
Minnie Pearl, and the man on Main Street didn't decide
on his own hook to buy "a new El Dorado mutual fund
which has since flushed half its assets down the drain."

Well, that is a handsome list of villains. I have the feeling that in Babson's part of New England the stocks they
put you into for not having common sense are the wooden
ones down on the village green that are very uncomfortable
for the hands and feet. In retrospect, there is nothing
wrong with Babson's list except that the villains do overlap
and the excesses are seen as totally within the industry.
There were, as we have seen, some macro-villains that also
helped to set the stage: there was the unpaid-for Vietnam
war with the concomitant inflation, and those responsible
for that; and there was the antiquated structure of the
securities industry, and those responsible for that. Four
of Babson's eleven villains were investment managers

guilty of one sin or another, and three were people in other roles in the securities industry proper—partners, analysts, salesmen—who ignored their professional responsibilities.

I brought Babson's list in here to show that there was a lot of finger-pointing within the industry, and that if you have a secret hurt, so did a lot of the professional managers. If you bought an "El Dorado mutual fund," you may have hurt right along with those managers.

Which brings up a pertinent point: suppose that all this business about the Federal Reserve and the market and the swings makes you too nervous. Suppose you want to leave it all to the pros. You go to your bank and let them manage the money. Or you buy a mutual fund. How would you have done? (For, after all, it should be pointed out that many funds were not "El Dorado" funds, and that the vast majority of American securities by market capitalization were not promotions but mature American companies. They may not have produced gains for their investors, but that may be due to other reasons having more to do with their own basic natures and the broader market forces.)

A simplistic answer has to precede the statistical one. If you bought a mutual fund that went up, you did well. There were such funds. If you bought one that went down, you did badly. There were such funds, too. And there were banks that made money for people, and banks that lost money for people, and investment counselors that did the same. This point is brought up for a very obvious reason: you have to do something with the money, and just because you invest it does not mean you have to be the median or the average. Somebody has to be first and somebody has to be last, and one hopes to be closer to the former than the latter.

Now to the sources. They are familiar to those in the industry that care about such things, and they include the obvious: *The Institutional Investor Study Report of the Securities and Exchange Commission,* especially Volume 2; *The Comptroller's Staff Reports* from the Office of the Comptroller of the Currency; *Bank Trusts: Investments and Performance*; and the work done by several academic institutions, notably the Wharton School of Finance at the University of Pennsylvania. From the latter came the best-known statistical job: sponsored by the Twentieth Century Fund, it is published as *Mutual Funds and Other Institutional Investors,* by Irwin Friend, Marshall Blume and Jean Crockett. In addition, there are a number of academic papers, usually heavy in mathematics and statistics, published in such professional journals as the *American Economic Review,* the papers of the American Statistical Association, and so on. And you can take your own samples from the Lipper computer runs of funds, since those have been done and the Weisenberger statistics from the mechanical age. For various reasons, I have had to go through much of this material as it came out, and I have talked, though not extensively, to the authors.

This battery of citations is a defensive measure, for—as you might have guessed—the news is not so good, and some very well-paid manager might just come up to me in the shuttle line at the airport and swing if we say that managed funds with well-paid managers do about the same as a totally random portfolio. For that is what the statistics say, and we are back with our old friends from the freshman course, the random walkers. Here is a key sentence from the Wharton study led by Irwin Friend:

Virtually all the published government and academic studies have indicated that the investment performance of mutual funds in the aggregate is not very different from that of the stock market as a whole.

The Wharton study compared the mutual funds with random portfolios in New York Stock Exchange stocks:

> Mutual funds as a whole in 1960–68 seemed to perform worse than equally distributed random investments in New York Stock Exchange stock, but, except for low-risk portfolios, did better than proportionally distributed random investments.

It isn't necessary to go into the comparisons with the funds here—whether the random portfolios were weighted or unweighted (the Wharton people tried both) and the so-called beta coefficients, or degrees of volatility, in the portfolios. For some of the period of the Wharton study, the higher-risk funds—those so asperically charged by Babson—helped the overall performance of the fund industry, because the Wharton study ended in September 1969, before those funds took their biggest bath, and a horseback guess would be that by factoring that in now, you would once again come out about even. These statistics do not count the sales commission of the fund (if it has one), so if you pay that, you have to start that much further behind.

In other words, a random portfolio is just as good as the average mutual fund. Chicago's Harris Trust tried another way: comparing the funds with the Dow Jones average and the Standard & Poor's 500 stock average, for the twenty-five years ending in 1970. For half of that time, the median common-stock fund came in last, behind the averages. "There is no evidence," says Professor Friend, "that any group of funds can beat the averages."

Of course, you cannot buy a statistically random portfolio, even though your portfolio may have a very random look about it. And you cannot really buy the Dow Jones average or the Standard & Poor. If you are going to buy a fund—or the equivalent slice in a bank-managed common trust—you have to buy that, and you hope that your fund or your bank is at the top of the list, helping the team against the randoms, and not at the bottom.

There is at least one other important point in the Wharton study from the potential fund investor's point of view. Adjusted for risk, the performance correlation in funds between one time period and another is zero. Professor Friend's words, expressed also in the study: "There may be no consistency in the performance of the same fund in successive periods."

In other words, a fund that performed well in 1966 and 1967 may not perform well in 1969 and 1970.

This is important, because many new investors came to buy funds for the first time, or were sold them, within the last five or six years. The funds that took in the most money the fastest from investors were those that had the hottest records for a short period of time previously. The investors who in 1967 and 1968 bought funds that had shown big increases in the year or two previous did unusually badly, worse than they had any statistical right to expect. Gerry Tsai's Manhattan Fund, up 39 percent in 1967, went down 6.9 percent in 1968, 10.15 percent in 1969, and 36.80 percent in 1970. The Gibraltar Growth Fund, ranked third in 1968, ranked 481st in 1971; it threw in the towel and was taken over by the Dreyfus organization. Insurance Investors Fund, ranked fourth in 1968, ranked 317th in 1971. The Mates Fund, ranked first on some lists in a disputed finish in 1968, ranked 512th out of 526 funds in 1971. (Statistics by Arthur Lipper Corporation)

The conclusions seem obvious. If you want to buy a fund, buy it, do not be sold it. There are magazines and publications—*Forbes* among them—which rank mutual funds over a period of years in all kinds of markets. You do need more than a year or two to judge a record. There are funds, and fund-management organizations, that have performed well for their investors over many years, consistently, in good markets and bad. And there are independent investment counselors who have done even better. It does take some investigation, however, a small enough price to pay.

As a group, the professionals did not have a very good time through what happened. Some of them even suffered personally, which is to say that they checked out.

CAUTIONARY TALES

3:

REMEMBER THESE, O BROTHERS, IN YOUR NEW HOURS OF TRIUMPH

USUALLY it is the customers who suffer more. That is the point of the very old story about the visitor being taken around the waterfront, and having the yachts pointed out—That is Morgan's yacht, that is Gould's yacht, and so on—and the customer says, "But where are the customers' yachts?" The brokers make as much money selling for customers as buying for customers, the reasoning goes, so it doesn't matter.

That was not always the case this time. The customers could get busted right to zero, but some of the brokers managed to make it well below zero.

The two incidents I felt most personally among the casualty lists did not involve brokers; I just don't know many brokers. Of the broker's misfortunes in a moment.

One summer night I had a drink with a gentleman who was on his way back to Texas, from which place he had sprung with a reputation for open-handed daring. For a brief period he was well known, and he had been in one of our seminars, a happy new millionaire. Now the hedge fund he was running seemed to have evaporated, and rather than hang around New York he decided he had better get his toes back in the good ol' Texas dirt and see if he could find himself again. We talked about some of the things that had gone on, and he looked at his watch. He said he'd better be off to the bus terminal. *The bus terminal?* I have nothing against buses, but that is a *long* bus trip, and I offered to lend him $41.05, the difference between the air coach fare and the bus fare. He turned it down. "I don't know when I could pay it back," he said. "Anyway, it's a good way to see the country."

Shortly afterward, I got a call from another gentleman I had met once but did not know. Could he speak to me confidentially? He could. Had I heard what happened to his firm? I gathered it was busted. It was, he said, and so was he, and he was selling his wine cellar. He knew I was interested in wines, so naturally he thought of me.

A wine collection can be just as valuable an asset as a stamp collection or a spoon collection or what-have-you. Somebody who has paid attention to his wines not only has vintages that have appreciated, but has those that can't be found anywhere on the open market. They have all been bought and many of them have been drunk, so they are unobtainable at any price. I listened intently, pencil in hand. I expected him to say he had, say, three cases of that, a prize case of something else.

"I have four bottles of La Tâche 1962," he said.

"Four cases of La Tâche," I repeated. "Very good. What do you want for those?"

"Not four cases," he said. "Four bottles. I want thirty dollars a bottle. Well worth it."

"Go on," I said.

"I have three bottles of Chambertin-Clos de Bèze 1964."

I began to get very depressed.

"Tell me the cases," I said.

"I don't actually have cases," he said. "Of course, I could put twelve bottles into the same box and make up a mixed case."

He read me the rest of the list. All excellent wines, obviously picked with great care over several years. But they were individual bottles.

"Listen," I said, "that's a very nice collection. But even pricing it generously, your whole cellar is only worth about six hundred."

"Make it six-fifty and it's yours," he said.

"You just can't be that broke," I said. "In Texas a man can only be busted down to his house and his horse. There must be something in some statute in this part of the country that says a man can only be busted down to his last twenty bottles."

"I owe the money," he said. "Do you want it or not? I may have other buyers."

"If I was ever busted down to my last six-fifty," I said, "and they came for my wines, the day before I would go down in the cellar and pull the corks and have a festival they would talk about for fifty years."

In fact, I proposed just that: I would bring a large Brie, some splendid French bread and a corkscrew, and we would invite a convivial group, charge admission at the door, and do justice to the last remaining assets.

That idea didn't sell. A buyer came along who bid up—$730, I believe—and the wine collector watched his bottles depart one by one.

"What do you do all day?"

I asked this of Dan, who had run both institutional accounts and an in-house fund at a leading institutional brokerage house. Dan's background was impeccable:

Princeton and the Harvard Business School. He had been at the firm about seven years, and as of the Big Bear, was in his late thirties. His portfolios had been volatile, to say the least; some of them had performed quite spectacularly earlier in the decade, but he had paid the price for the volatility in more recent markets. His personal account showed the streak of a true gambler: stocks were rarely leveraged enough (that is, the profits didn't move fast enough unless he borrowed and bought more); usually he was into calls and sometimes into commodities. While he was a partner, or stockholder, in the firm, it was decided—"mutually," he said—that they should part company.

"It was very pleasant at first," he said. "The only time I'd ever had off from working was vacations, timed to benefit the kids, and so on. Now I picked them up at school every day and helped with the marketing. I decided that with Wall Street in a convulsion and contraction this was no time to go looking for another job. I read *The New York Times* every day. I mean I *read* it. I used to spend ten minutes with the papers. I found I could spend three hours with the *Times* alone. I didn't tell very many people I'd left—I didn't think that would help.

"Then it was summer and I went to the park with the kids every day. Summer is vacation time, and people don't know whether your vacation is in June, July or August. So they just assumed I was on vacation.

"I went to one or two job interviews, but it was plain that going to work at that moment would not be advantageous. I never knew whether I would have gotten those jobs, but I think I would have had a good chance. But they wanted me to relocate—one to Hartford, one to Toronto. I wasn't ready to do that. Furthermore, I began to ask myself what I wanted to do for the rest of my life. Maybe I'd had enough of the financial world. Maybe I'd go into government.

"Fall was a bit rougher. The kids went back to school, and obviously I couldn't go sit in the park any more. I went on a couple more interviews that didn't promise much."

I asked Dan what he was living on at the time. He said he gradually sold off some of his stocks, and he had sold the stock of the firm in which he had worked. He made a few turns in the market. I asked Dan's wife how she liked having him around all the time.

"At first I liked it a lot," she said, "and even on balance I liked it. If your husband has been working long hours in an absorbing job, with some travel, it's nice to have him around for lunch and to help with the marketing and to get to know his children. But he did get discouraged from time to time, and then I really had to be careful with him. He could have real flashes of depression and anger. Don't ever cross him on *The New York Times,* by the way. He knows everything in that paper."

Eventually, which is to say about sixteen months after he and his job had parted company, Dan became a financial consultant to a governmental agency. He had decided not to go back to Wall Street.

"That whole place," he said, "is just devoted to making a lot of money. And I wanted to make more than anybody, really to pile it up. You don't need all that much. What was all that about, anyway?"

It was, as I said, some of the brokers who managed to make it well below zero. The only way their customers could have gone more broke than that would have been to borrow more than was legally available. The principle was very simple. A gentleman would go to work for a firm and, his eye on the golden apple, strive for years to become a partner. He would work late, take out-of-towners to the hockey games, land accounts, put a syndicate together, or whatever one had to do to become a partner in his particular area. Then one day the partners would come to him and say, Rodney, you've made it, you can have fresh orange juice on a silver tray at eleven every morning.

There would be some legal mechanics. If the firm was worth $10 million and they had decided to make Rodney a 1 percent partner, then he would be expected to put up $100,000. He could then start earning a very handsome share of the partnership. Of course, if he didn't have the $100,000, the partnership would lend it to him. Sort of a fringe benefit.

In the recent unpleasantness, firms that got into serious trouble often asked their partners to put up more money. Or various other lenders were called in, and their money would have to be repaid before the partners had a partnership. If the whole effort failed, the firm might be merged away on very unfavorable terms, such as $1.50 per desk, 75¢ per chair, and zip for the partners. The trouble is, that $100,000 loan would still be listed as a personal liability for Rodney. In the old days, he would have gone to debtors' prison or to Australia.

One unlucky gentleman to whom I was introduced had worked for years at a distinguished firm. But his efforts were not rewarded with that golden apple of partnership, and he got another offer, this time a partnership at Goodbody & Company. Goodbody quite happily loaned him the partnership money, and for a year or two he reaped the handsome rewards that Wall Street partners reap. Then, as we have seen, Goodbody got deeper and deeper into trouble, and finally, with numerous midwives and witch doctors attending, Goodbody got merged into Merrill Lynch at $1.50 per desk, and let us say quickly that everybody breathed very hard on Merrill to do it since Goodbody was so large there was practically no one else that could swallow them. Our gentleman found himself without a job—he did get another one—but along with him went that loan he had signed. "My life is very simple," he said. "I am fifty-four years old, I have three children in school and college, I have a job, no assets, and I owe five hundred and forty-five thousand dollars."

The way this works can be illustrated with the story of a man we shall call Phil. Phil was in research, and at forty-five, he was making $75,000 a year at one of the leading retail brokerage firms. Phil did well and they offered him a partnership. To buy the partnership, Phil put up $6,000 —Phil did not come from a moneyed family—and the firm loaned him $30,000. The firm at that time had a capital account of $4 million. The only problem was that the liabilities of the firm seemed to increase geometrically. The figures showed that the partnership was deeper and deeper in the red, and so was Phil.

"I had an East Side apartment and three kids in school, boarding school," Phil said. "In February or March of 1970 the senior controller showed me the real figures, which even the senior partners weren't up on. In fact, as the firm started to go, we began to get monthly financial statements that broke down the loss per partner and said at the bottom, *Please remit,* or something like that."

Phil tried to get out of his contract. "You couldn't get a lawyer on Wall Street in those days," he said. "They were all afraid of retribution. I finally got a kid I knew on the *Harvard Law Review*—not even a lawyer—but there was nothing I could do. I owed the firm three hundred and fifty thousand dollars. It was just too ridiculous to think about. I mean I thought about it, I still think about it; I couldn't pay them a thousand, much less three hundred and fifty thousand."

The firm went busted—it was reorganized, let us say—

and Phil found himself on the sidewalk for the first time in his life.

"You go through various psychological things when you've been laid off. You begin to doubt your ability. All sorts of things. Even at that, I was luckier than some. There was one partner who had inherited his money. He had put up all the money as a subordinated lender to the firm, and he had made a handsome return out of it, playing golf with the president. He lived in a big house, owned chauffeured limousines, had never thought about money a day in his life. His wife is sixty-two years old and she just went to work. *How can a man like that start wearing Thom McAn shoes?*

"I job-hunted for a while. My bank account was down to eighty dollars, my wife divorced me—she was going to do that anyway—and I started on marrying my second wife. Then I broke my hip moving furniture for her. It was really pretty depressing. It's not that your friends desert you, it's that they don't know what to do with you. When you're back, they call, but while you're out, they don't call, and you don't call them because you don't want to put them in an awkward position. There was one job I really wanted, and when I was turned down, it really toppled me. I think the guy who interviewed me was really interested. Then he asked the opinion of a senior man and the senior man said, Nah, he's a has-been. Or maybe he said shopworn. Even now, when I hear the expression 'has-been' or 'shopworn,' I cringe."

Phil got a job with another firm, I would think somewhere in the $15,000 to $20,000 range. He still has his $350,000 debt, but he doesn't think about it quite so much any more. "I'll tell you one thing," he said. "It's like having to pay a percentage of your income as alimony. It cuts down on your ambitions."

The Great Winfield is on the casualty list even though he retired with a considerable fortune. Winfield went to Wall Street in cowboy boots and jeans, had his own firm, and made a reputation as a tape-trader, which is to say he watched stock symbols dancing across the screen, bought those that danced well, sold those that did not dance well, and so on. He also sometimes promoted companies of dubious virtue, and once he got me involved in a cocoa scheme that I reported on some years ago.

I thought Winfield should be on the casualty list because without his firm and his audience he no longer had quite the same aura, and because I sent him an account which went down 90 percent, a notable score even for those years. Winfield had gone all the way up in Leasco, but his accounts also went from 67 to 11 in that stock, and then he found a company in Brooklyn that rebuilt old air conditioners. Somehow it got rechristened Atmospheric and Pollution Controls—did it not, after all, cleanse the atmosphere and control pollution, roomwise?—but the stock went from 26 to 6. Many years ago, Winfield had bought a ranch in Aspen, Colorado, because he liked to ski and he liked the West, and now the ranch's borders were sprinkled with condominia—just his luck. He had a hot hand in good years, but it was gone, and according to him, so was the business.

"It was a great business for a while, but it's over. Over, over. The government, the SEC, they've ruined it. There won't even be any more characters like me."

In his heyday, the Great Winfield was noted for his bubbly confidence. "This is a stock," he would say, "that is going from ten to two hundred." Solitron Devices had done just that; the new one would be backed with the same conviction. In the Great Winfield's philosophy, what one should do in the market was to find a Kid with a Hot Hand, one who really *needed* to win, and let him find the stocks that would go up ten times in a year. That was what he liked: ten times in a year.

I saw the Great Winfield once after he had left his firm. He was now, at forty-seven, a graduate student in art history at Columbia. He had a Pan American stewardess—he was always partial to Pan American. I picked up the list on his desk.

Columbia Gas
Virginia Electric Power
Texas Utilities
Southern California Edison
Southern Company
American Electric Power
South Carolina Electric and Gas

"What the hell is this?" I said. *"Utilities?"*

"That's my portfolio," he said.

"The Great Winfield in *utilities?"*

"Don't laugh. That portfolio is going to double in only twenty years. Maybe fifteen. Riskless. A sure thing."

"You used to have stock that doubled in a week."

"Things change, m'boy, things change. We have to recognize them when they do."

On a trip, I stopped by the office of Irwin the Professor, the master architect of computer-based technical analysis. Irwin's professing included computer applications, management sciences and some advanced mathematics, but he spent more time with his own companies than he did with his students. Irwin's companies have names in their titles like "computer," "decision," "application," "technology," and so on, and he works in a new office building about three blocks from the university. Irwin's computers monitored stocks: the price, the volume, the percentage move. Then they determined the stock's Behavior Pattern. Once the computer knew the stock's Behavior Pattern, it knew when to buy and sell—the ultimate in technical analysis and charting.

Irwin's computer had certain anthropomorphic qualities.

"When we first put the computer on the air," he said, "we asked it what it wanted to buy and we couldn't wait to see what it reached for. It said, 'Treasury bills. Cash.' We couldn't get it to buy anything. So we checked out the program again, and while we were checking it out, the market went down. Then we asked it again. The computer insisted on staying in cash. We begged it to buy something. 'There must be *one* stock somewhere that's a buy,' we said. You see, even computer people are victims of these old atavistic instincts from the pre-computer days. The computer just folded its arms. It wouldn't buy anything. Then, just when we were worried that it never would buy anything, right at the bottom it stepped in and started buying. The market started going up, and the computer kept on buying. Then one day it came *and asked us for margin*. It wanted to keep buying. So we gave it some margin. After the market went up some more, it sold out a bit and came back to being fully invested."

A brokerage firm had signed up Irwin's computer and was selling the service to customers. On my trip, I asked Irwin how the computer portfolio had done. Irwin said it had gone down 30 percent in the bear market, and that the broker had canceled the service. Another casualty. I asked what had gone wrong with the computer.

"Nothing," Irwin said. "Nothing was wrong with the computer. It was the *people* we had tending it. They kept interfering. They made interim judgments. They couldn't leave the program alone. It's *people* that are the problem. The computer couldn't have lost thirty percent by itself. The computer was fine."

I asked Irwin what he was up to now. He said the computer program was being refined. He was tinkering with it all the time. Meanwhile, his other computer programs for industry were doing all right. Of course, Wall Street was not too flush, so Irwin didn't know when another brokerage firm would spring for wiring up his computer.

"But we're running it on our own," he said, "and the computer is doing very, very well. It is outperforming the market. And our system is getting better every day. It is almost people-proof. It really wasn't the computer's fault, those losses. The computer will be back, you'll see. You can't turn back the tides of history."

Seymour the Head has to go on the casualty list for losing $10 million, but he says that does not make him unhappy. That is because Seymour is following the Way, and money is only a chimera anyway.

I met Seymour in the mountains of Mexico. He was the talk of Cuernavaca, or at least of the endowed Americans of Cuernavaca. They were sure he was a fraud or a con man or at least some superior kind of nut. He said he had been a respectable Los Angeles lawyer, but that he had quit that; he *claimed*, they said, to have bought and sold $300 million worth of stock the previous year; he *claimed* to have made $15 million and to be the biggest individual trader on the New York Stock Exchange, all the while operating long distance from Mexico and the Bahamas and Nepal, where he owned a monastery.

"If Seymour likes you," said the friends, "you get the ultimate gift. Seymour has a hundred lamas from his monastery say prayers for you for one hour."

So they trotted me along to meet Seymour, to unmask the impostor, to expose the fraud, because how could this character with the wild gleam—his hair down to his shoulder blades, wearing a jump suit and no socks—how could this character be anything he said? A hippie speculator? An acid-head arbitrager?

It was all true, of course, a little hard to take because of
the manic gleam and the long, stringy hair and the sandals,
but there I was, the Berenson of the Mountains, and
Seymour was real, formerly a respectable Los Angeles
lawyer with a respectable wife and child, who discovered
arbitrage, mind-blowing chemicals and a new life style all
at the same time. Goodbye, law practice; goodbye, wife
and child; goodbye, socks and ties. If Seymour went to a
directors' meeting in New York—for Seymour was on several boards—a secretary would pull out some socks kept
specifically for him; Seymour would put them on for the
directors' meeting and take them off afterward, returning
them to the drawer. That was the extent of his compro-
mise. He was not going to live a materialistic life; he was
going to feel Beautiful and do good things and help people, meanwhile playing the arbitrage game to finance it all.
David the Bond Man at TPO, Inc., and the traders at Bear
Stearns learned to answer the phone any time of day or
night, and if it was a character sounding slightly stoned
calling from Nepal, *take the order*.

So Seymour borrowed $100 million, all from banks, mar-
ried the most beautiful and serene Chinese girl you have
ever seen, and sought Inner Peace. We went to lunch at
Seymour's rented mansion in Mexico and had a Wonderful
Chocolate Cake for lunch, a Cake to Help Peace and
Understanding and Bring Love, and with Seymour giggling
wildly, like a Renaissance prince watching his palace visitors get tipsy, the guests ate the chocolate cake, and we got
back from the Tuesday lunch Wednesday night—Sara Lee
should have that recipe, it does something to your sense
of time. Seymour said the experience was Beautiful, and
we had such a good time that he had his hundred lamas
in Nepal say *two* hours of prayers for me, which had no
noticeable effect on my portfolios.

There is supposed to be minimal risk in arbitrage,

because you are buying and selling the same thing, only at different times or different places. If company A and company B are going to merge, and B sells slightly higher, you could buy A and sell B, all with borrowed money to make the effort worthwhile. The only risk is that it doesn't come off quite right, and that is what happened to Seymour in a very big arbitrage. Seymour dropped about $10 million, but his life style did not change one whit; he never wrote checks or paid bills anyway—his brokers did that for him. Seymour said he had been too rich anyway, and stayed quite cheerful. He had put the initial money up for a vaginal douche called Cupid's Quiver. There are vaginal douches and vaginal douches; apparently this one was the first with *flavors*: strawberry, raspberry, champagne and so on. The chic ladies' magazines took the ads for it, McKesson and Robbins took over the franchise, and Seymour was above water again.

Seymour said that the same group had made an unsuccessful attempt in trying to market a flavored jelly for homosexuals; I never knew whether to believe him, but in his new incarnation Seymour didn't believe in lying. He still sponsors an ashram in Arizona, and the monks must still be praying for him in Nepal because I saw him once in the south of France, wearing a pair of dirty white pants and carrying a hairbrush and some Tibetan art the monks had shipped him. He said he had just gotten off a plane, and that was all his luggage—the hairbrush and the Tibetan art—because he wanted to be a free spirit. He never made plans and would never commit himself for more than twenty-four hours, because he wanted to live in the *moment*, in the Now, and go where he wanted when he wanted. We went to look at a villa for rent that used to belong to Mrs. Heinz, the ketchup one. Then he made two very-long-distance telephone calls and disappeared again.

We heard later that he had gone to Montreal to borrow

some money—$10 million or so—to buy some bonds, as usual carrying his hairbrush and nothing so soiling as currency. Seymour borrowed the money, then realized he could not even get back to the airport, so he asked the banker for an additional $100 for cab fare. Then we heard he was trying to start an astrology fund, with none of the usual stuff about "this mutual fund specializes in growth situations"; the managers would all be picked and would operate by the signs under which they were born. Six months later I got a call early in the morning from Seymour: he had an arbitrage scheme so complicated it would result in a perpetual tax loss, but when your Curaçao corporation received the loan from your Bahamian corporation, you wrote off the loan from your Panamanian corporation and got the money back. I said I couldn't follow it. Seymour said that was all right, he would call some other time; right now he was going to Ecuador to look at some pre-Columbian art, and he did.

There is a final character on the casualty list, and that is me. A man has to be part of the actions and passions of his time. right? The path he chooses does not matter. Having done that stuff about the Black Horsemen, I was not about to buy for myself any fried-chicken stands, chains of nursing homes, fancy conglomerates, the so-called gambling industry or National Student Marketing. I saw it all coming—yes, sir—and I bought the safest stock anybody could buy. I bought a Swiss bank.

4:

HOW MY SWISS BANK BLEW $40 MILLION AND WENT BROKE

IN early September of that bad year, 1970, I was riding into New York on one of the Penn Central's surviving trains when a story in *The Wall Street Journal* caused some hot flashes and palpitations. Nothing alarming; in 1970 it was impossible to read *The Wall Street Journal* without having hot flashes and palpitations. This story was not even on the front page, and I am sure was passed over by many of the newspaper's readers. UNITED CALIFORNIA BANK, read the headline, SAYS SWISS UNIT INCURRED LOSSES THAT MAY HIT $30 MILLION. Swiss unit? United California Bank? That was *my* bank!

I don't mean it was my bank in the sense that the Bank of New York is my bank because I have a checking account there, or that people have a friend at the Chase Manhattan because that is where they owe the payments. I mean *it was my bank because I owned it.* There was no public stock in this bank; it was the biggest, solidest and safest investment I had ever made. A lockup, as they say. And only months after I bought this hunk of the bank, my judgment seemed to be confirmed. The majority interest was bought by the great United California Bank of Los Angeles, one of the fifteen largest in the United States, second largest bank on the West Coast, itself the flagship bank of Western Bancorporation, *the largest bank holding company in the world.* Big brother.

> Clifford Tweter, senior vice-chairman of United California and president of its parent, Western Bancorporation, last night declined to explain how the loss occurred. He said he hoped to be able to provide more data once an audit at the Swiss bank is completed. That would be within the next few days, he added. "We think we should speak in general terms at this time," Mr. Tweter said.
>
> The troubled institution, United California Bank in Basel, is 58% controlled by United California Bank . . . the other 42% is held "by a variety of investors, mostly individuals," Mr. Tweter said.

It was a good year when I bought into my Swiss bank. I had a popular book on all the best-seller lists. Now you take the average American male who has a fat year or a windfall, and there are a lot of ways to spend the money in tune with fantasyland. He could buy a beautiful sloop (not to mention yawl, ketch and cutter) and cruise around the world. He could get fitted for a Purdy in London or a Wesley Richards .375 and go shoot an elephant in Kenya while they are thinning out the herds. He could buy a pro football team—or at least part of one—and buy and sell 280-pound tackles, and have a modest little speech prepared when the television cameras roll into the locker room amidst the victory whoops, the champagne and the wet towels. Not me. I had to buy a Swiss bank. Overexposure to early Eric Ambler, I guess, when if you really wanted to know what was going on, you certainly didn't watch the newspaper headlines because they didn't tell you anything; you watched the rise of the dinar and the fall of the drachma, and those barely perceptible flutters told you that Peter Lorre and Sidney Greenstreet were in a compartment on the Orient Express on their way to Istanbul. They were looking for Demetrius, and you remember the trail led right back to Switzerland, good old Switzerland, where the master spy was in his château playing a Bach fugue on his magnificent organ.

So it wasn't all safety and solidity that attracted me, though what could be safer than a Swiss bank? It was a hedge against the troubles of the dollar, and a friendly place to call upon in Europe, and the prospects of a lot of fun, and maybe even a very good investment to boot. The United California Bank of Los Angeles didn't buy into the bank because of Eric Ambler. American business was expanding in Europe. There was big merchant banking to be done. American banks were expanding in Europe—opening branches, chartering banks. Dollars had piled up overseas and there was a big business in Eurodollars. American banks sought to start banks in Europe, but that was hard, and took time; if they could buy one, that would put them right in the middle of the action. We junior partners were delighted when the United California Bank took over; obviously our bank was to be part of the big expansion in Europe. We were in for a great ride.

When I got to my office that September day the story came out, I dialed 061 35 94 50, the number of the bank's office in Basel. I remember that I was worried but not stricken. No one likes to see his biggest investment have a bad year. But with the great United California Bank as a senior partner, could anything really go seriously wrong? It was like owning a great ship in partnership with Cunard. The *Titanic* is unsinkable. If you hear that it has had a little brush with an iceberg, you are annoyed that maybe some paint has been scraped off and now the damn thing is going to need a new paint job when it gets to New York.

After only a few moments, 061 35 94 50 answered, but the bank's office seemed to be in some confusion. I asked for Paul Erdman, the thirty-eight-year-old American president of the bank. Previous calls had gone right through, the voices across the Atlantic sounding clearer than a local call. Both Paul Erdman and his secretary seemed not to be there. There was some chattering in German on the other end.

Finally a male voice said, "Mr. Erdman is not here. He is not with the bank any more."

Since when? I wanted to know.

"Since yesterday," the voice said. I asked where I could reach Erdman, and the voice said to try him at his home in Basel, which I did. Erdman sounded cheerful as usual.

"I've resigned," he said. "But I'm staying on as a consultant. There's a bit of a mess. Maybe you heard."

I told him I had just read about it, and what exactly was the problem?

"There's a shortfall in the trading account of thirty million dollars."

Thirty million dollars?

Unlike American banks, Swiss banks act also as brokers, and can trade for their own accounts. The assets of our bank were reported to be $69 million at the end of 1969, but of course there were liabilities against those assets. The capital of the bank was less than $9 million. A loss of $30 million would have busted not only our bank but two more the same size, except for our giant parent. I brought this up.

"UCB will keep the bank open," Erdman said. "They have to—their reputation would be damaged if they closed it."

Where is the thirty million dollars? I wanted to know.

"It's lost," Erdman said. "We lost it trading. A commodities trader lost it."

"Listen," I said. "I have seen guys lose one million dollars. Two millions dollars, even. But there is *just no way to lose thirty million dollars.* No way."

"Well, it's lost," Erdman said. "The UCB will make it up. You're going to suffer some dilution. But the bank will go on."

"How come you resigned?" I asked.

"The buck has to stop somewhere, and I was in charge," he said.

At that point I began to feel some sympathy for Erdman. For me the bank was an investment: for him it was a personal creation, something he had spent years building up. I said, "This must be tough."

"I'm all right," he said. "I'll be at the bank tomorrow, helping to clean up the mess."

But he wasn't. Shortly thereafter, the Basel police picked Erdman up, as they did all the directors of the bank who were in Switzerland. The two directors they did not pick up were the chairman of the board, Frank King, who was also the chairman of the United California Bank in Los Angeles and, in fact, of the Western Bancorporation, and Victor Rose, a vice-president of the Los Angeles bank. Both of them were in Los Angeles. It seemed somehow very Swiss to put the board of a bank in jail. I never heard of it happening here.

Erdman was to spend ten months in the Basel prison, much of it in solitary confinement. Habeas corpus is an Anglo-Saxon institution. In Switzerland they can keep you in jail as long as they see fit, for investigation. The Swiss say it's very efficient.

I called Erdman's house a few days later, and talked to Erdman's attractive blond wife, Helly.

"It's like a nightmare," Helly said. "No one will speak to me. They won't let me talk to Paul. I am afraid the house is being watched. It's like a bad criminal show on TV."

How could they simply hold someone without a charge?

"This is not the United States," Helly said. "There is a long phrase, *Verdacht der ungetreuen Geschäftsführung.* I don't know how to translate it." Helly was a native-born Baseler, but she spoke good English. "I think," she said, "it means *Suspicion of Crimes Against a Bank.*"

I couldn't think of anything like that in English.

"There isn't," she said. "In Switzerland this is very serious. More serious than murder."

That, incidentally, is true. Long jail sentences do not meet the Swiss standard of justice. There is a gentleman at this moment in the Basel jail who caved in his wife's skull with a blunt instrument. She was a nagging wife, he said, and she liked to boss him around. One day he had had all he could stand, and he dispatched her. Then he went downtown and mailed a letter. Murder one, five years, with a year and a half off for good behavior. In Switzerland almost everybody gets off for good behavior, because almost everybody is well behaved.

On September 16, 1970, at 2 P.M., the United California Bank in Basel AG closed its doors and posted a notice on its premises at St. Jakobsstrasse 7. According to the papers, the losses were closer to $40 million than $30 million. Representatives of the United California Bank in Los Angeles presented a plan to the Swiss banking authorities in Bern. They would, they said, make good to the depositors and creditors. In a report to its own stockholders, the California bank explained that a great international bank has deposits from other great international banks, and if it were to welsh it couldn't continue in business. The loss, it said, would be treated as an ordinary and necessary business expense, and it applied to Internal Revenue for a tax saving of half the loss. Furthermore, insurance might cover $10 million. On the New York Stock Exchange, Western Bancorporation went down two and a half points, and then back up two points. In 1969 Western Banc had had a net profit after taxes of a bit more than $60 million, so a $10 million or even a $20 million loss, while quite an inconvenience, was not a serious impediment to doing business.

Western Bancorporation was a publicly traded company; the United California Bank in Basel was held privately, by the Los Angeles bank and a few of us faithful junior partners. No one called the junior partners—at least no one called me, and I certainly left my phone number in enough places. There seemed to be nowhere to get information. I called an investment officer I knew professionally at the UCB in Los Angeles. He clucked sympathetically, said he didn't know anything that hadn't been in the papers, and suggested that the best use for my stock certificates was as wallpaper.

"Write it off," he said.

"Off what?" I said.

Finally I began to play a little game. I would call the office of Frank King, the chairman of the United California Bank, and explain carefully why I was calling, what it was in reference to, and that it was a call from the junior partner to the senior partner. Frank King's office would say they would take the message and he would call back. Then he wouldn't call back. We tried this thirty-one times and then gave up. I had to conclude that nobody wanted to talk to me. We were, after all, in the same boat, and we did have something to talk about, but when there is trouble, bankers get very tongue-tied, and this incident was a real conversation-stopper, bankwise.

My calls were over several weeks. Paul Erdman's salary stopped instantly, and since his only real possession was the bank stock, Helly got a job as a secretary. Teams of auditors moved onto the premises of St. Jakobsstrasse 7, but no one had any clear idea of how $40 million could disappear from a modern banking institution. Especially a *Swiss bank*.

Paul Erdman was in a small single cell, with a toilet, a fold-up bed and a table.

My bank was busted.

Paul Erdman had come to my office one summer day in 1968. He was lean, tall and bespectacled. I forget now who sent him; we were seeking to expand our knowledge of European banks, and Paul Erdman was to tell us about the Swiss, who are not eager to tell about themselves. We went to lunch, and Erdman began to tell me not so much about the rest of the Swiss banking establishment—he would introduce me to someone who could do an even better job than he could—but about his own small bank in Basel. I liked Paul.

Furthermore, I have an interest—or a weakness—for and in small companies that have big ideas. You would never consider running General Electric to be *fun*. It might be something else, but not fun. But you take a couple of guys with a sheet of yellow paper and an idea, and the idea is right, and they have an itch to make something happen, to build something that grows—that's quite exciting. If it works, it's exhilarating and—though the word is inadequate—fun, almost as much fun as anything else you can think of. The odds against success are quite long: the idea does have to be right, and the money—enough money—has to be there, and then more money has to be available, and then you have to have the counter-strategy ready when the existing establishment feels the sting and starts to growl. And most important, you have to have the right combination of people, and they must all bring out each other's positive qualities to the optimum. This is hardest of all, because people are the most valuable resource of any quickly growing operation, and the fellow who first started musing on the sheet of yellow paper is likely to have a very big ego along with his imagination, and a corresponding lack of sensitivity to the people the company needs.

I suppose I have been involved in about a dozen of these amateur venture capital situations, and the record is no worse than anybody else's. It used to be, when the venture business was easier, that in the morning you expected to find a couple of your colts stiff, their feet in the air, but that one or two would turn out to be great winners, ten or fifteen for one, and that would more than make up for the losers. In the early sixties I was in a company that made radar antennae so successfully it went broke. It doubled its sales every year, and the Navy loved the antennae, but they sold for less than they cost, somehow, and the company ran out of money. It barely managed to sell its stock to the public before it went broke. Then there was the electronic grading machine that was going to be used in every school in America—a lot of them were sold before they found all the bugs in the machine—and the company that made the typewriter that talked back to three-year-olds when they pressed a key.

There was one outfit that was designed to relieve office overtime. No need to hire expensive temporaries for, say, peak insurance work: you just dictated into the attachment on your phone, and Dial Dictation would have it for you the next morning. The company hit some foul weather, and at night the president used to call me in California, where I lived at the time, to talk to me. Finally I asked him why he was calling me; I wasn't a very big stockholder and I wasn't a director.

"Nobody else will talk to me," he said.

There were a couple that worked: Control Data bought the laser company, and the company that made the radiation equipment for atomic tests not only made it to the public-offering starting gate but was given a very nice ride in the 1967 enthusiasm. So—no great fortunes, but a lot of interesting entertainment, and my basic conviction was still unshaken: you don't get rich owning General Motors, because General Motors has already grown up. What you should do with General Motors is inherit it. What you look for—at least before technology became a bad word—was "the next Xerox." A lot of people have gone down swinging trying for that one.

Typewriters that talked back to three-year-olds; attachments for telephones. I had never thought about a Swiss bank.

I took Paul to lunch at the restaurant of the American Stock Exchange, and he told me how he had started his bank.

"Swiss banks," he said. "The most common concept is the secrecy—numbered accounts, tax evasion, South American dictators, all that. But Swiss banks are universal banks. They operate everywhere and they are used to processing information from all over the world. But did you ever do business with a Swiss bank? Cold, formal, snooty, extremely cautious, very conservative, eh? I could see the age of the multinational corporation arriving, Polaroid and IBM building plants in Europe, Swiss drug companies expanding in the United States. The services offered by Swiss banks weren't up to those offered by American banks. I thought, What about an *American* bank in Switzerland, eh?

A bank that would have American management techniques and American aggressiveness, but that was operating in Switzerland under Swiss laws, with Swiss universality. With maybe some of the dynamic qualities of a top-flight British merchant bank, *eh?*"

Paul was an American, but enough of Basel had rubbed off on him so that he frequently ended his statements with a Baseler interrogative, *ja?* Certainly if anyone was going to start an American bank in Switzerland, Paul was uniquely qualified, except that, with hindsight, maybe his knowledge of bank operating procedures was a bit sketchy. *The Wall Street Journal* was to describe him later as "a personnel man's dream." He was born in Stratford, Ontario, where his father, an American Lutheran minister, had been called to a parish. Paul's father is now a vice-president and administrator of the Lutheran Church in Canada, responsible for such activities as Lutheran hospitals and Lutheran insurance. Paul was sent at fourteen to a Lutheran "gymnasium" boarding school in Fort Wayne, Indiana, and then to Concordia College in St. Louis, where he met Helly, a native Baseler.

After he graduated from Concordia in 1953, Paul enrolled at the School of Foreign Affairs of Georgetown University, thinking he might be interested in the foreign service. He worked part-time as an editorial assistant at the Washington *Post* and graduated with an M.A. in 1955. Still not sure of a vocation, but wanting to study abroad for a while, Paul and Helly returned to her native Basel, where Paul enrolled at the University of Basel; one of his professors there later remembered him as a brilliant student. He received a second M.A. and then a Ph.D. in 1958, and his dissertation on Swiss-American economic relations was published in 1959. His academic credentials got him a job with the European Coal and Steel Community; in collaboration with a German economist, a friend of his, Paul produced another book, this one in German, called *Die europäische Wirtschaftsgemeinschaft und die Drittländer,* a study on the European Economic Community. Now his visibility was such that the Stanford Research Institute of Palo Alto scooped him up as a European representative. For three years he commuted from Basel to the Stanford Research office in Zurich, but, he told me, "I wasn't there much. I was all over Europe, consulting on business problems. We did a study for Alfa Romeo on their trucks, another for a Dutch steel mill that wanted to know whether and how to build large-diameter pipe, and so on." Stanford Research moved him back to Palo Alto, but consulting began to pall. He wanted to do more. Through Neil Jacoby, dean of the UCLA Business School and a director of Stanford Research, he met Charles Salik, a San Diego businessman who had formed an investment company called Electronics International, Inc. Salik sent him back to Basel to monitor European companies, and then bought the idea of a brand-new, American Swiss bank.

"What'll we call the bank?" Salik asked, and after some toying with words such as Swiss, Universal and American, Paul suggested they call it the Salik Bank.

"Why not?" Paul said. "It was his money." Salik and his family put up $600,000, and the bank began in two rooms.

No one could accuse the Salik Bank of being formal or snooty. Paul himself hustled customers all over Europe, and at one time the bank claimed to be Basel's second biggest Swissair customer, even though Basel is headquarters for several of the world's great drug companies. The Salik Bank not only took deposits and made loans—short-term collateralized loans in this case—but like most Swiss banks, it dealt in portfolio management, commodities and foreign exchange. Its resources grew apace: from 13.7 million Swiss francs ($3.5 million) at the end of 1966, to 37.8 million

Swiss francs ($9.8 million) at the end of 1967, to 142.5 million Swiss francs ($37 million) in mid-1968.

Paul's particular interest was in currency speculation. In many ways, this is the headiest speculative game of all, for it involves anticipating the moves of central banks, watching the trade balances of countries, and assessing both gossip and political intelligence. Basel itself is an arena for such talk, because the Bank for International Settlements, the clearing house for nations, sits in an old converted mansion opposite the railroad station. The headiness of the speculation comes from the large sums and high debt involved, because one side of the transaction has a floor.

For example: let us say, as it was in 1967, that the Bank of England is committed to buy and sell pounds at roughly $2.80. That is where the value of the pound was arbitrarily pegged. But Britain has a trade deficit; no one wants to hold pounds; there are more sellers to the Bank of England than buyers. You decide that the pound is weakening; sooner or later it must be marked down to a level where international trade will once again support it, and where once again it will reflect the realities of that trading.

So you sell, for future delivery, a million dollars' worth of pounds. You have already sold them, so to deliver them you will have to buy them back at a future date. You have sold them at $2.80; you know that you can buy them from the Bank of England close to that price. You need put up only $50,000 or so; your only expense is the commission on buying and selling, and the interest charges on your obligation. You hope, of course, to buy the pounds back cheaper, marked down.

But ripeness is all. Those interest charges can begin to mount.

Analysts of World War II like to point out the influence

of *kendo,* the Japanese bamboo-stave fencing, on Japanese
military strategy. A lot of parrying, watching for the perfect moment, and then victory in one devastating, lightning
stroke—thus, Pearl Harbor.

Paul's mentality was something like that. Not for him a
slow, quiet, dust-covered compounding in some vault.

In the fall of 1967, Paul was watching the sterling situation closely. A number of customers of the Salik Bank sold
pounds for future delivery at $2.80. When Britain devalued
the pound to $2.40, the customers bought their pounds in
at $2.40 and delivered them, cleaning up. One client made
$80,000 over the weekend. The coup, the shattering *kendo*
stroke, had worked. Paul's reputation on currency matters
rose, and he enjoyed the role of the currency critic. He
wrote papers on gold and the dollar, signed by *Dr. Paul
Erdman, President, the Salik Bank, Basel.* Not only is there
something heady about currency speculation, but there is
an element of the ultimate judge when one in effect says
to a whole country: "Get your inflation in check and your
trade balances up, or down goes your currency." That is
the role not only of the Bank for International Settlements
opposite the railroad station in Basel, but the currency
speculator.

Paul also wrote for *The International Harry Schultz
Letter,* a breezy investment advisory letter from London
with Winchell-like tones:

"Hi-lo ratio is negative but mkt not ready for a real
kachunk . . . $ trading in Germany hectic . . . frustration
with biz expectations causing a rise in nationalism." While
the Winchell gossip might have been about starlets and
entertainers, Schultz's concerns trade deficits, currencies
weakening, and cryptic bulletins on world markets:

"*Austria*: sell into strength . . . *Holland*: buy, *Italy*:
avoid, *Japan*: hold (reread HSL 254) . . ."

Schultz had been a California newspaper publisher, and

is the author of several investment books, including one on Switzerland and Swiss banks.

Schultz's readers, called HLSM, for "Harry L. Schultz men," are a loyal group—"Take an HLSM home to dinner"—who buy HLS ceramic cuff links and spend several hundred dollars for a ticket to his seminars in London and Denmark. Schultz likes to compare the United States to ancient Rome in its decadence; in fact, he signs his letter "Slavius." Debasing of the currency is a favorite Schultz leitmotif; he considers it not the symptom but the *cause* of national decline:

"A people can only sink lower without a dependable store of value. Currency debauchery is the *sole* source of U.S. decline & decadence—just as it has been in every society of recorded history."

Schultz's letter was a boost for Paul. It ran his short articles, detailed in one-liners some of Paul's travels and thoughts, and even identified some customers for the bank. It was one of Schultz's tenets that in the face of the weakening dollar, investors should not hold cash in U.S. savings or bank accounts. Instead, they could profit from the revaluation of the harder currencies: the Dutch guilder, the Japanese yen, the German mark, and Belgian and Swiss francs. Accounts in a Swiss bank could, of course, be invested in any of those currencies, and in fact an account could be left in a Swiss bank in a time deposit and denominated in Swiss francs.

Because of the corruption of the dollar, the faithful also saw exchange controls coming. Soon you would not be able to take dollars out of the country. After all, the English had once roamed the world, and now they were restricted at the borders to a few measly pounds and could scarcely travel abroad. The same could happen to Americans; the faithful, by getting their money out ahead of the lowering boom, could assure their future mobility. They would still be able

to travel, to buy a house in France or a ski lodge in Switzerland; their foresight would be rewarded. Denuded of the
rhetoric, the faithful were, of course, right. The dollar has
been devalued, some say not for the last time. Specific
taxes have been laid on to discourage American investment
abroad, and the first limitations on transferring capital
abroad have been imposed. Your bank keeps a record of
each transfer into another currency of more than $5,000,
and in fact you are supposed to report any such transfer to
the IRS. Brand-new law. Presumably the IRS can thumb
through all the microfilm any afternoon it feels like looking for fleeing capital.

Schultz ran a short list of Swiss banks in his letter, with
the Salik Bank conspicuously on the list. After one Harry
Schultz seminar in London, an excursion to Switzerland
was formed, with Paul and his fellow Salik Bank employees
entertaining the excursioners in Basel. Paul said he did not
always agree with Schultz's apocalyptic notes, and he dis-
paraged some of the Schultz faithful as "right-wing Texas
kooks, who eat that stuff up," but he was glad to have them
as clients. For a small bank in Switzerland's second city, the
bank had an unusual number of Texas clients, and reportedly some of the clients became shareholders.

When Paul came to see me, he was not seeking another
shareholder; he was seeking a friend for the bank. He did
this naturally, as an active promoter, a selling president.
He sought friends everywhere, and found them. Economists, business-school deans, currency experts, commodity
dealers—all found him interesting and agreeable. He even
cultivated the press—unlike, I am sure, any other bank
president in Switzerland. Other Swiss bankers went to
lengths to avoid the press. Paul courted friends for the
bank everywhere. If he were asked to write an article on
currency for a magazine, he was glad to do that; if, as we

did, someone requested more information on Swiss banking, he would set us up with people who could help us.

But he could sense my enthusiasm. A dynamic young bank that had increased its resources by a factor of fifteen in less than three years—that was exciting to me. Coincidentally, the bank had grown so fast that it needed more capital, and it was just in the process of raising it. Paul himself had written the prospectus, and while the prospectus, representing a Swiss corporation, naturally did not need to be registered with the SEC in Washington, it was "just like a prospectus for the SEC, because we want to do everything right; we may come to the U.S. some day, and a New York law firm is going over it completely."

"It occurs to me," Paul said, "that you would be a very good shareholder for us to have."

I said I was very interested. We shook hands, mutually impressed, and Paul went back to Basel that evening. The prospectus arrived a month or so later.

"From the beginning (1965)," said the prospectus, "the Salik Bank was conceived as a bridge between conservative Swiss banking—characterized by extreme caution, stability, and a unique expertise concerning financial matters on a worldwide basis—and modern corporate and financial management techniques usually identified with the United States." The bank had, the prospectus reported, recruited talent in the fields of portfolio management, foreign exchange, and commodities, and a Swiss financial newspaper had reported that the bank was the fastest-growing banking institution in Switzerland.

The bank, the prospectus reported, acted as a broker and dealer in foreign exchange, metals and commodities. "This field of activity," said the prospectus, "is usually reserved to the large commercial banks, since the private banks of Switzerland seldom have sufficient expertise in this rather esoteric area of international finance." "The Salik Bank has sought," it added, "to move beyond the usual areas of money management offered by many of the more traditional private banks in Switzerland, and to provide 'total money management' by building its capabilities related to type of investments other than the usual stocks and bonds."

Little did I know, but those paragraphs contained the potential for disaster. But like the hidden figures in the child's puzzle—how many animals can you find?—my eye could not see anything but good.

The bank was also to open a subsidiary in Brussels; then within three to five years, there would be an international bank holding company, which could make other acquisitions "on a larger scale in other areas of Europe, as well as perhaps the Far East and even Australia."

The Far East and even Australia! The sun would never set on the Salik Bank!

I asked some of my pals on Wall Street for their counsel. I said I had a chance to buy a rapidly growing Swiss bank at a quarter over book value. Would they do something like that?

"How much can you get me?" they said, to a man, and they offered to take any left over. Of course, they were basically gunslingers, attracted to such situations. They didn't get any of the stock, but that didn't help them. The nursing home and peripheral computer companies they bought did just as badly. My enthusiasm grew. I decided to go to Basel.

When you land at the airport in Basel, you notice one thing right away. You're not in Switzerland, you're in France. Everybody wants to own land in Switzerland because of its stability, and that puts a premium on land. So the Basel airport is over the border in Alsace, a part of

France, halfway to the town of Mulhouse, and when you come out of the airport the freeway or turnpike has a big fence on each side, a nice sanitized corridor into Switzerland, uncontaminated by France.

You would have to say that as a European city, Basel is undistinguished but likable. Green trams seem to run everywhere. You can sit by the Rhine watching the barges and sip pleasant Swiss wines—or even pleasanter German ones—and there are some nice parks and squares. For a city whose main industry is a series of drug and chemical complexes, it seems remarkably clean. At first, when you walk the streets, you can't quite define what's missing, and then you realize: it's the garbage bags, spilling over on the sidewalks, that you see so consistently in New York and London. And where is the litter? Where are the wrappers underfoot, the cigarette butts, the old newspapers? I never could figure out whether everybody peel-strips their butts and throws the tiny shreds into a container, the way they bring you up at Fort Dix, or whether the Turks and Spaniards and Italians who clean Basel just do a good job.

Paul picked me up at the airport, and we had lunch with the gentleman who was to fill us in on the background of Swiss banking—the subject that had brought Paul and me together. And after lunch we went to St. Jakobsstrasse, one of the main thoroughfares of Basel. There it was at Number 7, all glass and metal and shiny, four stories of it: my Swiss bank.

Paul had worked with the architect, designing the circular staircase that connected two floors. Otherwise it looked like—well, what can you say? It looked like a bank —like an American bank, all open and bright and shiny, with tellers and people in shirt sleeves and calculators. Which is to say that it did not look like a private Swiss bank, with its corridors and guards and its general air of reticence.

We sat in Paul's office, with its impressive desk and conference area—the right dimensions for a proper *Bank-
präsident*—and I met a variety of people. Now I can only
remember one of them, and that is perhaps because I
met him a number of times later: Louis Thole, a pleasant,
blond Dutchman in his thirties, scion of an Amsterdam
banking family, who was going to handle the bank's
portfolio-management activities.

"The Deutsche mark looks a bit stronger," said one of
our staff.

"Let's buy another million Deutsche marks," Paul said.

Louis Thole wanted to know if I had looked at Japanese
convertibles. I hadn't.

"The Hitachis are coming next week," Louis said. "They
are beautiful. They are quite sexy."

"Silver," Paul said. "Silver is going to go through the
roof."

I knew the silver story.

"I'm doing a report on silver," Paul said. "The U.S.
Treasury will run out of silver at some point, and then,
whoom. We have a man in Beirut who is very good on
silver."

And gold—well, the world was not going to stand for
long for all these jerry-rigged paper currencies, depreciat-
ing every day as their governments printed more paper.

Then another pleasant gentleman came in, whom I will
call Alfred because I can't remember his name. Alfred had
with him the forms to open an account. I said I was going
to become a stockholder, not a depositor. Alfred said most
of the stockholders were also depositors, and didn't I know
all the advantages of a Swiss bank account?

I don't know what made me hesitate. Swiss bank accounts
seemed appropriate for Las Vegas gamblers, South American dictators, Mafiosi, and people with cash incomes—some
doctors, say—or with incomes abroad who weren't about

to tell the government their foreign earnings because they considered taxes a personal injustice. I didn't see myself as the holder of a numbered account. Where would I keep the number? Tattooed on my heel? And what would I put in the account, anyway?

"I don't need an account," I said. "I already have a checking account. In the United States."

Alfred looked a little weary. Obviously that was not the right thing to say. I began to think the other visitors to the bank must have arrived with cardboard suitcases full of currency.

"Look," I said. "I'm very excited by the bank as an investment, but I pay my taxes."

Alfred looked absolutely blank at that. I was still apologetic.

"My income," I said, "is totally visible, and they take the taxes right out. And anyway, if you don't want to pay your taxes right away in the United States, you put your money into tax shelters, and then you don't pay them—at least that year. All legal and approved by the government."

I had Alfred's interest.

"See, the United States Congress writes the tax laws," I said. "Then special-interest groups lobby for privileges."

I told Alfred about my cattle.

Alfred liked the Western flavor of the tax postponement, but it did not deter him.

"You do not have to have a numbered account," Alfred said. "You can have an account as public as you like. I am happy you like to pay your taxes. In Switzerland we feel that what happens between a gentleman and the tax agents of his own country is his own business. In Switzerland we cooperate fully with other countries in pursuing criminals, but by Swiss law tax evasion in another country is not a crime. But let me ask you: are you married?"

I was married.

"Happily married?"

Happily married.

"Now," said Alfred, "you are happily married, you have insurance on your house. You naturally believe you will always be happily married, but you know that statistics do not bear this out, especially in America. And we know what happens in American divorces. They are famous. The woman keeps the house, she continues to live the same life; the lawyers and the courts take the husband's income and permit him to live on seventy dollars a week, in poverty. You are happily married now, but no man knows the future, five, ten, twenty years away. You are an American; you like to pay taxes; if you do not want to pay taxes, you feed cows; you think you will always be happily married. But do you not owe yourself a little insurance?"

"What are you saying?" I asked.

"With an account here, you need do nothing illegal. You can pay your taxes, you can buy stocks on any exchange in the world, you can buy and sell commodities anywhere in the world, and *no one need know about it*. And someday, when your wife's lawyers are trying to take away the money you have worked for twenty years to build up, you will have a private reserve."

Alfred must have met Americans before. Like a master insurance salesman, he closed in. Even the happiest of husbands would have paused for a moment.

"Nothing illegal," Alfred said. "There is nothing illegal in trying to strike a more equitable bargain with your wife's lawyers. That is nothing to do with you and your government."

Now that the matter was not between me and the government but between me and my wife's lawyers, those sonsabitches who were going to make me live on $70 a week, I began to loosen up. I could see them, the ferret-faced wretches—Bardell and Pickwick, crackling at their rolltop desks, rubbing their bony hands together as they dispatched me to some roach-infested garret with winos lying in the hallway and junkies shooting up under a ten-watt bulb. Why? What did I do?

"It's not illegal not to tell my wife's lawyers?" I said, forgetting for the moment that my wife had no lawyers nor any need of them.

"You don't owe your wife's lawyers anything, do you?" Alfred said. "They are going to try to prove you a criminal —that is the nature of American divorce justice: one party must be a criminal, an adversary proceeding. A criminal in fiction, mind you—mental cruelty, lack of attention, what-have-you—things that would make a European laugh. When an American wife behaves in a manner that would cause her to be *shot* if she were married to a European, the American stands still like a patient lamb to be fleeced."

"I've seen some tough cases," I said. "A friend of mine just went through it. They left him one shirt and one cuff link."

"Another thing," Alfred said. "Your dollar is declining. Your Vietnam war is bleeding it. Your government mis-handled its finances. That is going to cost you dearly as a citizen."

"I've been saying that for three years," I said.

"Good," Alfred said. "Now, you pay your taxes, so you are already paying for your government's political sins, but why should you pay for its fiscal sins, when you yourself warned against them? Your account here will be in Swiss francs, so when the dollar falls apart, you will still have some currency with some value."

"Terrific," I said.

"Sign here," Alfred said, holding the pen out for me.

"Wait a minute," I said. "I don't need a number. Just a name."

"That number is for us," Alfred said. "Not secret. Your

own account in America has a number. All bank accounts have numbers. Computers can't work with Roman numerals."

"Okay," I said.

Alfred held the pen out. I signed the form.

"No secret number," I said firmly.

"As you wish," Alfred said.

I had a Swiss bank account. I put $200 in it.

"No alarm clock," I said. "No toaster? No bonuses for signing up? Do I get pretty checks? A winter scene?"

Alfred did not seem to know about the American banking tradition of giving away two-dollar appliances for new accounts, and he indicated as long as the account was that size I would probably not need checks. The bank charges for the various bookkeeping transactions of deposits and checks were higher than in the United States. Paul came back into the room.

"You have a new depositor," I said. "But no number."

"Good," Paul said.

"Now that I'm part of the family," I said, "tell me. Do we have any South American dictators as depositors?"

"Oh, for heaven's sake," Paul said.

"I bet we must have one Mafioso. What's a Swiss bank without at least one Mafia account?"

"For heaven's sake," Paul said, "we want to *go public* with this bank."

We walked out through the bank, and Paul pointed out various of the officers. One was working in a small room with a desk calculator. Paul said he was from a wealthy family; he himself was a multimillionaire. Then why, I asked, was he working in a bank?

"First of all," Paul said, "in Switzerland everyone works. We have no playboys. If you are going to be a playboy, you have to go to the south of France or to London or New

York or wherever they have that environment. Saint Moritz
is for foreigners. And second, in Switzerland you never
know how much money anyone has. There are families in
Basel whose net worth must be a billion dollars. But you
never know. If you ever get to anyone's house, and through
the front door, sometimes you see it on the walls—Picassos,
Renoirs and so on. And when they take a vacation they
take a good vacation—a safari in Africa, a visit to South
America and so on. But you must leave Basel to spend the
money. The houses are solid and square, not ostentatious.
In Switzerland it is not only the money you *have* that is
important, it is the money you *get*."

On the way to his house, Paul drove up to the cathedral,
and we stood in back of it, overlooking the Rhine. We
walked around among the gabled houses of old Basel, some
of them built in the fourteenth and fifteenth centuries.

"Basel's skills came from the Catholic persecutions,"
Paul said. "The Protestants who fled here had two skills.
One was that, not being Catholics, they could lend money
and change currencies, and that grew into banking. The
other skill was in dyeing, dyeing textiles. During the
nineteenth century the skill of mixing dyes grew naturally
into chemicals, and during the twentieth century there
was a natural transition from chemicals into drugs, and
that is how Basel became one of the great chemical–drug
complexes of the world."

Paul lived in a pleasant American-suburban-style house
with a cathedral ceiling and books in three languages over-
flowing the shelves. The house was located in a solid resi-
dential section of Basel. The Erdmans did not live elabo-
rately; they had an Alsatian girl who helped with the two
daughters.

"It's nice to have somebody for dinner," Helly Erdman
said. "In America you do that all the time. In Switzerland

you just don't do that. Visits inside the house are inside the family. You go out to dinner only to see your own relatives."

"Once a year," Paul said, "maybe you will go to someone's house—another banker, let's say. Then it is very stiff, very formal. Dinner jackets. You send flowers to the hostess ahead of time."

"The conversation is very stiff too," Helly said.

"There are no backyard barbecues in Basel that I know of," Paul said. "Switzerland is built on privacy."

We talked about the plans for the bank. There would be a branch in Zurich, and then another in Geneva, and a subsidiary bank in Brussels; eventually the bank would sell its stock to the public in Europe and spread its activities far beyond Switzerland.

"Paul is involved in every detail," Helly said. "I can't tell you—he even debated with the architect over where that stairway should go in the bank."

The next morning we went back to the bank, and I went over various reports on European issues and European currencies. I also used my new bank to make an investment.

The Bank for International Settlements is the international clearing house for the central banks of governments. It is through this bank that government currency swaps are engineered, and also through this bank a government that is going too deeply into deficit in its international accounts is told to shape up. The stock of the bank is held by the member governments: the United States, Germany, France, Japan, Italy and so on. Every once in a while there seem to be a few stray shares floating around, and so there was this day. For something like $1,100, I bought one share. Then the stockholders were the United States, Germany, France, Britain, Japan, Italy and Adam Smith. I think I had in mind going to a meeting of the stockholders, or having some conversations with them, but I never got around to it.

Paul had a present for me. It was a diseased cocoa pod; someone had brought it to him, and there had been a section on cocoa in my book which Paul liked. We took pictures of each other holding the cocoa pod in front of the Bank for International Settlements. In the light of what was to happen, it was the ultimate in irony.

I got on the train for Zurich. Swiss trains were supposed to run with the precision of watches; the train was to leave at 11:59, and I had just had my Swiss watch set. Starting at 11:57, I watched the sweep of the second hand. The train left ten seconds early.

In Zurich I had appointments with several major banks. Sometimes, peripherally, I would drop the name of my new bank into the conversation just to test the reaction. There wasn't much of one. Those that had heard of it didn't know much about it; one banker who had thought the bank was "very aggressive," which in Switzerland is not a term of praise.

In Zurich the visceral feeling I had about Switzerland and money began to be confirmed. Now, I do realize that a week spent in banks does not provide a very broad background for generalizing about a country. You could spend a week on the ski slopes and come away with a different feeling, or a week in the chocolate factories, or some time with watchmakers or with the cuckoo-clock guild. Nonetheless, there is something about Switzerland and money that makes it ultima Thule, the country that provides one definitive end to the spectrum. After all, why *Swiss* banks? Most Western industrialized countries have well-developed banking systems, and a number of countries—Lebanon, the Bahamas, and Uruguay—have imitated the Swiss system of secrecy. Lebanon even used the Swiss banking code as a model. Still, for its size and per capita income, Switzerland leads the world in this profession. Why? It is the Swissness of the Swiss, and it might be interesting to take a moment to see how they got that way. Even though my new bank was not very typically Swiss, it gave me a feeling of confidence against fiscal dangers unknown, a home away from home.

By rights, Switzerland ought to be one of the world's losers. The popular image of Switzerland is mountains, and the popular image comes pretty close to being right. Only 7 percent of Switzerland can be farmed, and the country can't feed itself. Unlike much of Europe, it has no coal, oil, gas, iron ore or other industrial amenities, and no access to the sea. It had, of course, William Tell, a symbol of pragmatism, technical competence and an unwillingness to be pushed around. Being mountainous, Switzerland had no large estates, no large convenient political divisions. Each valley community had to survive by itself. That led to a certain amount of hard-headedness. It isn't a Swiss proverb that says if you have an ugly face, learn to sing, but it might as well be.

In the late Middle Ages, the small Swiss towns found themselves astride a German–Mediterranean trade route, handling sugar, salt and spices, discounting the gold from Venice and the silver from the Rhineland. According to one author, T. R. Fehrenbach, the Swiss burghers also had little use for medieval Christianity. For the Swiss businessmen already honored hard work, individual effort and money, and medieval Christianity denigrated all of these things. *Gott regiert in Himmel und 's Galt uf Erde,* went a Zurich proverb, *Für Galt tanzt sogar de Tuufel.* "God rules in Heaven, and money on earth. Even the Devil dances for gold."

John Calvin and Ulrich Zwingli changed the course of Switzerland. Gold was the sober gift of God and work was holy. Calvinism's ideal was "a society which seeks wealth with the sober gravity of men who are conscious at once of disciplining their own characters by patient labor, and of devoting themselves to a service acceptable to God." (This is from Tawney's *Religion and the Rise of Capitalism*; so is what follows.) Calvinism is "perhaps the first systematic body of religious teaching which can be said to recognize and applaud the economic virtues." No longer was "the world of economic motives alien to the life of the spirit." Here is Zwingli, quoted by Wiskemann, quoted by Richard Tawney: "Labor is a thing so good and godlike . . . that makes the body hale and strong and cures the sickness produced by idleness . . . In the things of this life, the laborer is most like to God."

Thus banking became one of the Protestant fine arts. According to Fehrenbach:

> Zwinglianism did not reconcile Christ and Mammon. Zwingli and his rational spiritual descendants never saw any conflict. The Swiss did not learn to love money . . . The Swiss *respects* money, a very different thing. Respecting it, a Swiss pursues, handles, and husbands money as an end in itself, which is utterly different from German materialism with its emphasis on things or American status-seeking, with its drive for power or prestige . . . respecting money, the Swiss made its handling not a miserly trait but more a priestly calling. He erected ritual rooms and bare confessionals, guarded one and gave the other secrecy.

For four hundred years, the Swiss stuck close to the proverb, Money rules on earth. No political passions, no religious crusades. When the Swiss went to fight a war, it was somebody else's war. Something like two million Swiss soldiers left Switzerland to fight all over Europe—but always for money. The Swiss mercenary became a factor in the military history of the world.

Hard-headedness, pragmatism and a distrust of new ideas; if the Swiss had had General Motors, they would have erected a statue to Charley Wilson for saying that what was good for General Motors was good for the country. Feudalism and Catholic Christianity weren't good for business; nor was despotism, anarchy, nationalism, a strong central government, socialism, Marxism, and even female suffrage. All of those winds have swept over the mountains without effect. (Only recently did the ladies get the vote. But Switzerland is still a male-chauvinist-pig country. If community property is involved, any husband can request information on his wife from a bank, but no wife, for any reason, can get such information on her husband without his consent.)

Non-Swiss seem to have been affected most by two factors in the Swiss banking code. One is the Swiss attitude toward taxation. In the Zwinglian Protestant society, honesty was not only the best policy, but work and the reward of work were holy. There was no strong central government, only a confederation of states, so by any world standard, national taxes are not particularly high. Therefore you get what you pay for, and you pay your taxes; taxes are a part of duty, and duty is a part of life. In the 1300's, the Austrian Hapsburgs had made life tough for William Tell, and sent the nasty agent Gessler, still booed in schools. Swiss society is structured to leave the individual Swiss alone. No Swiss government has ever made the evasion of taxes a *crime*. Americans shook off the stamp tax and the tea tax imposed by the Crown and went on, independently, to taxes of their own. The Swiss, having gotten rid of the Habsburgs, saw no need to complicate life further: that lesson was learned.

Most governments in the world today cooperate with

each other in apprehending criminals—but only if they agree on the crime, or on what is a crime. A crime in Soviet Russia or in Mao's China might not be a crime in the United States. A tax matter in Switzerland is an administrative detail between the state—that is, the canton—and the citizen, not a crime. But if you rob a bank and send the money to a Swiss bank, the Swiss government is delighted to cooperate, take the lid off the bank account, check the serial numbers, and help send you to jail. Everybody agrees that bank robbery is a crime.

In the early sixties there was a scandal concerning a Texas promoter called Billie Sol Estes and a lot of missing assets. Some people thought that maybe some of the assets had worked their way into Swiss banks. But the U.S. government had slapped a tax lien on Billie Sol's assets, making the affair a tax matter, so as far as the Swiss were concerned, that was the end of it.

The other factor in the Swiss banking code that has endeared Swiss banks to foreigners is secrecy. But secrecy is nothing new to banks; in fact, the lack of secrecy is something relatively new, a part of contemporary nationalism. Roman banking law, Germanic civil law and the laws of the northern Italian states, where banking flourished during the late Middle Ages, all contained secrecy provisions. Europeans are still a little startled by the way an American department store—or worse, the American government— can call up your bank and find out your fiscal habits. Until the 1930's, a Swiss bank account was properly secret, but it was up to the Swiss banker to preserve the secrecy.

As Germans—particularly German Jews—began to send their money out of Germany under Hitler—Gestapo agents tried to follow the money. Some of them simply bribed or cajoled the employees of Swiss banks, but others came up with a more ingenious device: they tried depositing money in Swiss banks, in the names of various wealthy Germans.

The Swiss bank that accepted the Gestapo agent's ruse as a courier, and accepted the deposit, confirmed the fact that there was a bank account, and the unlucky German was whisked to a concentration camp, from which he asked the Swiss bank to send his money back to Germany, and then was tortured and executed. Much of the money that left Germany was never recovered and is still in the Swiss banks, and by now it belongs to the banks themselves, since under Swiss law if no one has claimed the deposit after twenty years it escheats to the bank.

The Swiss government was annoyed enough by the Gestapo's tactics to ratify the Banking Code of 1934, which made bank secrecy a part of the penal law. It took the moral burden off the banker by making it a crime to reveal any banking secrets, and it reassured foreigners that foreign deposits were protected by Swiss law.

The final appeal of the Swiss bank is not in the Swiss banking code, but in the Swiss banker. From his neutral perch, he has seen the world on the horizon go to war for seven hundred years. Castles are sacked in war, chieftains are scattered far, kings are deposed, governments fall, currencies become worthless, families break apart, wives leave husbands, husbands leave wives, children turn on their parents, mobs swirl in the streets—all like one of the Breughels in the Swiss museums. If governments were not corrupt, if paper currencies did not depreciate, if taxes were fair, if there were no wars, if humanity were not so fallible—if the world were like Switzerland—then there would be no need of Switzerland. But the world is like that, and if Switzerland did not exist, to paraphrase Voltaire, it would have to be invented. The money in the bank is there in solid Swiss francs, backed by gold. Never mind the people who brought it there; it is the money that is immortal, to be tended like a delicate flower by God's own anointed gardeners. Even that simile is not quite accurate, for it is more important that the money be *preserved* than that it grow. Thus the honored calling: to preserve the incremental lump, the evidence that somewhere, sometime, someone pleased God with some work that was rewarded: husbanding the lump—that stewardship is an elite-enough calling.

And, incidentally, very profitable. Can anything profitable be all bad?

I have had some time to think about the policing effects of the Protestant ethnic since my Swiss adventure. Clearly, something was lacking in the competence of Swiss accountants or in the Swiss banking system. Somewhere, some Swiss had not made the handling of money a proper priestly calling. Would I rather be policed by the Fed in Washington or by the ethics of the good Swiss bankers? The trouble is, even in Switzerland nobody really lives in fear of God, Calvin or Zwingli any more. Most of the habits continue in good shape, but the Protestant ethic leaks.

In the month following my first visit to the bank, Paul and Louis Thole came to New York. Paul was eager to get the bank established in underwritings—that is, to be one of the group selling securities to the public, a function usually done by brokerage houses in the United States. Paul also wanted the bank to get more deeply into money management, running portfolios for clients.

Those were the heady days of "offshore" funds, led by Bernie Cornfeld's IOS. The funds were headquartered in "tax havens" such as Curaçao and the Bahamas. These are countries equal to the United States, Britain and West Germany in legal status, but their laws governing taxes, investment policies and the ability to borrow on the funds were (and are) more relaxed than those of more developed countries. Paul and I talked about a hedge fund to be operated by the bank, as an additional service to its clients. We tried the hedge fund for a brief period on a "pilot" basis—that is, with a very small amount of money but with the pretense on paper that it was really full size. We washed around in some of the popular stocks of the tail end of the bull market, but it was plain to see that there was something nervous in the market: it simply did not behave with any degree of health. We discontinued the experiment after a few months with a small loss.

In the spring of 1969 I got a jubilant letter from Paul. Now the stationery was different: it bore the bold words *United California Bank in Basel,* in the same type face used by the United California Bank in Los Angeles. It also had a familiar monogram: UCB, familiar to me because I had once lived in California, and the UCB had a very catchy UCB commercial all over the television channels.

"Now we can proceed with a number of projects," Paul wrote. "You will see by our new stationery that we have changed our name and made a great step forward. The United California Bank has bought a majority interest in the bank. UCB itself is the flagship bank of Western Bancorporation, one of the biggest bank holding companies in the world. Frank King, the chairman of both the UCB and Western Bancorporation, has become our chairman, and I am vice-chairman. We have a number of very exciting plans."

But for the next year, I was not in very close touch. We ran a seminar on American investments at the Savoy in London, attended by a number of European institutions, major banks, mutual funds, and insurance companies from Britain, Switzerland, France, the Netherlands, Belgium, Germany and Italy. Paul and Louis came as invited guests, but I did not have much chance to speak to them.

In the spring of 1970 our Basel bank offered additional shares to its shareholders. I called Paul. He said things were going well, that the expansion was continuing, but that 1969 had been a disappointing year due to losses in

the securities markets. That was not surprising; 1969 was
not a good year anywhere. But now we had a new and additional important shareholder: the Vesta Insurance Company of Bergen, Norway, and through them, perhaps
twenty Scandinavian banks. Scandinavia was to be a new
and fertile field, and our Scandinavian shareholders would
send us a lot of reciprocal business.

Bear-market gloom was upon Wall Street, and brokerage
houses tottered. There wasn't much time to think about
Basel or the United California Bank, but presumably
things were going well. That was all I knew.

The Basel bank was indeed one of the fastest-growing
financial institutions in Switzerland. In the United States
such an image would have been welcomed; in Switzerland
it was considered not sound and a bit pushy. For one thing,
it was not easy to find qualified, competent people. Hiring
away from another bank is something not readily done in
Switzerland. To manage the bank's portfolios, Paul recruited Alfred Kaltenbach, an affable, nattily dressed Swiss
with uncharacteristic long sideburns.

But the prize catch was Bernard Kummerli, an intense,
near-sighted, rather olive-skinned foreign-exchange specialist. Kummerli was a native of Reinfeld, a small Swiss
town near Basel noted for its spa and medieval old section.
Kummerli's father was the banker in town. Kummerli had
been educated in the local schools and in a private Catholic
school, and then had worked for the Crédit Suisse, one of
Switzerland's Big Three banks. Paul found him at the
Bank Hoffmann, a smaller, private bank, where Kummerli
was the head of the department that traded currencies.
Kummerli was very ambitious. His reputation was that of
a walking computer, a man who could transact millions in
foreign exchange in his head, the essence of cool. Kummerli
is described as emotionless, which can scarcely be true for
someone with that kind of fire in his belly, but that was

the description extant. Kummerli could effect $10 million trades without the flicker of an eyelash. Three or four young traders came with Kummerli from the Bank Hoffmann, one of them Victor Zurmuhle. The *-li* or *-le* suffix in a Swiss name is a diminutive; Swiss-German abounds in diminutives. When Paul's trading department got going, Kummerli and Zurmuhle became known to the currency and commodity traders in Europe's financial centers as the "-li boys" or "Lee boys."

Paul had assembled a staff of young executives—almost all of them in their thirties—but not without some cost. The Big Three banks of Switzerland sent Paul a rather stiff, formal, four-page letter. It was not done to go raiding for employees, said the Big Three, and Paul was to stop it.

Kummerli arrived in mid-1968 and took a characteristic plunge into silver futures. The bank and some of its customers had already been into silver, and Paul had put out a letter in May suggesting that silver was a sale. But if his executives and his customers wanted to speculate—well, the customer was always right.

The rationale for the silver play was that the U.S. Treasury had stopped selling silver. Industrial uses of silver were growing. Therefore, with the U.S. Treasury no longer selling and industrial uses growing, silver had to go up. Right?

There was only one problem with that reasoning, and that was that the story was too old. Speculators had already anticipated all the events. I myself had culled out the dollar bills that came to me when breaking a ten or a twenty and saved the ones that said "silver certificate" on them, and in fact I had taken nineteen of them to the U.S. Treasury and traded them for a baggie full of silver. At this point there were no more dollar bills that were silver certificates, and the price of silver had in fact gone from 91¢ an ounce to $1.29, the price at the time that the

Treasury had stopped selling, all the way to $2.50, the point at which the Basel geniuses discovered it. But so had all the people who had patiently bought silver for years, awaiting just such a rise; certainly the last 30 percent of the rise had been sheer speculation. By the end of 1968 the speculators had begun to cash in, and silver was down to about $1.80. In a commodity trade, the cash the investor puts up can be as low as 10 percent, so a drop of 25¢ an ounce on $2.50 silver would wipe out the account; long before that, there would be margin calls.

By June of 1969 silver had dropped further, to less than $1.60, but the bank had recouped some of the losses by quick trades on both sides. For its own account the bank made back its losses, but its customers who had been in silver were, needless to say, quite unhappy, and some of them complained to Paul.

Since May 1968, Paul had disassociated himself from the silver trades. He believed, he said, in giving his staff full rein, in leaving them complete autonomy. Paul felt badly about some of the accounts with silver losses. "Those guys," he said of his staff, "put some people in who had no right to be in. Not exactly widows and orphans, but practically. That was wrong." Especially after his form letter predicting just such a decline. So the bank did an extraordinary thing: it *canceled some of the silver trades, taking the losses onto its own books.* "We looked over the list," Paul said, "and we figured if it was a sophisticated guy, he was big enough to take his own lumps. But some of the accounts weren't, and we took the losses ourselves." The losses on the silver accounts were more than two million Swiss francs.

If it had become known that my Swiss bank was guaranteeing its clients against loss, it soon would have become the most popular financial institution in the world. Yet the bank was to do this twice more.

Once it was in an over-the-counter stock called Leasing

F

Consultants, Inc., a Long Island computer-leasing company which financed aircraft and computer equipment. There was a plethora of such companies in the late 1960's; they based their existence on a bank loan for, say, an IBM-360 or a jet plane, something that could be readily leased. Then they sold the management of the company to the public. By the time Alfred Kaltenbach had found this company, it was already late in the game. Leasco, Data Processing, Financial General and Levin-Townsend were on their way to Mr. Babson's booby list. An analyst in Oslo, Norway, told our sideburned and nattily dressed Kaltenbach about Leasing Consultants, proving that distance from Roslyn, Long Island, lends enchantment. For the bank's account, Kaltenbach bought letter stock, which was restricted and which the bank could not sell for a number of years, at prices around $12 and $13 a share.

Not only did the bank buy Leasing Consultants for its own account, it circulated a report on its own stationery recommending its purchase. Nineteen of the bank's clients bought the stock through the bank. Unfortunately, Leasing Consultants went the way of many such companies. Its income had been overstated, and early in 1970 it admitted it. The stock dropped to 7. By August the company had filed for bankruptcy, and the stock was 37¢ bid.

Again, the bank was distressed at the losses of its clients. This time the major loss was in the bank's own account—in fact, the loss was to total $2 million—but the nineteen clients got their money back. In *The Wall Street Journal* Ray Vicker reported that "one startled customer" had said "this was the first time anybody ever reimbursed me for a bum trade."

Meanwhile, Kummerli had found a new field for his talents: cocoa futures. But by the time Kummerli was really rolling, our bank was part of the great United California Bank.

In 1968 Paul had been on a trip to the West Coast, and had looked up his friends from the Stanford Research Institute. Over drinks one night, Paul met Edward Carter, the chairman and chief executive of Broadway Hale, one of the nation's major department-store chains. Carter, who was on the board of both the United California Bank and its parent, Western Bancorporation, later called Cliff Tweter, the vice-chairman, who set up a meeting for nine the following morning. Tweter was joined by the senior vice-president for international affairs of the bank, Victor Rose, then sixty-five. Within ten minutes, according to Paul, Rose had said, "Can't we buy that bank?"

In October, shortly after my own visit to Basel, Paul had met Frank King, the chairman of the United California Bank, in the London Hilton. King, then seventy-one, had started as the assistant cashier of the first National Bank of Sparta, Illinois; he had been president of the United California Bank for twenty-four years. "We want to buy your bank," King said. King had three prerequisites: first, that the United California Bank in Los Angeles have absolute control; second, that Charles Salik and his family retain no further interest; and third, that the management team stay on. In January King came to Basel to look over the bank. There seemed to be no question of his fascination with Paul Erdman. In March of 1969 there was a handshake agreement between King and Salik, and the lawyers went to work. The deal was complete in May; the Basel bank was valued at $12 million. What the UCB sought, among other things, was the Basel bank's toe hold in Switzerland and Europe, and even more important, its dynamic young executives. "We bought the bank to get Paul Erdman," said a UCB official at the time. And according to Ray Vicker of *The Wall Street Journal*, King regarded Paul "almost as a son."

The United California Bank put two men on the board

of its new acquisition. Frank King became the chairman of the board, and Victor Rose became a director. The California bank was quite proud of its acquisition. It changed the name almost immediately to The United California Bank in Basel. In its glossy annual report for 1969, it discussed the acquisition of the Basel bank as high among its achievements for the year, and listed it as a subsidiary.

Paul had thought the affiliation with a powerful bank would bring in new business, but apparently it did not. Paul was to report directly to Frank King, and in their discussions they went over a potential international program. In particular, now that he had Scandinavian stockholders, Paul had planned his end run around the dominant banks of Scandinavia. There were no American banks in Scandinavia; now, with his new Scandinavian connections, he could meet middle-sized businessmen in those countries and recruit their accounts before they moved from their country banks to the major banks of the Scandinavian capitals.

At the time the California bank took over, it had sent in its own auditors, who reported how the bank had taken over the customers' losses on silver, and also that there was a substantial exposure on margin accounts. But this did not get in the way of the merger. In fact, according to Paul, there was little communication with the parent bank. "Occasionally," Paul said, "a visiting fireman from Los Angeles would come through. He would ask where the good restaurants were, and whether we would get him a reservation at the two- and three-star places over the border in France." There was no general plan, and no external budget, and only slowly did the Basel bank come on stream into the California bank's reporting system.

Meanwhile, Bernard Kummerli was on his way to buying *half the cocoa in the world*.

. . .

Even to this day, I find the incident which brought down the bank totally and personally incredible. I had received the write-up on Leasing Consultants, and in fact had asked Louis Thole where they had come up with such a turkey at such a late date. But no one ever told me our bank was going into *cocoa*. What was to follow was as bizarre an example of nature imitating art as could ever be found.

For, after all, I had been into cocoa a bit myself. That was back when the Great Winfield discovered cocoa trading. Occasionally in those more leisured days I would sit with him lazily watching stocks move, like two sheriffs in a rowboat watching the catfish in the Tennessee River. There was a lull in the market, and everybody was fatigued from some slide or other, and somehow the Great Winfield had figured that the world was about to run out of cocoa.

"And, my boy," I remember him saying, "when the world is just about out of something, the price goes up. The Cocoa Exchange is unregulated. A three-cent rise in cocoa doubles your money. It's going to be wild. Come along for the party." The cash you had to put up for a cocoa contract was small.

Why was the world about to run out of cocoa? Well, the African states that produced cocoa were having political troubles, and there was supposed to be an outbreak of Black Pod, a Dreaded Cocoa Disease. The farmers had been leaving the farms, and hadn't sprayed the plants. So I bought some cocoa contracts and began to root for everything that would bring about a world-wide shortage of cocoa. Was there an unconfirmed report of Black Pod in the far interior of Ghana? We cheered. Was Nigeria breaking up into civil war? That was good for cocoa prices —maybe they wouldn't get the cocoa to market. Cocoa was selling for 25¢ a pound, and all we needed was the farmers leaving the farms, riots, chaos, no spray for the cocoa, and some torrential rains to encourage the Black Pod, and cocoa would be at 60¢ and we would all be rich.

We even sent Fat Marvin from Brooklyn—five-six, two forty-five—to West Africa to find out what was going on. Marvin knew pieces of paper in the commodity markets; in fact, he had just recently gone busted trading the same. I had gone to Abercrombie with Marvin while he outfitted himself in a safari suit and tried on an elephant gun, because you never knew what you would need in Africa. We waited breathlessly for word from Marvin about our speculation, and got telegrams like

RAINING OFF AND ON

MARVIN

and

BRITISHER IN HOTEL HERE SAYS SAME NUMBER OF COCOA TREES AS LAST YEAR AND CAPSID FLY UNDER CONTROL

We did not know a capsid fly from a horse fly, but anything that ate cocoa trees was all to the good.

Eventually they brought in a nice medium cocoa crop, same as most always, in spite of civil war, chaos, riots, no spray for the cocoa trees, and the Dreaded Black Pod. Marvin returned, having had one adventure where he was dunked naked into warm oil by some of the locals. Cocoa prices did not go up and we lost our stake. I wrote that story and it was not only in *The Money Game*, it was also in *Das grosse Spiel ums Geld* (more or less the same thing in German), and in fact, Paul and I had taken those pictures with the cocoa pod in front of the Bank for International Settlements.

The problem—or one of them—with our cocoa venture was information and its interpretation. There were some serious players in the game—Hershey, Nestle, and M & M

—and they bought real cocoa and knew a capsid fly from a Black Pod, and I have to assume they knew more than we did, because they are still in business. So I wrote that the next time the feeling came over one that there was money to be made in commodities, one should go to a nice beach and lie down until the feeling went away.

But Bernard Kummerli hadn't read that cautionary tale.

When I was trying to find how my bank could have evaporated into the soft summer air so quickly, a vice-president of the United California Bank in Los Angeles said, "You know, this is all just like your own story about cocoa."

It was, and in spades. Unfortunately, I do not have all the pieces, because they take their time about trials in Switzerland, and Kummerli was still in the Basel jail and the authorities there showed absolutely no interest in letting me swap yarns with him. For Kummerli followed the trail of Fat Marvin, at a distance of a couple of years, even though the admonitory and avuncular lessons were already in print.

Paul had not changed his policy of letting his staff have free rein, even after the stubbed toes in silver. "Everybody makes mistakes," he said.

Our bank had already dabbled in cocoa for the accounts of some of its customers. "A few contracts, nothing more," Paul said, and in the noble tradition of our bank, when the market went against the clients the bank, of course, took over the losses. "Small stuff, only a hundred thousand dollars or so," Paul said. "I thought we had only a few contracts." All that, according to Paul, had been audited by the United California's Bank's own auditors when the Los Angeles bank bought the majority interest.

The bank, of course, was eager to have a coup. It had a reputation for brilliance and aggressiveness, and Paul's own style was the *kendo* stroke. The mistakes in silver and the securities market needed to be made up.

Somebody must have told Kummerli the world was about to run out of cocoa. With Fat Marvin's trail scarcely cold, Kummerli took off for Ghana to become an expert. Later I asked Paul what Kummerli had done in Ghana.

"Damned if I know," he said. "Drank a lot of beer. I think he got to know some of the fellows who were experts, commercial attachés, people in the cocoa trade, and so on."

In mid-July of 1969, there was some sort of inter-departmental intrigue going on in the commodity department of our bank. Kummerli was on vacation, and the other one of the Lee boys, Victor Zurmuhle, came to Paul to report that Kummerli had been speculating. According to Paul, Zurmuhle discovered three thousand cocoa contracts, all betting on chaos, riots, no spray, and Black Pod. What did they do? "We traded them out." Heretofore there had been no limits on the commodity traders; now Paul told the young Swiss accountant on his staff, Helmut Brutschi, to set controls. Apparently Brutschi never got started, and even Paul, out on the frontiers wooing the Scandinavians, began to realize that better operational controls were needed. He hired such an officer from a Swiss unit of National Cash Register, but "he didn't work out." And by the time another such officer was brought in, this one from the Volkesbank, the books had been doctored.

When Kummerli returned from vacation in August 1969, he promptly fired Zurmuhle. Zurmuhle, he said, had been speculating without authorization.

What follows is perforce a bit hazy, and it may safely be said that probably no one knows exactly what happened. Since the bank closed its doors teams of auditors have been sorting out the Byzantine mess, and to compound the usual Swiss secrecy, a trial is impending and much of the information belongs to the prosecuting attorney, who is tight-lipped even for a Swiss and a prosecuting attorney.

Somewhere along the line the United California Bank in Basel bought 17,000 cocoa contracts—*seventeen thousand* cocoa contracts—with a face value of $153 *million*. That is quite a chunk for a bank with a net worth of $8 million or $9 million. The contracts were sold by major commodity brokers: Merrill Lynch; Hayden, Stone; and Lomcrest of London. Normally, brokers would not extend a total of $153 million in credit to an institution with $8 million in assets, but our stationery did say that we were the United California Bank in Basel, and the United California Bank itself had assets of more than $5 billion.

Our bank's exquisite timing extended to cocoa. It managed to buy at the highs, something like 48¢ a pound, and the market promptly began to erode. By June of 1970 it was close to 30¢ a pound, and on 10 percent margin, the bank had lost three or four times its stake, maybe more, and was desperately insolvent, except for whatever its California parent cared to put up.

Only, nobody knew it, since by now the books were really doctored. "The balance sheet was undeniably falsified," said Max Studer, an auditor from the Swiss Society for Bank Inspection. But the chicanery had begun before. The bank had not exactly taken all its loss on the Leasing Consultants fiasco. "That was just too big a loss," Paul said. "No one writes off five million Swiss francs in one quarter. That was too big a hunk. You spread it over a longer accounting period. It would have looked very bad." What Kaltenbach did was to get a letter from the Norwegian firm that had first recommended the stock, promising to buy it at its $25 cost, even though by then the stock was down some 40 percent. In return, the bank promised to make good the Norwegian firm's purchase so that they would lose no money on it. In other words, the two institutions would trade worthless pieces of paper. "The Norwegian guarantee is meaningless," Paul told the California bank. "As long as it keeps the auditors happy," said L.A. Apparently that was all right with the California bank.

The auditors were a company called Gesellschaft für Bankenrevision; the auditing firm itself was owned by two of Switzerland's Big Three: the Swiss Bank Corporation and the Crédit Suisse. Not only were the auditors happy, but they approved and certified a balance sheet that was already short by about twenty million Swiss francs.

Kummerli and crew rather desperately tried to straddle cocoa as it fell; some auditors, that is, tried to minimize losses by contracts covering short-term fluctuations with different delivery months, but even the straddles misfired. On the rare occasions there was a cocoa profit, that went onto the books. When there was a loss, the confirmations went into Kummerli's desk drawer.

Later—in fact, the day after Paul got out on bail—I asked him how, in an age of computers and organized record-keeping, all this had been possible.

One mistake, he said, was that the commodity department ran from under the same roof as the foreign exchange trading and the money desk, where interbank deposits were made and accepted in a multiplicity of currencies. "The Big Three banks controlled the foreign exchange market," Paul said. "We were very aggressive. We had built up until we were fifth in Switzerland, and we were turning over five billion Swiss francs a day in exchange. The bank's own positions in currencies, forward and spot, added up to more than two billion dollars. When you have that much out, nobody cares much about a few million dollars." The brokers who sold the UCB cocoa contracts were paid out of the foreign exchange department. The California bank had spot-checked its bumptious subsidiary, and suggested that maybe a position of $2 billion in foreign exchange was a bit much for a bank that size; it suggested that perhaps only $1 billion in foreign exchange be held.

Paul and I sat there on an apartment terrace in Basel discussing this just as if we were management consultants analyzing the process.

"Say," I said, "you remember the thing I wrote about cocoa?"

"Sure," Paul said. "That was good."

"You remember you gave me a diseased cocoa pod as a present when I first came to Basel?"

"Sure."

"You remember what it said at the end of the story? That there are serious pros in cocoa? Hershey and Nestle and like that? When you are tempted to speculate in cocoa, *lie down until the feeling goes away.*"

Paul shrugged. "These fellows said they knew what they were doing."

"How about Kummerli? Did he read that story?"

"No, it wasn't out as *Das grosse Spiel ums Geld* yet, and Kummerli didn't read English."

For the first time, I lost my temper.

"He bought the cocoa in English, didn't he?" I said.

There was an awkward silence and the cordiality dropped away.

"He bought the cocoa in English." Paul shrugged again. "I'm sure he never read the story."

We went back to discussing the decline and fall.

How could it happen, I asked, in a modern, twentieth-century Swiss bank that so much money could disappear unchecked, simply by putting the losses into a desk drawer? After all, this was not a robbery, not an embezzlement, and as far as was known, no money actually went in anyone's pocket.

"We should not have combined the commodity money

market and foreign exchange departments," Paul said again. "That made it too easy to cover by simply listing a time deposit from another bank. And if a department gives an order, the confirmation should go somewhere else, to be double-checked. Every position in the balance sheet should be verified, and it wasn't."

"Shouldn't the outside auditor come in and check, at least once or twice a year?"

"They should, but Swiss auditing firms only care that the numbers you give them match up, not that there is anything behind the numbers. There's one more thing."

"What's that?"

"The chief executive of a bank should know the operations side of a bank—all the procedures, the accounting processes, and so on. I thought I had people covering that, but I didn't, and I certainly didn't do the job myself."

I wanted to know what Kummerli's motivations were. I could see how anyone could bite on the cocoa story; I had myself. After all, in any given year, the world can run out of cocoa, although it has never happened yet. But from there to putting the losses into a desk drawer, and thence to busting a bank, is quite a step.

"I think at first he wanted to impress his own traders. He had a big ego, a reputation for being very smart. When the losses were a million or two, he just couldn't admit it. He was like a man at a roulette table, doubling up and doubling up again, waiting for the final double up that would break him even. Finally—I don't know, maybe he saw the handwriting on the wall and decided as long as he was going to get nabbed at some point, he would put something away for the day he got out of jail. I don't know. To do that he would have had to have confederates somewhere else, someone working in one of the commodity houses."

One day in the summer of 1970 Paul was preparing to go

on vacation. At that point, he had condoned the jiggle of Leasing Consultants, and knew that there was speculation going on in commodities, but the depth of the trouble lay ahead. He stopped by the office of the bank's chief accountant, who said he had a question. It was a small piece of pink paper with a debit of twenty-five million Swiss francs. The accountant said it must be a mistake; Paul hadn't a clue.

"I knew something was wrong," Paul said. "I knew I should stay and sort it out. But the family hadn't had a vacation in a long time."

One of the items on Paul's desk was a partial translation of the annual report, done internally. Foreign exchange, foreign currency and margin positions for commodities had been lumped together in one big number. There was that mysterious pink slip for twenty-five million Swiss francs, apparently a realized cocoa trade. Paul deleted the reference to "margin," in the report, even though it had already circulated in German and had been approved by the Swiss Banking Commission. "Why wave a red flag if you don't have to?" Paul said. "We needed time to clear things up."

The family took off for Marbella, Spain, but Paul did not enjoy his vacation.

"I didn't sleep very well," he said. "I had a tummy ache."

Paul decided that the vacation just wasn't going to work, with unanswered questions floating around. Why had that accountant given him a chit for twenty-five million Swiss francs and then asked what it was? What else was wrong?

"Something wasn't right, and I wasn't facing it," Paul said, a bit belatedly. Back to Basel went the family and behind Kummerli's back, Paul started a low-key investigation. There were, it seemed, huge losses in the commodity department. So, according to Paul, he called Kummerli in, and something like the following dialogue took place:

Paul: What's going on?

Kummerli: Losses, losses.

Paul: I know losses, but how much?

Kummerli: I don't know.

Paul: Why not?

Kummerli: I lost control. I just lost control.

Paul: How much are the losses? Five million?

Kummerli: More than that. I lost control.

Paul: Ten million? Fifteen million?

Kummerli: More than that, I think.

Paul: *Twenty* million?

Kummerli: Somewhere around there, I think.

And Kummerli kept muttering "Losses, losses" and "We lost control."

At twenty million, not only was the bank gone but so were one and a half more banks the same size. Paul decided that he had better carry the message to Los Angeles personally, and he caught the daily Swissair early bird from Basel to Paris and then an Air France flight over the pole to Southern California.

Paul and Helly checked into the Century Plaza in Los Angeles. Neil Moore, a senior vice-president of the UCB, met them. "Don't give me the details," Moore said. "Just tell me the loss, down to the penny."

On Sunday, August 30, Frank King led the group of UCB officials who met with Paul in a conference room at the Beverly Hilton. The president of the bank, according to Paul, was philosophical. "Win some, lose some," he said. The one concern everyone seemed to have was to keep the affair secret to avoid a run on the bank. "How many people know about this?" Paul was asked. "Can we keep it all a secret?"

The bank's chief auditor was worried about the extent of the loss. "We could handle five million dollars," he said.

"But twenty million—twenty million could mean trouble even for Frank King."

Two days later, Paul and Helly and Neil Moore and an attorney for the bank flew back to Basel. "Nobody said much across the Atlantic," Helly recalls. Outside auditors went to work on the bank's books; the losses seemed to be closer to $30 million than to $20 million. In Los Angeles, Paul had tendered his resignation, but he was to remain as an executive and consultant to "straighten the mess." The idea was that the bank would remain open, still the United California Bank's Swiss unit; the parent would work out a scheme to protect depositors and creditors.

On September 6 there was a board meeting of the United California Bank in Basel, but Paul did not stay long. He was asked to leave the room and told that he was fired. "I went home and had a Scotch."

The UCB officials went to the Swiss Bank Commission in Bern, and presented their plan to reimburse the depositors and creditors. The Swiss Bank Commission naturally was worried about the reputation of Swiss banks; the word around Basel was that once that was protected, they were glad to see an American-owned bank get a black eye; now it would be easier to keep the foreigners out of Switzerland. The details of what went on between the UCB officials and the Swiss Bank Commission are not known; again, there were rumors that the commission told the UCB that if it would make good and get out of Switzerland, it would be kept out of the trial to follow as much as possible. On September 10 the bank suspended operations, and on September 16 at 2 P.M. it posted notices on its doors saying it was bankrupt.

The United California Bank in Basel AG was by no means the first Swiss bank to go broke. In the Depression of the 1930's, three of the top seven Swiss banks folded, just

as banks everywhere did. Swiss banks were overinvested in
Germany, and suffered from the German inflation of the
1920's and the rise of the Nazis, and then from the impact
of World War II on their German investments. In more
recent years, the Germann Bank had folded because of bad
loans, and the Aeschen Bank and Arbitrex on speculation,
and the Seligman Bank had bought a huge tract of land
south of Rome without clearing the building permits, and
expired, suffocated by illiquidity. So busted banks were
not new to Switzerland.

But my bank goes in the almanac. That is the biggest
Swiss bust ever.

Paul was about to come down to breakfast on Wednesday, September 9. He was wearing loafers without socks
and was in his shirt sleeves when two Basel policemen
appeared at the door. They said he was wanted for questioning. Paul expected this; he would be there, he thought,
two or three days. The Basel police also picked up the
Lee boys, Kummerli and Zurmuhle, as well as Helmut
Brutschi, the accountant Beat Schweitzer, Louis Thole and
Alfred Kaltenbach.

Paul was shown to a cell with a toilet, a fold-up bed and
a table. The schedule went like this: lights on at 6:30 A.M.,
and a broom handed through the door. At 7:00 A.M., a mug
of cocoa and some bread, the mug reached for at 7:30.
Occasionally a half-hour in the exercise yard was offered;
then lunch through the door at 11:00. "Lunch was not so
bad," Paul said. Dinner—soup and black bread—came
through the door at 5:00, and the lights went out at 9:30
P.M.

At 8:00 A.M. every morning, the warden came by and
asked through the door if everything was all right.

The Basel prison itself is a grim seventeenth-century
building, downtown, with small windows high above the

floors. Even though no charges had been brought against him, Paul was not allowed to see a lawyer. He was permitted to write two letters a week, and allowed one visit of about fifteen minutes per week from his wife. The expected questioning did not materialize for weeks.

Then there would be a key turning in the door, and a guard would escort him to another building for interrogation. I asked if the guard was armed. "He was armed with a dog," Paul answered, but that was all. Paul faced the investigating magistrate across the table.

"What happened?" asked the investigating magistrate.

For Helly, life was, if anything, even more difficult. She was, first of all, without means, since the family's assets were all in the bank. She got a job as a secretary with a pharmaceutical firm, and moved the girls and her Alsatian help—who volunteered to stay without pay—to a small apartment.

"I was scared," Helly said. "Because no one in Basel would talk to me. I thought the house was watched. People were afraid to call me on the telephone. It was like a bad criminal show on TV."

Later, some of Helly's Basel friends were to say that it served her right for marrying an American, and that an American so aggressive had to have unsound practices and was therefore getting what he deserved. Some of the Baselers suggested this was a good time for a divorce. "Basel," Helly said, "is not a pleasant place for a woman alone with children, especially one whose husband is in trouble." When Helly was not working, she was trying to get Paul released on bail and talking to lawyers, but it looked as though, if bail ever were to be set, it would be one million Swiss francs, or about a quarter of a million dollars. That would be far beyond anything she could raise. The general feeling was that Helly's husband had committed a crime

so unspeakable it could barely be discussed. Murder, at
least, was comprehensible. But Paul was still not charged.
In Switzerland a citizen may be held on suspicion for three
weeks, with the three-week periods continuously renewed
if the authorities feel they need additional investigation.
Paul was to spend ten months in the Basel prison—most
of it in solitary, all without bail and without being charged.
When his lawyer inquired, he was told that the charge
would probably be *Verdacht der ungetreuen Geschäftsführung,* which turned out not to be Crimes Against a
Bank but Suspicion of Untrue Management. To which
Urkuendenfälschung, Falsification of Documents, was
added.

Later I asked a Swiss lawyer about the process. "This
is not an Anglo-Saxon country," he said. "We do not have
the doctrine of habeas corpus, nor the underlying idea of
innocent until proved guilty. The job of the investigating
magistrate is to determine as far as possible the truth, and
if you hold a citizen in jail and permit him to talk to no
one, only the investigating magistrate, that is quite efficient."

What, I asked, if the citizen were innocent?

"If he is innocent, then he receives justice," the Swiss
lawyer said. "He is paid his former salary for his jail time.
If his salary is sixty thousand dollars a year, then he is
paid that. And of course, if he is guilty, the time he serves
counts, and for good behavior it counts half again, and
the sentences are not as long as in the United States."

"At first, I was glad it was over," Paul said. "And I
really thought I would be there only a week or two. I was
guilty of negligence. No doubt about that. But that doesn't
mean I should spend years in solitary, *eh?* After a few
weeks I could see if I just sat in that cell I would become
a vegetable. So I established a strict discipline. After sweep-

ing my cell, I did half an hour of calisthenics. Then I asked for a typewriter. I decided that as long as I was in jail and in solitary, I would write a novel."

Paul, of course, was not an ordinary prisoner, he was an uncharged bank president. And the Basel prison was no Attica. Spartan it might be; but it was also Swiss. In Switzerland you get what you pay for. Paul paid for subscriptions to *The Wall Street Journal,* the *Financial Times* of London, the *Economist,* and the *Neue Zürcher Zeitung,* the leading Swiss newspaper. He also paid for the rental of a television set.

"Within a short time," he said, "I was as well informed as I have ever been in my life. Except for the uncertainty, I enjoyed the rest."

It was not only a seventeenth-century jail, it was a seventeenth-century prison life, like Captain MacHeath in *The Beggar's Opera,* who could send out to the best restaurants for his meals and even for Polly.

"You can send out for meals only on occasion," Paul said, "if you pay for them. In Switzerland, you can have what you pay for."

Meanwhile, back at the ranch in New York, I did what any aggrieved citizen would do. I called a lawyer. Several, in fact. It should, I figured, be interesting. After all, this was not just a sour investment, a stock that went down. This was a *crime.* The management of the bank was all in jail. For crimes there is some sort of justice.

The reaction of the great Wall Street law firms was very interesting, enough to inspire a certain amount of cynicism, if you are inclined to be cynical about lawyers. They acknowledged there was a case, but scuttled away like rabbits through the brush because of their own banking connections. I was as popular with the Wall Street lawyers as a Black Panther.

One friend said, "Listen, don't think we don't take

unpopular cases. Why, we represent ex-Nazis out of Spandau—rich ex-Nazis, I grant you. We represent Greek shipowners who are so far beyond any national laws they think a law is an insult. But you're talking about an action against a *bank*. We represent a major New York City bank. This is a major West Coast bank. They do a lot of business together. Our New York City bank pays a lot of the bills, and they wouldn't like us in this. Sorry, baby, but go away."

I called Abe. I should have done that first anyway. Abraham Pomerantz is sixty-nine, portly, and has a nice white mane. He is also the name that scares banks most, not to mention mutual funds and other financial institutions, because Abe is the Ralph Nader of the investment business. There are differences, of course. Ralph Nader lives in a boarding house and operates from a pay phone down the hall. Abe lives in a penthouse and operates from the senior partner's corner suite of a prosperous midtown law firm. Ralph Nader burns with righteous zeal; Abe thinks there are many defects in the society which can be corrected through legal action, and he gets enormously well paid for the corrections when they work.

One day in the early 1930's, when Abe was a struggling young lawyer, the widow of his high school gym teacher came to see him. The widow Gallin's husband had left her twenty shares of the National City Bank. Once they had been worth $400 a share, and now they were worth only $20 a share. "I remember telling her there was no law against losing money," Abe said, and the widow Gallin went away. Then the Senate Committee on Banking and Currency, identified usually by its counsel, Ferdinand Pecora, began to investigate the skulduggery that had gone on in some of the nation's board rooms: the excessive compensation, the dealing in corporate assets, and so on. Charles Mitchell and some of the directors of the National City Bank seemed to be high on the list, in a famous case adequately chronicled elsewhere. Abe filed suit on behalf of the widow Gallin against National City Bank—and hence its stockholders—in a derivative action, so called because the stockholders derive their rights from the shares in the corporation they own. The stockholder who brings the suit brings it on behalf not only of himself but of his class—that is, his fellow stockholders.

The courts awarded the widow Gallin $1.8 million, of which Abe—and the lawyers and accountants who worked on the case—took $472,500. Abe became a champion of the minority stockholder. The Chase Bank was next; that was $2.5 million for a Mrs. Gertrude Bookbinder.

Abe went on to test the way mutual funds used the commissions derived from buying and selling their portfolios to pay for the selling of their funds; excessive sales loads for mutual funds; using the commissions to buy research, and so on. In the courts, he questioned the way banks use the commissions from their trust departments to gain deposits for themselves. Eventually he even got to the drug companies on the price-fixing for tetracycline, which resulted in a judgment against the drug companies of $152 million. Since it was impossible to pay back the individual consumers of the drugs, that amount was spread out among the health departments of the fifty states. Most of Abe's efforts, though, were in the securities and investment fields, and the structure of that industry was hardly the same for having known Abe.

So I called Abe. Normally, and at this stage of his career, Abe does not take phone calls from private citizens, however grievously wounded, but in our peregrinations through the securities business, our paths had crossed. Abe had already read about it in the papers. He told me to come right up. "Makes me feel young again," Abe said.

I had made up a list of questions. If a big bank bought a little bank, and hence had the power to hire and fire people, and in fact the right to name the whole board, weren't they responsible for proper procedures? They did have that power; they had, in fact, fired the president in ten minutes one Sunday, without even telling us junior partners. So wasn't the big bank guilty of *ungetreuen Geschäftsführung*, even if they weren't guilty of *Urkundenfälschung*? And the outside auditors certified all the *Urkundenfälschung* and the *ungetreuen Geschäftsführung*; Price Waterhouse and Peat Marwick had gotten into a lot of trouble for less. Weren't the auditors liable too? And the board: naturally, the board.

But when I went to see Abe, he was in a sober mood. He had read through some research, and he looked up from the papers.

"If this had happened in this country," he said, "this would be worth a hundred million dollars as a class action. But it happened in *Switzerland* and everything in Switzerland is a secret. We don't even know who the stockholders are. Switzerland is a very backward country. They have never heard of a class action. So the answer to all your questions is yes. Yes, the board is clearly liable, but the management of the bank is in jail and clearly busted, except for the two Californians from the parent. And yes, if it were *here*, the auditors would be culpable. And yes, if it were *here*, the controlling bank would have a liability. But it wasn't here. So I can't take the case, but I like you and you like me, and out of all the people that the UCB doesn't want to have overhanging the cleanup of this, the two of us have to be at the top of the list. I have a reputation as an ogre in this field, and so I will write them on my ogre stationery, and we'll offer them your stock, at cost. Maybe they'd like to buy out a partner, just to clean things up. Their name was all over the prospectus, after all."

But the United California Bank didn't seem eager to

buy any more stock. We got a stiff letter from O'Melveny and Myers, the lawyers for the United California Bank. The entity to which we referred, they said, was a *Swiss bank*. Funny it had the same name, but clearly, how could they be involved?

"I was afraid of that," Abe said. "You see, that's the trouble. This whole damn thing is *in Switzerland.* The Swiss won't even tell you the telephone number. You'll have to sue in Switzerland, and the trouble with that is, there is no bank left in Switzerland, so there's nothing left to sue. And the United California Bank itself is in Los Angeles."

"Is there no justice?" I asked.

"That's a metaphysical question," Abe said. "I don't know if there is or isn't justice, but I do know one thing: there's no class action in that damn backward country over there. You know, I had a client once who put me into a sure thing in commodities."

"What happened?" seemed to be the proper inquiry.

"I lost my shirt," Abe said. "I've never made a penny on an investment. It's good I've been lucky in the law."

While I was pondering the fickleness of justice, and its limitations at natural boundaries, Paul was typing away in his cell.

After a while, the stringent regulations relaxed a bit. Paul was allowed to go to the prison library. But he found it disorganized. He got permission to use some of the other prisoners in reorganizing and cataloging the library. "Furthermore," he said, "there are people of other nationalities in the Basel jail—Yugoslavs, Spaniards, Englishmen. There's nothing for them to read." Paul wrote to the ambassadors of thirteen countries and asked them to donate old books to the Basel prison. Some of them did. When the reorganization of the library was complete, the warden of the prison gave a dinner for the library task force.

"He and his wife served it themselves, and we had a very acceptable wine," Paul said.

One by one, the bank's management was released from prison on bail. Louis Thole had a nervous breakdown, was released, and went to Belgium. In the early summer of 1971, Paul was released on bail of half a million Swiss francs, raised from Harry Schultz, Helly's family and some friends. Paul went to England to work for the Harry Schultz letter. All the prisoners were out on bail except Kummerli, and the word was that Kummerli—pending, of course, his guilt or innocence at trial—would be in custody a long time. Paul had had one confrontation with Kummerli before the investigating magistrate. Kummerli said that everyone knew the books were doctored, and that he got his orders from Los Angeles. "He might as well have said from Joan of Arc, or Jesus," Paul said. There was some speculation around Basel as to whether Kummerli had really gone off the deep end in jail, or whether this was a foxy act so that he would be allowed to serve his time in a mental institution rather than in prison. There was also some talk about Frau Kummerli, who was bombing around town in a flashy Mercedes. There is a phrase in Schwizer-dütsch which translates as "green widow." A green widow is one who obviously knows where some of the green is for which her husband is serving time.

The investigating authorities sent questionnaires to all the commodity brokers who dealt with the UCB Basel in cocoa. All were returned except the one from Lomcrest in London.

I went over the prospectus once more, masochist that I am. There it was, "the bridge between conservative Swiss banking and modern corporate and financial techniques, usually identified with the United States."

The present situation, then [it said], is that the Bank is

a subsidiary of United California Bank of Los Angeles, a bank with total assets of $5.2 billion at the end of 1969. United California Bank is, in turn, affiliated with Western Bancorporaton, the world's largest bank holding company, embracing twenty-three full service commercial banks located in eleven western states of the United States. United California Bank itself is the full owner of an international bank in New York City, and has branches, representatives or affiliates in England, Belgium, Switzerland, Spain, Lebanon, Japan, Mexico and Greece. It has direct correspondent relations with important banks throughout the world.

The music began to rise again. The sun would never set on our fast-growing Swiss bank. I was trying to abstract some lesson from the experience, but I knew that if tomorrow someone brought me the fastest-growing financial institution in Switzerland, with that kind of affiliation, and with a dynamic young management, I would probably do it all over again. There was one thing that bugged me above all others.

"When I called you," I asked Paul, "and asked you how the bank was doing, at the time the bank was raising more capital, you knew that all was not well, and you didn't say a word."

"We were opening new branches in Zurich and Geneva," Paul said. "We were going to have banks in Brussels and Luxembourg. We had a little problem with the balance sheet, but who would have thought we couldn't work things out?"

I asked Paul what he was going to do next.

"I don't think I'll be the president of a bank," he said. I didn't think so either.

"I'm going to finish my book," he said.

I read the first sixty pages of Paul's novel. Belatedly,

maybe I did learn something. It was set in the near future. The world was involved in a financial crisis. Treasury officials from various countries were flying from capital to capital. Among the characters were a Russian from the Narodny bank, a titled Englishman from the Bank of England, a bluff American, a safe-cracker named Sammy, the Basel police, and a stiff, austere Swiss banker who was about to pull off an audacious and entirely legal currency coup which would result in a profit to his bank of one billion dollars. *One billion dollars.* The greatest *kendo* stroke of all time.

5:

SOMEBODY MUST HAVE DONE SOMETHING RIGHT: THE LESSONS OF THE MASTER

HAT we had hoped to do in the soberer days of our Swiss bank was to create some Supercurrency in Europe. Before the bizarre events, we had hoped the plan would go this way: our bank would prosper and grow, then it would offer some of its shares to European investors (and also to Americans if they would pay their government's penalty tax). Then the shares would be traded, probably in London and Brussels and Zurich, and we would have a Supercurrency. We could buy other banks and other services with Supercurrency instead of cash, and any time one of the stockholders wanted a chalet or a new cuckoo clock he would peel off a few shares of our Supercurrency. It would be *Swiss* Supercurrency, too, and as the dollar had troubles, that would make a *Swiss* Supercurrency sell at an even bigger premium.

Some of the creators of Supercurrency came to grief, and so did many of the traders in it. But not all, by any means.

The casualty list was typical, but not universal. There were those who kept their counsel and their cool.

There is only one Dean of our profession, if security analysis can be said to be a profession. The reason that Benjamin Graham is undisputed Dean is that before him there was no profession and after him they began to call it that. He came to Wall Street in 1914; twenty years later he published the first edition of *Security Analysis,* the first and reigning textbook in the field. Big, black and forbidding, it has gone through four editions. Generations—plural now—of analysts have grown up with Graham and Dodd, as it is called—Dodd being David Dodd, the Columbia professor who was and is coauthor of the book. Graham himself taught at Columbia on and off for eighteen years and also at UCLA. When Graham arrived on the scene, a security analyst was a statistician, an ink-stained wretch wearing a green eyeshade and sitting on a three-legged stool, who gave figures to the partner in charge of running that day's pool. Now there are examinations and learned analyst societies and the appellation C.F.A., or Certified Financial Analyst.

That makes Graham dean, but it would not necessarily make him respected in the downtown canyons, since professors of finance rarely move stocks, and respect is today's buck, after all. But Graham was also an active investor; he put in about twenty-odd years at it, as the head of his own investment company, Graham-Newman, which was considered a very smart outfit one generation ago, and he retired a very comfortable multimillionaire. Graham is now seventy-eight, and travels to his houses in Majorca, in the south of France, and in La Jolla. That makes him respected, in addition to making him Dean.

One day I got a letter from the good Dean, who was at

his house in the south of France. It is a nice letter, and so characteristic of the Dean that you might as well read it all; it tells you a lot in a brief moment.

"LA CHAMPOUSSE"
42, AVENUE DE MARSEILLE, 42
AIX-EN-PROVENCE

—Sept. 6, 1968

Mr. "Adam Smith",
c/o Random House,
New York City.

Dear "Adam Smith",

This is an appreciative note about *The Money Game* from the chap you call "the dean of all security analysts". I read your book with a great deal of enjoyment, and with admiration for your many-faceted culture. Also, it gave me a lot of information on what has been happening in Wall Street since I left it some years ago.

I think I understand pretty well everything in the book that's in non-mathematical English. However, your Greek on p. 25 gave me a bit of trouble. The second part is evidently a version of the well-known "Quem deus vult perdere prius dementat". (But your text has $\phi\tau\alpha\nu$ instead of $\delta\tau\alpha\nu$.) Does the preceding part mean "When a beam falls every man gathers wood?" If so, your $\delta o\nu\delta s$ must be changed to $\delta o\kappa\delta s$.) And where does the quotation come from?

Thanks in advance for your reply, and sincere congratulations on your book.

Benj. Graham

P.S. Also: shouldn't it be Mme. Récamier instead of de Staël (p. 221) and Hinzelmenschen for—menshen (p. 270). That's for your next printing.

You know something right away. Nobody messes with
the Dean as far as the classics are concerned. To many
Wall Streeters, Horace is the guy who works in the cage
in the back room tallying the margin accounts. Benj.
Graham has always been a classicist; the prescript to
Security Analysis is a marvelously apt quotation from
Horace's *Ars Poetica*:

> *Multa renascentur quae iam ce cidera, cadentque*
> *Quae nunc sunt in honore vocabulae . . .*

> Many shall be restored that now are fallen and many
> Shall fall that now are in honor.

It is nice to hear good words from the Dean, even with
the ruler-taps on the wrist. We did have to have a special
printer for the great quotation, and any good proof-
reader would have realized that φταν should have been ὅταν.
Hinzelmenschen should certainly have a *c*; you can't catch
them all. (I did, however, mean Madame de Staël, not
Madame Récamier.)

After some further correspondence the good Dean came
to town and we had breakfast at the Plaza. Graham is a
short, dapper man with a vague resemblance to Edward G.
Robinson. He was in town, he said, to see a publisher
about the new translation of Aeschylus he had just com-
pleted, and then he was going to see some of his grandchildren. When we met, the market was sliding, and the
performanceniks were in their final throes. I asked him
what he thought of what was going on.

"Oh, I don't keep up any more," he said. "I only own
one stock, and the rest is all municipal bonds. But these
periods have come before. As it was written once, *hoc etiam
transibit,* this too will pass."

What was the one stock?

"That's just left over, Government Employees Life Insurance; we owned the whole company at one point. I don't even keep up with that. I've reached the stage where I'm just giving things away, not trying to make more."

We talked about events since the last edition of *Security Analysis*. Benj. Graham had an idea he wanted to talk to me about: a new edition of *The Intelligent Investor* was forthcoming, that book being more or less a distillation of the textbook, *Security Analysis,* only for the layman. Graham wanted me to work on it, more or less by long-distance correspondence with him. I could send the relevant chapters to Aix-en-Provence or Majorca or La Jolla, and he would send them back again.

"There are really only two people I would want to work on this," Graham said. "You're one, and the other is Warren Buffett."

"Who's Warren Buffett?" I asked.

That, as it turns out, was a rather extraordinary question at the time. Extraordinary because I knew most of the highly visible professional money managers of the time; they spoke at seminars, delineated their theories, dressed up and trotted out their favorite industries and their favorite stocks. I didn't know Warren Buffett. He was not in the chain letter for Four Seasons or Viatron, or even for Control Data or Polaroid.

That, of course, would have made him atypical but not remarkable. What was remarkable was that Buffett was easily the outstanding money manager of the generation, and what was more remarkable was that he did it with the philosophy of another generation. While the gunslingers of the sixties were promoting each other over drinks at Oscar's, then going back to their offices so they could watch the tape, Buffett was compiling the best records in the industry *from Omaha, Nebraska.* No quote machines, no ticker, no Oscar's, no chewed fingernails, no tranquilizers, no Gelusil, no backgammon after the close, no really big spectacular winners, no technological companies, no conglomerates, no "concepts." Just pure Benj. Graham, applied with absolute consistency—quiet, simple stocks, easy to understand, with a lot of time left over for the kids, for handball, for listening to the tall corn grow.

Buffett, it's true, did not manage a public fund, so he was not subject to the pressures of salesmen wanting to sell the fund. While he made his record with the philosophy of another generation, some of his big winners were also well within the growth-stock philosophy. He did not have a committee to deal with, and he did not have a boss. He kept himself out of the public eye, though for most of his career the public eye would not have been on him anyway. If he bought so much of a company that he controlled it, he was willing to step into the business. All of these factors freed him from more typical restraints.

His partnership began in 1956, with $105,000, largely supplied by uncles, aunts and other assorted relatives. It ended in 1969 with $105,000,000, and a compounded growth rate of 31 percent. Ten thousand dollars invested in the partnership in 1957 would have grown to $260,000. Over that time, the partnership *did not have a single losing year,* and it gained in the years of severe market declines, 1962 and 1966 among them. The partners in the Buffett Partnership received a letter annually telling them the goals of the partnership, and the same consistency ran through the ten or so letters.

The money managers of the sixties habitually took a record of one or two hot years, gave it to the salesmen, and let them bring in the people. Buffett's record ran for thirteen years and wasn't merchandised in any way; in fact, as the partners began to see the success, they wanted their own relatives in, and Warren couldn't accommodate them because this was a private partnership of limited members.

Warren Buffett was a far more logical choice than I was to work on Graham's new edition, and indeed, he did do some work on it, though he and Benj. Graham, pupil and master, did not agree on everything, and Warren is acknowledged but doesn't share the authorship. Shortly after I met Graham, Warren came to town and we had lunch, and this was followed by other similar meetings and a rather desultory correspondence until finally I went to the west bank of the Missouri with my various marked-up Graham texts. There, in the Heartland, Warren and I went over the lessons of the Master to see what was still relevant, like two scholars over the Scripture.

Having compiled his record, and having made both himself and his partners quite comfortable, Warren did another unusual thing: he quit. They hung up the jersey and retired the number. He was then thirty-nine. He said that it was getting harder and harder to have good ideas, and of course his own drive had been somewhat dimmed by his own success, since he had then twenty-five million dollars or so to his own name, and there are other stages of life. Of the scholars and the Scripture in a moment; Warren's own story serves as such acute counterpoint to what was going on at exactly the same time elsewhere in the financial world that it is worth telling on its own. I find a certain nostalgia in this triumph of Middle America; it seems almost to have taken place in another country than the one which experienced the Vietnam war, a changing morality, student riots and a burgeoning military-industrial bureaucracy.

Warren was born in Omaha, the seventh generation of Buffett in that city since the first Nebraskan Buffett opened a grocery store in 1869. Warren's father was a stockholder, but his main interest was in politics. In Omaha in the 1930's, stockbroking cannot have been an overwhelmingly

G

fascinating occupation, though it must have exposed Warren to the atmosphere early on: Warren remembers chalk-
ing the board on his father's office as a boy. Howard Buffett
ran for Congress five times, serving four terms as a Republican from Omaha, and Warren moved to Washington at
twelve. He was already interested in the market the way
some lads used to be in baseball averages. And he was
interested in business. He had, of course, that prerequisite
for all business success stories, a paper route; he delivered
the Washington *Post,* which enabled him twenty-five years
later to tell Katherine Graham, the owner, that he had
once worked for her. Together with a friend, he also had a
business delivering and servicing pinball machines in
barber shops. That was good for $50 a week; the paper
route was good for $175 a month, and Warren saw no
reason to go to college. It interfered with business. His
father prevailed, and he went to the University of Pennsylvania's Wharton School of Business and Finance for two
years. He wasn't exactly turned on by it: "It didn't seem
like I was learning a lot." After two years he transferred
to the University of Nebraska, and by taking an accelerated
course, was out in another year.

At Nebraska, Warren had still another business: he sold
golf balls. Once he showed me his ledgers, his net worth
carefully calculated, all on lined paper in cramped round
handwriting: his first stock purchase—three shares of Cities
Service Preferred—and the golf-ball business. The ledger
itself looks like what Horatio Alger might have donated
to the Baker Library at the Harvard Business School. The
net worth starts very, very modestly: the initial capital,
after all, is merely the proceeds from the paper route, the
pinball-machine servicing, and the selling of golf balls.
Warren was also into the market, although his older sister
had to sign the appropriate papers, since he was not yet
twenty-one.

"I went the whole gamut," he says. "I collected charts, and I read all the technical stuff. I listened to tips. And then I picked up Graham's *Security Analysis*. That was like seeing the light."

Warren went off to the Columbia University Business School to study under the Master, and when he graduated he worked for Graham-Newman for two years, commuting from White Plains. He had married Suzy, an attractive blond girl from Omaha, when he was twenty-one. Graham-Newman was further training in the same principles, but Warren did not like the pace of New York or the commuting. In 1956 he returned to Omaha and started his partnership; all his partners were relatives or friends. The partners were to get a return of the first 6 percent of the profits, and the profits in excess of that were to be split, with one quarter to the general partner, who comprised the entire operation.

For the first six years, the office was an upstairs bedroom in the rambling house Warren had bought for $30,000, located in a relatively unfashionable section of Omaha. "This was the fashionable part of Omaha maybe forty years ago," Warren said, when we drove out to the house. "Now everything's moved on much further west. I think most of my neighbors make ten to fifteen thousand a year. You can be anywhere in five minutes from here." The house is on a pleasant, Midwestern, tree-shaded street; it looks like the same section of Kansas City or Indianapolis or Des Moines; you would need only a jalopy and some high school youngsters and that street and those trees and those houses to have a 1947 *Saturday Evening Post* cover. Warren's house is a rambling affair, more rambling because the Buffetts added on another room when they wanted to, and an indoor paddle-ball and handball court. The house is full of books, and the walls of posters (*War is unhealthy for children and other living things*); it is the obvious gathering place for neighborhood children. The Buffetts have two children in Central High School (one of them is named after Benjamin Graham), where Warren's father and grandfather went, and one at the University of Nebraska. Suzy works energetically for Planned Parenthood and for the Panel of Americans. Among all the books is a shelf on Bertrand Russell. Warren can quote Bertrand Russell almost as well as he can quote Ben Graham.

Obviously, as the Buffett partnership grew, so did Warren's contacts on Wall Street, and some of those contacts must have asked him why Omaha, for his answers show the question has occurred to everybody.

"I can be anywhere in three hours," Warren says, "New York or Los Angeles. Maybe a little longer, since they took the nonstop off. I get all the excitement I want on those visits. I probably have more friends in New York and California than here, but this is a good place to bring up children and a good place to live. You can think here. You can think better about the market; you don't hear so many stories, and you can just sit and look at the stock on the desk in front of you. You can think about a lot of things."

"What did Ben tell you?" Warren asked before dinner one night, as I stirred my Scotch and he stirred his Pepsi-Cola.

"He told me *medius tutissimus ibis*," I said, "which he explained is what Phoebus Apollo told Phaëton about chariot-driving, and the bum didn't listen. You go safest in the middle course."

"That's Ben all right," Warren said. "Gee, Ben really knows languages. Ben really liked learning things. The one thing he didn't care much about was money. I don't think Ben ever knew how much money he had."

To win, the first thing you have to do is not lose. That is my own distillation of one of Graham's first principles. It

sounds absolutely simplistic. Of course you shouldn't lose
if you want to win. There is more to it than that. This is
a rational statement in a rational world, even though
Keynes once said there was nothing more disastrous than
a rational investment policy in an irrational world. And
it excludes all the people who really do want to lose,
because their parents once told them they were losers, or
for whatever psychological fulfillment they might get.

Graham does not do much to feed the fantasies of those
who would, say, turn five thousand into a quarter of a million. He starts with the supposition that your money is at
risk; the first thing you must do is not lose your money,
even before you think about making more with it. The
joys of compounding are there if you keep your stake growing, but all you need have is one year in which you give
back half, and your program, at the same growth rate, must
stretch out years and years longer. And he is not sanguine
about your ability to judge the market, or even to judge
individual stocks.

Everyone knows that most people who trade in the
market lose money at it in the end. The people who per-
sist in trying it are either unintelligent, or willing to lose
money for the fun of the game, or gifted with some uncommon and incommunicable talent. In any case, they
are not investors.

A great deal of brain power goes into this field, and
undoubtedly some people can make money by being
good stock market analysts. But it is absurd to think that
the general public can ever make money out of market
forecasts. For who will buy when the general public, at a
given signal, rushes to sell out at a profit?

Too many clever and experienced people are engaged

simultaneously in trying to outwit one another in the market. The result, we believe, is that all their skill and efforts tend to be self-neutralizing, or to "cancel out," so that each experienced and highly informed conclusion ends up by being no more dependable than the toss of a coin.

Graham had little faith that even stock market analysts themselves could, as a group, prove consistent winners:

> We once likened the activities of the host of stock market analysts to a tournament of bridge experts. Everyone is very brilliant indeed, but scarcely anyone is so superior to the rest as to be certain of winning a prize. An added quirk in Wall Street is that the prominent market analysts freely communicate and exchange their views almost from day to day. The result is somewhat as if all the participants in a bridge tournament, while each hand was being played out, gathered around and argued about the proper strategy.
>
> Modern stock market movements, in fine, are the result of a concentration of tremendous skill in a limited area, where profits can be made by smart people only at the expense of other people who are almost equally smart.

The metaphor is very much like Keynes' market metaphor of musical chairs. You can see why I was the wrong choice to work on the next edition of Graham. In Graham's view, the stock market is what the game-theory economists would call a zero-sum two-person game: that is, one person wins what the other one loses, as in a gin rummy game, or one team wins over another team, as in a bridge game. But my own apprenticeship was geared to the recognition of small, rapidly growing companies. The company was worth $20 million when it was small and $600 million after it grew up. Someone else did not have to lose in order for you to win. Of course, over a long period of time, and with enough participants, there is a zero-sum game simply because there is a buyer for every seller. (This concept, it should be added, is relative to the market. If the whole market moves up, then the losers have lost only relative to the winners; they still may have more than they started with. Conversely, if the market moves down, even the winners may have less than they started with.) Mathematicians everywhere are undoubtedly working on the final and complete equation for the whole thing.

Well, all right, *not to lose* is a very good ambition. It will be hard for optimistic young tigers to bother with, or even people looking for increments to their life from the market other than the ones they might rationally expect. How not to lose?

"There is one important proviso," Graham wrote. "The shares must be purchased at reasonable market levels. That is, levels that are reasonable in the light of fairly well-defined standards derived from past experience."

Nothing wrong with that. Some of Graham's critics say that properly applied, this would have kept him out of most of the market from 1949 to 1969, because the market levels never looked reasonable in terms of the way they had looked from 1929 to 1949. IBM, for example, was never right to Graham; a dollar of 1949 earnings on IBM was valued "3.4 times as liberally as a dollar earned by Atchison, and 4 times as a dollar earned by Atlantic Refining . . . the price itself of IBM precludes the *margin of safety* which we consider essential to a true investment." IBM, said Graham, was a speculation; it might turn out all right, but that was speculation.

To Graham, a stock had Intrinsic Value. In the Dark Ages of the Thirties, it was not so hard to find Intrinsic Value. Some companies were selling for less than the cash they had in the bank, and many for less than their true book value, or for their cash and net assets. You could buy a stock for $10, and that share of stock would have behind it $10 in cash. Ideally, you would buy a stock for no more than two-thirds of its Intrinsic Value. That way you would have a Margin of Safety—a stock selling at two-thirds of its Intrinsic Value would have to be counted as depressed. It might not rise immediately from that discount from Intrinsic Value, but sooner or later it would have to.

> One might wonder why, if the market undervalues the issue at the time he purchases, it should not continue indefinitely to do so and perhaps even increase the measure of undervaluation. There is no theoretical reason why these unpalatable results could not occur. The comfort and encouragement to the intelligent investor are to be found in practical experience. In the long run, securities tend to sell close to a price level not disproportionate to their indicated value. This statement is indefinite as to time; in some cases the day of vindication has actually been deferred for many years.

You can see why Benj. Graham never sold like *Anyone Can Make a Million* or *How I Made $2 Million* and so on. Telling a game player that he might make some money in two years is like betting him on how tall the corn will grow and then letting him sit on a camp chair in the corn field watching it. And in the long run, Keynes said, we are all dead.

Benj. Graham would never buy a growth stock, or what has been recognized as a growth stock, because growth stocks seemed to be betting on a future market judgment and the continuation of those growing earnings. The growth stock would not turn out to be one after all, and one has only to look at the "growth stocks" of the fifties—

chemicals and aluminums—to realize that growth in many, probably most, companies is not a permanent stage, but a dramatic burst in early adolescence.

But, of course, in other instances growth was quite real. Not only would Benj. Graham have steered clear of IBM in 1949, he would have avoided it at any time, and IBM has been the source of many fortunes. The same could be said of Xerox, Polaroid and innumerable other growth companies. They simply do not look like the value is there; it is certainly not there in assets, related to market value; it may be there in patent protection or reputation, but how do you measure that? Money has been lost in growth companies which stopped growing, and at market peaks, it has been possible to pay too much for even the true growth companies. The growth companies rarely have the cash in the bank, and the more true the growth, the more they have deprived both their own current profits and current balance sheets to the benefit of some future payoff. And as the companies get more technical, the assessments become more difficult. Sperry Rand preceded IBM into computers, and American Photocopy preceded Xerox into copying, and it was possible to lose handsomely in either case. All you can say is that there are multiple theologies.

Another of Graham's tests was the Value to the Private Owner. Would a private purchaser pay the same price as the market? In depressions, or market bottoms, a private purchaser could find great bargains that way. The rest of the time he would not pay cash and debt; there would be too much of a premium assigned by the market to future earnings or good will or a future buyer even more eager. The private owner would have to have Supercurrency of his own or not pay.

In any case, the investor was to ignore the market, the current price quotation:

He need pay attenton to it and act upon it only to the extent that it suits his book, and no more. Thus the investor who permits himself to be stampeded or unduly worried by unjustified market declines in his holdings is perversely transforming his basic advantage into a basic disadvantage . . . price fluctuations have only one significant meaning for the true investor. They provide him with an opportunity to buy wisely when prices fall sharply and to sell wisely when they advance a great deal. At other times he will do better if he forgets about the stock market and pays attention to his dividend returns and to the operating results of his companies.

Dividend returns! Dirty words to an aggressive investor in the fifties, and certainly to a swinger in the sixties. Happiness when stocks decline!

And ignore the market! Not watch the tape? Not trade stories? Not press the buttons on the quote machine.

Benj. Graham was studied with respect by generations of analysts, but not with affection. What was one to do all day, if the market was to be ignored? That would not get you rich. How could anybody ignore IBM? How smart could somebody be if he had missed IBM—not because he didn't know about it, but because he had considered it, measured it and turned it down?

Graham was well aware that he was himself selling at a discount from Intrinsic Value. Through a number of editions of *Security Analysis,* the final sentence to the "Summary of the Valuation of Common Stocks" warned that "our judgment on these matters is not necessarily shared by the majority of experienced investors or practicing security analysts."

But the judgment *was* shared by one bright student. Warren sat in his bedroom office, reading through the manuals—the statistical manuals of Moody's and Standard and Poor's. There are all the statistics, the balance sheets, the debt, and the contingent reserves, and slumbering on the forest floor, if you could but recognize them, were the truffles.

"I always knew I was going to be rich," Warren said. "I don't think I ever doubted it for a minute. There was Western Insurance *earning* sixteen dollars a share, and *selling* at sixteen dollars a share. There was National Insurance selling at one times earnings. How could it miss?"

Warren wrote to his partners every year, and what he wrote was in line with the teachings of Benj. Graham. "I cannot promise results to partners," he wrote, every year.

> What I can and do promise is that:
>
> a. Our investments will be chosen on the basis of value, not popularity;
> b. Our patterns of operation will attempt to reduce the risk of permanent capital loss (not short-term quotational loss) to a minimum; and,
> c. My wife, children and I will have virtually our entire net worth in one partnership.

The foundations of the operation were almost straight from Graham: "Never count on making a good sale. Have the purchase price be so attractive that even a mediocre sale gives good results."

There is this about Graham: If you have bought at less than True Value, if you have a comfortable Margin of Safety, you are going to sleep better. Then, as the stock starts to work its way up from the discount from its Intrinsic Value to that Value, you will have a gain, and when gains compound, you do very nicely. Warren's letters to his partners usually carried a small table to show how compound interest, the growth of money from the increment, can grow. Here is a compound interest rate table showing the gains from $100,000, compounded at various rates:

	4%	8%	12%	16%
10 years	$ 48,024	$115,892	$ 210,584	$ 341,143
20 years	119,111	366,094	864,627	1,846,627
30 years	224,337	906,260	2,895,970	8,484,940

Now, you can do better than 4 percent at a savings bank. And a 16 percent gain—two points on a ten-point stock and pay the taxes—does not seem unusual as a goal. But look what happens toward the right-hand corner! It is hard to believe that the professional managers running hundreds of millions in the late sixties ever looked at such a table, or they would not have been able to declare confidently that they expected to do 20 percent a year. Eighty times the original stake is better than any professional I know has done with other people's money in the last thirty years. The point is that a 16 percent compound can be a pretty exciting figure.

Over a long enough period of time, the effect of compounding can be a bit ridiculous and you can play any historical game you want. The Manhattan Indians sold their island to Peter Minuit in 1926 for $24. Who got the better deal? Well, at $20 a square foot, Peter Minuit's island is now worth $12.4 billion. Could the Indians have gotten 7 percent, they now would have more than $225 billion, and they would be twenty times better off. Or take Francis I—the French Francis I—who is reported to have paid four thousand écus for a painting called "Mona Lisa." Local scholars translate that écu rate out at about $20,000. Had Francis been able to find, in 1540, a 6 percent after-tax investment, his estate would be more than $1,000,000,-000,000, a quadrillion, three thousand times the U.S. national debt. (Try that on your art dealer the next time he says art is a hedge against inflation.)

You do have to have a very long life in order to enjoy

the greatest benefits of the compound table. Warren wrote them up for his partners to illustrate "the enormous benefits produced by relatively small gains in the annual earnings rate . . . every percentage point of investment return above average has real meaning."

Warren had a relative, not a finite, goal from the beginning of the partnership: it was to beat the Dow Jones averages by ten percentage points a year. If the market was up 20 percent, the partnership should be up 30 percent; if the market was down 30 percent, the partnership should be down only 20 percent. Because of the investment approach, it would be easier to beat the Dow in a down market than in an up market, which was the reverse of the very aggressive so-called swinging managers. The record demonstrates that: in the five years that the Dow was down, the partners were up, and the Dow was comfortably beaten by ten percentage points except for two years in which that average was up rather sharply.

All through the sixties, Warren stayed away from the stocks that dominated the financial headlines and provided the excitement in the board rooms. The partners bought an old textile company called Berkshire Hathaway because its net working capital was $19 a share and their cost was about $14; they ended up owning most of the company, and Warren put new management in.

"While Berkshire is hardly going to be as profitable as Xerox, Fairchild Camera, or National Video in a hypertensed market, it is a very comfortable sort of thing to own . . . we will not go into the businesses where technology which is way over my head is crucial to the decision."

In some of the partnership's investments, the partnership did end up controlling the company. A second category was "work-outs"—that is, situations in which a merger or reorganization has already been announced. Usually the market has recognized the first ninety-five cents on the dollar in such a case, but even the last 5 percent, two or three times a year, on an annualized basis, builds up to a respectable compound.

The major category of the partnership's investments, however, were in the Undervalued category. Here the market was ignored, unless it was presenting something at an unusual price. Benj. Graham had instructed his students to think of themselves in partnership with a Mr. Market. Every day, Mr. Market tells you what he thinks the business is worth. Some days Mr. Market is feeling very optimistic, and is willing to offer you much more than your share of the business is worth. Some days he is very depressed, and he is willing to sell you his share for less than it is worth. All you have to do is know what the business is worth.

"Ben was right," Warren said. "The market is a manic-depressive. That's why you can't buy and sell on its terms. You have to buy and sell when you want to." After a while, around Warren, you begin to get a feel for business, as opposed to stocks moving.

We are driving down a street in Omaha; and we pass a large furniture store. I have to use letters in the story because I can't remember the numbers. "See that store?" Warren says. "That's a really good business. It has a square feet of floor space, does an annual volume of b, has an inventory of only c, and turns over its capital at d."

"Why don't you buy it?" I said.

"It's privately held," Warren said.

"Oh," I said.

"I might buy it anyway," Warren said. "Someday."

That phrase—"That's a good business"—I heard several times, always applied to something solidly managed, with a secure niche, plenty of capital and a respectable return on invested capital. Sometimes, it was the "ethnic banks" in Chicago, which have forty or fifty thousand passbook savers so loyal they will drive for miles even after they have moved away from the neighborhood; sometimes it was a Tennessee or Illinois bank that simply earned a very respectable return.

One example can serve very well in this idea of the undervalued stock. In the first part of the 1960's, American Express was involved in the financing of some salad oil that turned out not to exist. A number of institutions were badly hurt, and several Wall Street houses whose commodity departments had participated went broke. American Express was sold from a high of 62⅜ in 1963 down to 35.

"American Express—the name only is a great franchise," Warren said. He went into Ross's Steak House in Omaha and sat behind a cashier, to see how many American Express chits showed up after dinner. He made a tour of the Omaha banks to see whether the scandal had affected confidence enough to discourage the sale of American Express traveler's checks. "American Express had over eighty percent of the traveler's-check market nationally, and nothing could shake it." Warren bought American Express at its darkest hour, and in fact the partnership owned 5 percent of the company at one point. Amex went from 35 to 189 in the following five years.

The same reasoning went into Disney in 1966. Disney was selling about $50 a share. "On that basis the whole company was selling for $80 million. But *Snow White, Bambi* and all those other cartoons had been written off of the books. They alone were worth that much. You had Disneyland to boot, and Walt Disney as a partner for nothing." While Warren bought Disney for its basic value, the market picked it up and carried it into the leisure boom. And while Warren's reasoning was from Graham, both Disney and American Express were soon to be growth-stock favorites. "If the stock doesn't work in one context, sometimes it works in another. Sometimes the conglomerates would come along and bid for one of our asset value plays."

By 1967 Warren was beginning to think that maybe he would not run the partnership forever. He was, of course, less hungry. But also, as he wrote to his partners, "I am out of step with present conditions. When the game is no longer being played your way, it is only human to say the new approach is all wrong, bound to lead to trouble, and so on . . . On one point, however, I am clear. I will not abandon a previous approach whose logic I understand (although I find it difficult to apply) even though it may mean forgoing large, and apparently easy, profits to embrace an approach which I don't fully understand, have not practiced successfully and which, possibly, could lead to substantial permanent loss of capital."

Warren cut the expectations of his partners by about half. "Philosophically, I am in the geriatric ward," he wrote. "We live in an investment world populated not by those who must be logically persuaded to believe, but by the hopeful, credulous and greedy, grasping for an excuse to believe." Those were the times when fund managers expected to do 30 percent a year, and when a hundred-percent gain could be expected in a computer stock, a franchising chain or a passel of nursing homes.

A leading investment manager of a billion-dollar fund had delivered himself of a statement that money management was a full-time job, not only week by week and day by day; "Securities must be studied on a minute-by-minute program."

"Wow!" Warren wrote. "This sort of stuff makes me feel guilty when I go out for a Pepsi."

Many investment funds far outperformed both the Dow and the Buffett Partners in the heady atmosphere of 1967–68. Most of them gave much of it back the following years. The Buffett Partners were up again in 1969, against a loss of 6 percent or so in the Dow, but Warren was through. The ideas were coming harder.

"In retrospect," Warren said, "maybe a convulsive period like the thirties provided Ben with his environment. A period when securities are really unpopular leaves a lot of bargains to be discovered. But for almost thirty years now, people have been combing and recombing, and I'm not sure how many bargains remain. There will be some, from time to time. But now there are so many security analysts—even though most of them are wedded to other theories, the ranks of security analysts have really multiplied in one generation."

There was yet another difference brought by changing times. Graham had originally divided his investors into "aggressive" and "defensive." The defensive or passive investor was concerned with maintaining his principal and securing a return on it. The aggressive investor was to be rewarded for his attitude toward risk. If the defensive investor could expect, say, 4½ percent return, then the aggressive investor would expect 9 percent; presumably the defensive investor would be in a combination of bonds and solid stocks, and the aggressive investor in undervalued situations. But over the years, bond yields rose, and the possibility of stock gains declined, closing the gap.

"The Fortune 500," Warren said, "yields about eleven percent as a return on its own invested capital. If you paid out half and reinvested half, the return to an investor in the forty percent bracket would be six to seven percent, and you can get that in a tax-free municipal."

There's no question that the Ben Graham approach was evolved in another era and designed for that time. Corporate managers in the thirties and forties did not fear inflation, they feared going broke. They wanted a cushion against adversity, and sometimes that impulse led them to

piling up cash far beyond their needs. Rather than reporting not only all their earnings, but even earnings they did
not have—as became the fashion in the sixties—they
actually hid their earnings through a variety of devices and
reserves so that they would have something for the lean
years. Now corporate managers, fearing inflation and also
wanting to look good on a quarterly earnings basis, leveraged their companies. Meanwhile, conglomerates already
leveraged sought out the remaining cash-rich companies.
So there is not as much Graham material around as there
once was, and yet the market does provide it from time
to time.

Warren introduced me to another Graham disciple.

"He has no connections or access to useful information,"
Warren wrote. "Practically no one in Wall Street knows
him and he is not fed any ideas. He looks up the numbers
in the manuals and sends for the annual reports, and
that's about it. He is a very family-oriented fellow: he
probably spends more time thinking about children than
about stocks."

There followed a list of stocks, about half of which I
had scarcely heard of. The Rutland Railroad? The New
York Trap Rock Company? *The Union Street Railway of
New Bedford*? Jeddo Highland Coal?

Clearly the fellow had never been to lunch at Scarsdale
Fats, and was probably not around after the close at
Oscar's.

The record was not spectacular; it plodded away, beat-
ing the Dow Jones average by a few percentage points, not
as wide a margin as the Buffett Partners, but up 17 percent
compounded over fifteen years. I made a lunch date with
Herbert. We stopped at the checkroom with his raincoat
and briefcase. He waited until the briefcase was stashed
away. You couldn't, he said, be too careful.

"I didn't get to go to college," Herbert said. "I went to

work in the Depression because my folks didn't have any money, and I worked as a runner on Wall Street and then in the cage, tallying stocks."

Herbert took a Graham course at night at the Institute of Finance. "Ben really loved to teach," he said. "He could have made a lot more money if he hadn't been so interested in teaching."

Herbert operated just as Warren said he had. He never looked at rising stocks. He looked at the list of new lows in the paper every day. "Look at the steels," he said. "No one wants them. Will they go bankrupt? How can an industrial country not have a steel industry? Look at American Can under thirty. Can they keep that dividend?"

"I'm not very bright," Herbert said. "I can't compete with all the bright people, and especially the ones who have college educations, who have been to business school, who have lots of corporate contacts. I don't know anybody. I have to buy what I'm comfortable with. These fellows that buy, even Procter and Gamble and General Electric, why, those stocks go *up and down* all the time. I just wouldn't be able to *sleep* at night if I owned stocks like that."

What was Herbert buying?

"Well, there's one issue of Penn Central bonds," Herbert said. That was a bit breathtaking. The Penn Central is very busted. "The Pennsylvania Railroad is bankrupt," I said. "The value of the stock is negligible. The value of the bonds is questionable. It will take twenty years to straighten out. What you should buy is Shearman and Sterling, the lawyers, who will get all the money for the next twenty years."

"I know," Herbert said. "But there is one issue of Penn Central bonds that is collateralized by the Pittsburgh and Lake Erie Railroad. I wrote Irving Trust and asked them, did they have the collateral behind the bonds, and they said yes. They don't pay interest on the bonds, but when they settle the case, I think they will, and meanwhile the interest is in a special account at Girard Trust, twelve, thirteen, fourteen percent. It may take a long time, but I can sleep at night. I'm not in a hurry. Things always take longer than you want them to."

Had he really owned the Union Street Railway of New Bedford?

"Oh, yes. They had a lot of cash. It took quite a while to liquidate, but it worked out very, very well."

Warren bought a weekly newspaper in Omaha, where he seems to be as popular as the Cornhuskers' winning coach. He also bought part of the *Washington Monthly,* a small circulation magazine on political affairs. He is interested enough in newspapers to have made a bid for the Cincinnati *Enquirer.* Considering the Cornhusker background and his father's service as a Republican congressman, it is a mild surprise to find him a Democrat, and in fact a number of Democratic hopefuls have found their way to Omaha to talk about issues and the future. Warren says he has no political ambitions. Most of the millions amassed by the Buffett Partnership will go to a foundation, because there is no point in ruining the lives of children—children at Central High—by leaving them an uncomfortable amount of money. We had a long discussion one night about the uses of money. "What would *you* do with twenty-five million dollars?" he asked. For he had, he said, everything he wanted: the house was enough house, and Central High was good for the kids. He didn't like travel; he might be uncomfortable where they didn't speak English. He wanted to do things in the public interest, but while the problems had been well articulated, there were no great original solutions. One thing he did in Omaha was to join the Jewish country club.

"I ate lunch in the Omaha Club—that's the downtown

club—and I noticed there weren't any Jews," Warren said. "I was told 'they have their own club.' Now there are Jewish families that have been in Omaha a hundred years, they have contributed to the community all the time, they have helped build Omaha as much as anybody, and yet they can't join a club that John Jones, the new middle-rank Union Pacific man, joins as soon as he's transferred here. That is hardly *fair*. So I joined the Jewish club; it took me four months—they were a little put back and confused, and I had to do some convincing. Then I went back to the Omaha Club and told them that the Jewish club wasn't totally Jewish any more. I got two or three of the Jewish-club members to apply to the Omaha Club. Now we've got the thing cracked."

In introducing me to Herbert, Warren had also, to my mind, described himself. "He never forgets," he said, "that he is handling other people's money, and this reinforces his normal strong aversion to loss. He has total integrity and a realistic picture of himself. Money is real to him and stocks are real—and from this flows an attraction to the 'margin of safety' principle."

After our Omaha session, I participated in a seminar with about twenty leading money managers. I brought up Graham.

"That old stuff," said one of the managers. "Graham is all right, but it's really just a lot of platitudes, interspersed with forty-year-old industrial gossip."

Then, after this particular four-day seminar, I reported the discussion on Graham to Warren. He took it for granted that Graham would be, as it were, selling at a discount, but his loyalty was undiminished.

"Graham's teachings," he wrote, "have made a number of people rich, and it is difficult to find any cases where those teachings have made anyone poor. There are not many men you can say that about."

IV:

Is the System Blown?

1: THE DEBASED LANGUAGE OF SUPERCURRENCY

W HEN Benj. Graham was not communicating in Latin or Greek, he depended on two other languages: English and numbers. The numbers—income statements, balance sheets—told you how a business was doing, what its strengths and weaknesses were, and what its characteristics were; in short, they were a mirror of activity. A good analyst could look at a cash-flow sheet like Toscanini looking at a score—Beautiful, beautiful, *tum tum de tum* . . . wait! Wait! Where are the flutes? *Tum tum de tum,* FLUTES! But when Toscanini looked at the score, he could make certain assumptions. If the score said C sharp, that meant it was a C sharp, whether played by a flute or a tuba. Beethoven did not put into the score: C sharp, except that the Composer has elected to defer certain notes and to leave some out because this year they do not sound so good; we should have three good flute players by this time next year (see footnote 13), and Counsel believes the

Composer has a meritorious defense and nothing will have a material effect on this melody except maybe. . .

Investors now have a problem that is more severe than in the days when Benj. Graham would take his students through a balance sheet. The numbers may or may not mean what they say, and there is a crisis in the language. The power of the Supercurrency is so strong and its rewards are so great that numbers go into constructing the best Supercurrency picture and not necessarily into mirroring activity.

There are all sorts of students of the marketplace, and numbers of differing portfolio strategies. Let us take one of the most deceptively simple, which is to look for growing earnings. The first thing to cheer your heart, if you are a growth fan, would be a neat stepladder earnings pattern:

1965	1966	1967	1968	1969	1970	1971
.93	1.25	1.49	1.68	2.08	2.40	2.71

Beautiful, beautiful, what harmony. That happens to be Xerox, which made a lot of people a lot of money.

In the old days, some investors did not want small companies which might or might not grow up to be Xerox. These small companies needed all the cash they could generate, so they did not pay dividends. Some investors wanted dividends. Pension funds did not even keep large percentages of stocks in their portfolios; they bought bonds. They knew the interest rate on the bonds, and that the bonds would pay the interest for many years, and that would take care of the pensioners when they retired.

But gradually, as a small growing company kept growing, more conservative investors became interested. A bank trust department here and there would nibble. A mutual fund might buy some. Not only would the earnings keep growing, but the premium that people would pay would grow. The adventurous investor would take the early risks, and then sell to the more prudent investor who required more convincing.

Then two things happened. One we have already seen in the history of the sixties; the prudent investors got just as aggressive as the old risk-takers. They did not wait for a stock to become a seasoned and proper and judicious fiduciary holding. All of a sudden there were ten thousand security analysts scouring the backwoods for those earnings patterns, and fifty thousand salesmen were eager to call everybody and tell them to buy.

The second thing that happened was quite amazing. Growth? Is that what they want, growth? Is that the highest price Supercurrency? Is that how it's done? Wow!

The supply of growth companies grew to meet the demand. Now, common sense, that great Yankee virtue, will tell you that there is one Xerox, not seventeen. But everywhere you looked, there was a company with a neat stepladder of growing earnings. Some of them kept the neat stepladder right up to the day they filed for bankruptcy. (Skeptics can look at some of the popular institutional holdings, such as R. Hoe, as well as the ones already noted on Babson's booby list.) Magic! Growth companies everywhere! You want growing earnings? We got growing earnings. Make our stock go up, then all our stock options are worth a lot.

Obviously, all the earnings were not growing like that. But did not the numbers imply precision? Did not the numbers, then, represent reality? They did not, in many cases. The world is not the way they tell you it is. The numbers represented a lot of imagination at work in a popular arena. But, you say, this is *business.* You make a widget for x dollars, and sell it for y dollars, and in there somewhere is the profit, and then Price Waterhouse comes in and signs the statement. It says, We have examined the books of Universal Widget, and they conform to generally accepted accounting principles. *Generally accepted accounting principles.* It is safe to say that for a generation no one knew what those four words meant. Leonard Spacek is a senior partner and chairman emeritus of Arthur Andersen & Company, one of America's Big Eight accountants. Here is Leonard Spacek on generally accepted accounting principles:

> How my profession can tolerate such fiction and look the public in the eye is beyond my understanding. I suppose the answer lies in the fact that if your living depends on playing poker, you can easily develop a poker face. My profession appears to regard a set of financial statements as a roulette wheel to the public investor—and it is his tough luck if he doesn't understand the risks that we inject into the accounting reports.

That is the senior partner and chairman emeritus of one of the most prestigious accounting firms in the world. Everybody knows the odds on a roulette wheel.

Translated even further, it means that if you see Universal Widget reporting $1 of earnings, that $1 can be 50¢ or $1.50, depending on which way they are playing the guitar that week. Where does all this flexibility come from?

Well, you could change your depreciation from accelerated to straight line. If your depreciation charges are higher, then your profits are lower, so to increase profits, decrease depreciation. A couple of years ago Armco Steel did just that. Its president, William Verity, said, "The move was a defensive ploy designed to get the stock up and out of the reach of asset-hungry conglomerates and other acquisition-minded folk." Of course, some future year your furnaces may be falling apart, and you without a cash reserve for new furnaces, but in the long run we are all dead—let's get the stock up now.

You can change the valuation of your inventories. You can adjust the charges made for your pension fund. You can make a provision for taxes on the earnings of a subsidiary or wait until the subsidiary remits a dividend to the parent. You can capitalize research instead of expensing it. You need not go as far as the gentlemen at the United California Bank in Basel to avoid showing losses; there are legal means at hand. You can defer the costs of a new project until that project brings in revenues; if the project never comes off, you will take a bath some future year. There are, in addition, other "discretionary expenses."

There is a phrase for this philosophy. It is called *Après moi, le déluge,* or as Scarlett O'Hara said, "I'll worry about it tomorrow." If you do manage to get your stock up, you can go out and buy another company which has some assets and some earnings but whose stock has not gone up. Then you can play with pooling and purchase, although not as much recently as in the good old days. With the newly purchased company tucked in, you can keep the game going.

All of the devices described are generally done with an eye on the stock, not on what might be considered economic reality. The stock market cares about current earnings; they took our old, quiet System and ran it right into the ground. "No one objects to a ruling," said James Needham, when he was an SEC Commissioner, "as long as it improves the earnings. If you touch the X-ray the other way, they scream."

Conversely, if you have a bad year, if the write-offs begin to catch up with you, if your stock is down anyway, then you gather up all the sins you can find and lump them all into the bad year. This is called "take-a-bath accounting," even by the accountants. The idea is that as long as your stock is down, you might as well get all the bad news for several years in each direction out of the way, cancel the old option plan, vote new ones, and hope the stock will go up again next year.

Two notes before we take off on the accountants. The first is that it is business itself that wants to write the books this way. Accountants may sign the statements as independent professionals, but they want the accounts; that is how they make their living. So if you are an accountant and you choose not to go along with reporting all the income but deferring all the cost, the businessman is likely to say, "Get lost; I'll get myself another accountant. A more cooperative one, who understands me." This is called "shopping for accounting principles."

The second note is that once again, there are some honest men and some honest businesses. James Needham, who is an accountant as well as a former SEC commissioner, and who is now president of the New York Stock Exchange, said there were less than fifty serious errors in nine thousand statements filed with the SEC. Only twenty-two out of *Fortune*'s top 100 companies, said he, showed discrepancies between what they reported to the public and what they reported to the SEC.

(Yes, there are differences. Companies report on 8K and 10K forms to the SEC, and on the grounds that the SEC needs more information than the public the information may be not only more extensive, but different. The 8K form now requires that companies also report whether any change in the auditor has taken place and whether that change involved a disagreement in accounting principles. The auditor who has been canned is supposed to say whether he agrees with the reason for seeking another auditor. That leaves the public with only two problems. One, disputes are not likely to be carried as far as the SEC, and two, the security analyst—much less the average investor—is hardly likely to spend his afternoons in the gloomy vaults of the SEC library. It is not easy to get 8K and 10K reports.)

The trouble with saying that most of the businesses report fairly is that it leaves the public with a question: Which are the ones that don't? All the numbers look alike, and it requires a full-time professional accountant to ferret out all the nuances.

It was not always this way; that is, there was not always this attention to hyping up current income. A generation ago, it used to be the other way around. There were far fewer stockholders, and the stockholders were much more likely to know the business, perhaps even to control it and hence to know the auditors. Management liked to pile up cash, as a reserve against leaner years. They did not *want* to report income. The stock market was sleepy; besides, the stock market valued assets and dividends, not reported income. If you reported big profits, your unions would ask for more money. The tax man would ask for more money. Your shareholders would expect a bigger dividend.

Gradually this changed. The Internal Revenue Code of 1954 had some regressive features: tax shelters, investment credits, declining balance methods of depreciation. Labor unions stopped looking at the published data and based their demands on what they could get, not on what the figures showed might be a slice of the pie. For the most part, they got much of what they asked for, and the corporation simply raised its prices, and we were on the way to cost-push inflation.

Shareholders began thinking that if you could get the stock to go up by plowing the dividend money back in, dividends were for old ladies. The corporation discovered that the more it borrowed, the higher the earnings and the higher the stock, so it began to leverage.

The trend finally culminated in the late 1960's when conservative managements were punished for their conservatism. If you carried your patents at zero, if you had written off everything and piled up the cash—if, in short, you had built up your assets—you were vulnerable to a company with no assets and a fast-moving, high-priced stock. Your own stock would have a one-shot jump when the offer would be made, but then you would be swallowed up into the company with the sexy paper, and history was to prove that those companies were ranking members of the booby list in the decline. Asset-rich insurance companies were a favorite target: thus Leasco took over Reliance Insurance, National General took over Great American, and so on. LTV, the vehicle of Jimmy Ling, took over the famous old packing firm of Wilson, and the famous old steel company of Jones & Laughlin, in the famous "redeployment of assets" on the way to its troubles.

Not all managements liked the trend, but once it got going, few were strong enough to buck it. "I wish to hell the stock market didn't want to see the earnings go up all the time," the chairman of a hotel chain told me. "Business just isn't like that. Every year is not always bigger than the last year, and we have to bend things around a lot to get them to come out right." Why not report it the way it is? "Then the stock would go down, and we'd be at a disadvantage vis-à-vis our competitors in hiring executives, making new hotel deals, and so on. If you could get everybody to go along at the same time, we'd do it."

Some people began to suggest that maybe reported profits weren't the way to measure a company. Perhaps it should be cash flow, or return on investment.

The worst sandbagging for an investor came not necessarily when the numbers danced around before he bought. That was nothing compared to the bath handed to innocent investors when the numbers were changed *retroac-*

tively. Universal Widget says it earned 50¢ in 1969, $1 in 1970, and $1.50 in 1971. You buy in, and then they tell you, Sorry, we've changed our accounting; we didn't earn that at all. Put a little *d* in front of those numbers for deficit. Let not the investor take off an hour for lunch; by that time the stock may have gone into one of those screeching dives that pulls out only at treetop level, à la Certain-teed and F & M Schaefer.

Shouldn't the investor get the same information as the SEC? Some of the accountants think that too much information would confuse the poor fellow. Philip Defliese, the managing partner of Lybrand, Ross Brothers & Montgomery, one of the Big Eight accounting firms, said thus: "Would you want things like maintenance and repairs in every annual report? Or rents and royalties? A layman has access—he can go to a library, most business libraries have these things. Or his broker can get them for him. If a man is going to invest and do a research job, then he should be doing the same kind of job the analyst is doing."

As sophisticated investors got bagged, some of them began to take shots at the accountants. Did not Peat Marwick certify the Penn Central? Was not that the distinguished name of Price Waterhouse on Minnie Pearl's Fried Chicken, later Performance Systems, later busted? Was not that Arthur Young's name on Commonwealth United? Did not the New York Stock Exchange itself sue Haskins & Sells, another Big Eight accountant, for certifying the busted New York Stock Exchange firm of Orvis Brothers? What did it mean to have a distinguished accounting name on reports?

"Nothing," said Thornton O'Glove, an accountant who writes a newsletter on accounting for a Wall Street firm. "The signature is worthless."

That is pretty strong stuff, so one does have to remember that the majority of companies play it quite straight. For those interested, there are articles galore (I have used some of them here) in The *Financial Analysts Journal,* in the accounting magazines, and in *Barron's* and *Forbes.* John Childs of Irving Trust has written a very expensive, technical and complete little book called *Earnings Per Share and Management Decisions.*

The ultimate responsibility in all of this was given by Congress to the SEC. Here is part of Section 19 of the original Securities Act of 1933, worth recalling just for the majesty of the Old Testament prose. It's also worth recalling that the title states, "An Act to Provide Full and Fair Disclosure." The italics are mine.

> The Commission shall have authority from time to time to make, amend, and rescind such rules and regulations as may be necessary to carry out the provisions of this title, including . . . *defining accounting, technical, and trade terms used in this title.* Among other things, the Commission shall have authority, for the purposes of this title, *to prescribe the form or forms in which required information shall be set forth, the items or details to be shown in the balance sheet and earning statement, and the methods to be followed in the preparation of accounts, in the appraisal or valuation of assets and liabilities, in the determination of depreciation and depletion, in the differentiation of investment and operating income, and in the preparation . . . of consolidated balance sheets or income accounts.*
>
> The Commission or any officer or officers designated by it are empowered to administer oaths and affirmations, subpoena witnesses, take evidence, and require the production of any books, papers, or other documents which the Commission deems relevant or material to the inquiry.

So that is where the ultimate authority lies. But the SEC,

whose payroll is an infinitesimal percentage of thaᴛ of the CIA, could not possibly police all of American business. It bounced the reporting responsibility to business itself and to the accounting profession.

But is accounting a profession? Could one be disbarred, or tossed out, for malpractice? For whom does the accountant work, the investor or the management?

Most important: Is there any consistency in reporting? In 1938 The American Institute of Certified Public Accountants set up a Committee on Accounting Procedure "to narrow the areas of difference in corporate reporting." In 1959 it set up the Accounting Principles Board to succeed that committee.

The proponents of uniformity question whether any investor can make a decision when all the numbers are so different. How can the same Boeing 727 be depreciated over ten years by one airline and over sixteen by another? The defense says that it is management's prerogative to decide, that accounting is an art, not a science, and too much rigidity wouldn't be good either.

The Accounting Principles Board put a committee to work on the metaphysical questions of accounting: What is "economic reality?" What is "current value"? What is "fair value" on a balance sheet? What should the objectives of financial reporting be? Can accounting provide what is needed? Should there be industry standards, with the discrepancies reported? Do differing circumstances justify the discrepancies?

The sway of the Accounting Principles Board is far from firm even within its own profession, and it remains to be seen whether the clients will go along. Each reforming rule is greeted with squawks from the owners of various gored oxen, and in fact early in 1972 the Accounting Principles Board was sandbagged by its own clients when Congress passed an investment tax credit. Industry went in and lobbied for that credit to be allowed as a one-shot, one-year boost to profits; the accountants wanted the credit spread over the life of the equipment, and they were easily beaten.

That dispute was followed by one over "full cost accounting" in the oil industry. We need not go into the harrowing details. Full cost accounting, said Stanley Porter, a partner of Arthur Young & Company and author of a book on petroleum accounting, would produce "instant earnings" for those companies that adopted it, and leave the more conservative companies facing the "erosion of their investment standing" by comparison. Yet full cost accounting spread like the Dutch elm disease.

Within months, the Accounting Principles Board was just about out of business. The American Institute of Certified Public Accountants was devising another body, a Financial Accounting Standards Board, to replace it, which would include some non-accountants and which might be full-time and professional. So the whole business is still enveloped in clouds of dust.

What is the investor to do? Short, of course, of getting the attention of his congressman—itself hardly likely, since accounting is rarely one of the gut issues in an election. I asked the question of many of the concerned people. Professor Abraham Briloff of the City University of New York thought accountants should subscribe to a Nuremberg Code and should refuse to carry out orders that were improper or morally wrong. One member of the Accounting Principles Board said to me: "We are the Establishment, and if we do not work quickly to change things, the whole thing is going to come down." David Norr, a Wall Street member of that board, wrote: "Accounting today permits a shaping of results to attain a desired end. Accounting as a mirror of activity is dead." Even the legal profession is wary, lest "generally accepted accounting principles" not represent full enough disclosure. The *Review of Securities Legislation,* citing *SEC v. Banger Punta Corp., U.S. v. Simon,* and *Gerstle v. Gamble-Skogmo,* warned: "Counsel must beware of blind reliance on the adequacy of financial statements, both as a whole and in particulars. There are many situations in which such statements, even though competently and carefully prepared, and in accordance with generally accepted accounting principles, must be supplemented extensively lest the statements themselves become instruments of deception."

Still another board member worried that Ralph Nader and the forces of "consumerism" might seize the issue, although, he said, "the public itself doesn't give a damn. The public is a greedy lot: give them two years of a good market and they'll be back." Another professor of accounting wanted the professional consumers of the financial information—institutions and their analysts—to refuse to buy the production until standards were satisfied.

The charges of the critics still echo, and they include such phrases as "fiscal masturbation," "massaging the numbers" and "corporate fandangles." The head of one of our major drug companies put it quite succinctly: *"One good accountant is worth a thousand salesmen."*

And yet, and yet—all of these exceptions take for granted that there is truth and it can be made to work. Even the accountants' critics can sometimes see progress, though they then say it's not fast enough. If you look to Europe or Japan, the accounting is nowhere near as full nor as precise. In Britain, whence much of contemporary accounting grew, some of the work done is even better, but it is done on British companies with their own sets of problems.

Accounting should chart the ebb and flow of activity so that non-accountants can take it for granted. It is scarcely fair to ask everybody to be an accountant. Yet the way things are, few investors will be able to unravel the nuances themselves. The accounting profession should earn the investor's confidence, but in the meantime an individual investor has to get help from the brokers who get commissions from him. Somewhere in the brokerage firm there have to be sophisticated buyers of information.

You can, of course, get the annual report, and throw the thing away if there are fifteen footnotes or if the notes are incomprehensible.

Ultimately, there is only one defensive quality that can serve as protection, and that is common sense. Does it really make sense to believe that this cigarette company is increasing its earnings 30 percent a year? Does it make sense to believe that in an industry as easy to enter as shell homes, this producer is going to continue earning 50 percent more every year? If the company is in a number of different businesses, did it really generate the earnings, or did it buy them, or did it borrow them?

There are enough things to worry about in life already, but there is no choice but to say be skeptical and on your guard.

2:

CO-OPTING SOME OF
THE SUPERCURRENCY

ALL right, the numbers dance around sometimes, but it is the only wheel in town. You still need some of the M_3 because it is so much higher octane than M_1 and M_2. What we all should have done was to find a grandfather who sold his ratchet company to that great fount of Supercurrency, IBM. Then all this would be academic. Granddad's ineptness we can lament, and it is hard to create Supercurrency because you have to go through the whole diaper stage with a new company. And we are not going to get in on the first batch of freshly baked Supercurrency in each company because that is when the insiders sell to the outsiders, and we are outsiders. But at some stage we must successfully co-opt some of the stuff just to get out of the prole ranks of the M_1's. Maybe we can just buy something that will go up a lot. After all, a $5,000 investment in Avon Products in 1950 would have grown to $2.3 million, roughly, today, and $5,000 in the Haloid Company that year would today be Xerox and about $3 million. You only have to find one such plum. Is that still possible for an individual?

If you ask this question inside the securities business, you get two answers.

The first is from the New York Stock Exchange and the retail firms who have many branch offices and deal directly with the public. They say that the public has equal access to information, and that individuals have invested successfully for years and will continue to do so.

The second answer comes from the investment professionals, who think the day of the individual investor is over. "There used to be individual investors in mortgages," one said. "Your grandmother might have held a mortgage on somebody's house, a mortgage on a house maybe in another town brought to her by a mortgage broker who knew she was looking for an income. That doesn't go on any more."

Earlier, we looked at a convulsive period for the whole structure: the banking system that absorbed a run on commercial paper, and the investment community which absorbed—barely—the collapse of undercapitalized brokerage firms. It survived. The structure shuddered a lot but stayed intact, and has now been bolstered. Within the structure, however, changes continue to take place. Institutions continue to increase their share of the trading markets. (Much of the public stock, remember, comes from the conversion of the family company to Supercurrency, and that tends to stay locked up in trusts.) Here is what has happened, the institutional share of trading (in average shares per day):

1952	800,000
1955	1,300,000
1960	1,600,000
1965	3,500,000
1971	15,900,000

Plainly, the days of Mr. Smith in Portland, Oregon, selling to Mr. Jones in Portland, Maine, are mostly gone, and so is everything that went along with Owning a Share in America. In order to increase their share of the market, many small investors had to institutionalize their investing.

When I think of the individual investor taking to the field these days, a quarterback called Harry Theofilides comes to mind. (He comes to mind because a sportswriter called William Wallace did a column about him; otherwise he would not come to mind.) Harry Theofilides was five feet ten. He played with the Redskins until Vince Lombardi came, but Lombardi was not about to have a quarterback who was only five-ten. Harry Theofilides was cut, and went to the Jets, where he came off the bench in a game against the Giants, pumped the team to three touchdowns, including a couple of touchdown passes, and hit for something like seven of nine the following week against the Vikings.

"Nobody ever beat me out," said Theofilides. He was cut for Al Woodall, who is six feet five, and went off to the Edmonton Eskimos in Canada.

"Ever since I've been in football," Theofilides said, somewhat bitterly, "I've been told I'm too short, that I can't see over the defensive linemen. Well, who can? Defensive linemen, *when they come at you with their hands up, they're over seven feet tall*. Nobody can see over them. You do a quick slide into the *gaps between them* and then you look. Sonny Jurgensen told me he could never see; he just threw the ball where he thought the receiver ought to be."

The individual investor has to be considered about five-ten on the investment field, and there are a lot of other people out there who, with their research and their computers and their staffs, are over seven feet tall with their hands up. The odds against a superior performance by an individual investor have to be considered to have gone up markedly since the people who are seven feet tall with their hands up have come onto the scene. It was easy enough for Mr. Jones in one of the Portlands to sell quietly to Mr. Smith in the other one; they were at least the same size.

Plainly, for a great number of investors, safety and a passive return are one course. The gap between the passive return, which doesn't want to accept risk, and the aggressive return, which will accept it, has narrowed considerably. The return from a tax-free municipal approaches the average return on the bulk of industrial stocks. Utilities, unexciting as a part of the game and facing financing problems, still are assured of revenue growth. Some of them have partially tax-free returns, and have a tradition of increasing their dividends every year.

A second course is to buy the so-called great companies and not sell them. This is the course of the University of Rochester, which has had a remarkably successful investment portfolio. The university, being an institution, has a long time horizon; it is prepared to take the sudden downdrafts these stocks face in bad markets because it feels that over the course of a generation it will achieve a superior return. Rochester has large positions in Kodak and Xerox, both of which are in the university's backyard, and some of which were given to it. The individual still faces the question, What is a great company? because great companies become mature and not-so-great. Early growth is an invitation to competition, and the growth companies of one era are not always those of the next. Nonetheless, it is possible, by concentrating on some of the characteristics below, to find companies which can be held for a long time.

Both of these courses assume the ability to leave the game element behind, entertaining as that may be.

Finally, a minority of individuals, those with some time

and the proclivity to do their own work, can do very well. For the people who are seven feet tall with their hands up are that way for everybody—even themselves—and nobody anywhere can see over them. You will have to take a quick step and look in the gaps between them.

But a time may be coming in which it would be possible to be successful with just the old tenet that used to work, *anticipate the institutions.* While institutions are big and muscular, their records are not all that awesome. Furthermore, their managers talk to each other and tend to run in packs, like beagles. All you have to do is find the scent before the beagles do.

For institutions, too, have been burned. They love the security of a front-running company with growing earnings, and they are wary of small companies because they cannot move in and out of them well in size. If you can find the smaller, growing company and sell it to the institutions when it gets a bit bigger, you will have stepped into the gap between them. That sort of front-running means the stock can go onto the Approved List of the banks, and a trust officer can put it into his accounts without being criticized.

You will be, by now, paying some attention to the accounting, and you will be listening hardest to your own common sense. You will have husbanded your time and not wasted it on those industries—about 80 percent of them—that do not have favorable characteristics in the long term. Very likely, the company you find will be financially strong, so that it will not have to sell more stock or borrow unfavorably. It will have a leading edge in its key products and the capability of improving that edge, through research if that is the way it is done. It will have control over its own prices, and a labor component low enough not to be a problem, or at least controlled labor costs. It will be in an area that common sense will tell you is growing. All of these things will have contributed to its nice profit margins and its profits.

All of these factors can be the ones to look for in finding something adolescent that is bought to be sold. If in addition, the company has something unique that makes competition difficult, you may have a great company that can be held.

In the 1960's it was fashionable to look to high technology for all of these characteristics, as well as for the something unique. Xerox and Polaroid were protected by rings of patents. But the lead time in patent protection is diminishing; if one polymer is patented, there may be a similar one which works equally well. Further, virtually everybody in the investment business underestimated how much the government flow of research and development money meant, even though the best of the pure companies (as the two above) were not dependent on that. In Avon Products, it was the sales force that was so hard to duplicate.

I have a bias about this particular philosophy which you should correct for, because it is the one that served best when I was first learning. A bunch of us sat at the knee of one of the great apostles of the Growth Theory, a man who went out to the mutual funds and pension funds and preached the true gospel. Since then we have learned that those growing earnings can be such a security blanket to the buyer that he pays too much for them, so even when the stepladder is true and the company is going to maintain the growth, it pays to buy them at the low end of the swings in their price–earnings ratios. Periodically Mr. Market gets manic. A true growth company may swing from selling at twenty times earnings in a bad market to forty-five times in a hypertensed market, and it does pay to wait for the troughs.

Anyway, we sat at the great man's knee, and then we

went out to apply the theory. We would wait tensely while the mentor graded our papers. I bring this up because I remember bringing in a stock that provides the perfect example of what an individual can do by himself. The mentor had bid us study Gillette. The mentor held up a pack of Blue Blades, very dramatic. "This will double, and if you *know* a double, you can do better than that." People used up the Blue Blades, threw them away, and bought more. Gillette dominated its market with an army of salesmen. Its displays were on every drugstore counter, and it was going into other grooming items.

What else was like Gillette? We were to go out scouting. I took a careful walk around a drugstore, and then I went to the manuals, and then I brought my stock to the mentor and waited for my very good grade.

I had a stock called Tampax. It had no debt, no preferred, and plenty of cash. Its product was a leading product. It was like Gillette in that you used it, threw it away, and bought more. It had flexibility in the pricing. Its profits grew every year. I wanted an A for my idea.

I got a B, and I protested.

"It's a very good little company," said the mentor. "I suppose Kimberly-Clark or Scott could compete with it. But what is so unique?"

"What is unique is that when people go to the drugstore, they don't know the name of any other product," I said. "Like Kleenex. Tell me the name of what else competes with Kleenex. A generic name is better than patents."

The mentor wouldn't change my B to an A.

"It's a solid B," he said. But the earnings grew perhaps 15 percent a year; we were looking at technological companies whose earnings grew 50 percent a year, making oscilloscopes and particle accelerators and other patented, super-sophisticated stuff, protected by patents and by technical staffs with hundreds of Ph.D.'s in physics.

"Yours is a population-growth stock," said the mentor. "I don't see why it's ever going to grow considerably faster, although that fifteen percent could compound. Texas Utilities and Coca-Cola increase their earnings every year too, and those stocks are already on the approved lists of all the banks."

So I didn't buy Tampax at 5, adjusted for splits. The mentor was right for that time: the technology stocks moved much faster. A couple of years later the pace accelerated, so that their patents were no protection, and then there was price-cutting in some of the products. Some of those technological companies are far bigger today, and some are treated as cyclical companies. But Tampax is around 120. I feel dumb every time I think about it.

There are numbers of other examples of front-running, solidly managed companies in growing fields with some sort of edge about them. Some of the ones that worked in the recent past were as easy to understand as Johnson & Johnson, Band-Aids and baby powder, and McDonald's, the ubiquitous hamburger stands. MGIC, the Mortgage Guaranty Insurance Corporation, filled a conspicuous gap in mortgage insurance. Not only did these companies make it through the sixties and the Big Bear, but they are up better than a 1000 percent from their lows of a decade ago. (That doesn't mean they are necessarily headed for that in the decade ahead.)

You have plenty of competition in looking for the outstanding steady growers, but you only need one for real success, and you can be sure that if you find one, somebody —a nice bank probably—will buy it from you at a premium some other time, even if you are only five-ten and the other fellows are seven feet tall with their hands up.

3:

BETA, OR SPEAK TO ME SOFTLY IN ALGEBRA

THERE is no System in the market, and there are many approaches that work. The generation now in command has had just time enough to learn that at some point any of them can fail. It is a bright generation, so that discovery was damaging to its self-confidence. This generation entered the sixties full of beans. The generation ahead of them on Wall Street had clearly been paralyzed by the memory of the Great Depression. The new generation had moved in with the appropriate lack of inhibitions. The older generation had lacked real, serious security analysis. Now there were ten thousand security analysts. The older generation had relied on country-club information and a few statisticians with green sleeve garters. Now there were computers to screen and filter, to assemble a stunning variety of comparisons and ratios, to do charts and measure relative strength. The financial rewards for the new generation were great, but that was only right and proper for gentlemen and ladies of business-school education, rational intelligence, daring and perception.

Then along came a severe test and took away not only some of the profits, but some of the scientific and self-confident aura of the whole business. The security analysts turned out to be just as wrong as they were right.

Writing in the January–February, 1972, issue of the *Financial Analysts Journal*, the director of research of a large institution assessed statistically the research which went to institutions. That is research presumably painstaking and not horseback, aimed at a sophisticated audience. The results weren't much different from the Standard & Poor's averages, and were summarized as "consistently mediocre." Some were good, some were bad, and taken all together they weren't so handsome. (The article may have been a bit unfair in that it was based on published material. The best work of the best security analysts goes unpublished. Analysts are paid indirectly with the commissions of clients, and those clients are quite likely to make up a list—a short list, at that—of the analysts and the firms they want to reward. If an analyst has a bright idea, it is going to go first to his biggest client, and then to his next biggest, and so on. By the time it gets to the nth client, or into print, it has lost much of its value, but it is only from print that surveys and evaluations in the *Analysts Journal* can be made.)

Not only did the work of the security analysts follow the price of the stock more than the course of reality, but much of the technical apparatus also blew its tubes. The performance of the funds has already been discussed, and in aggregate, the performance of the managers left something to be desired.

The more sensitive and alert money managers were the ones to engage in some self-questioning. Notes from portfolio-manager seminars reveal a change in the tenor of the meetings over a course of four or five years. As the jackets came off and the drinks were poured in the earlier meetings, the questions ran to: All right, what's hot? What do we buy now? How long have we got? By recent times, the questions had taken on a Kierkegaardian tone—at least so far as this field is concerned—full of doubt and musings. What is a portfolio, as opposed to a list of stocks? Can portfolios be managed as portfolios? Does anyone do it? What is a buy? What is a sale? Which one do you concentrate on? Can anyone outperform anyone else? What is risk?

The last question got asked a lot after some of the portfolios went down 40 percent. After all, why pay a professional to lose 40 percent of your money? Maybe something was wrong with the whole process: assessing where the economy was going, making some sort of market judgment, letting the security analysts scout their stocks, and building the portfolio, with the portfolio manager using his experience, judgment, rational intelligence, intuition and *Fingerspitzgefühl*. Maybe that was the wrong way; maybe there was something missing from the process. Maybe that something was risk, the opportunity for loss.

A headlong race to include the risk factor in all the calculations began, even though the professionals for years were accustomed to speak of the downside risk. But maybe you could *quantify* the risk, so that you wouldn't have to depend on the portfolio manager's judgment. Thus was born what came to be called the beta cult, after the Greek letter beta, β. Beta stood for the measurement of market risk through the variability of the rate of return, and thus could be considered a component in capital asset pricing theory. The beta cult gave Wall Street a new jargon to toss around. A dozen Wall Street houses offered beta measurement services, some taking full-page ads in *The Wall Street Journal* and *The New York Times* to announce their discoveries. The math and computer people had a quick re-surgence, and some senior people growled, as did Lemont Richardson of Booz Allen, "These people with math and computer backgrounds who think they can assign precise degrees of risk to five or six decimal places are nothing but charlatans."

You have to start somewhere with beta theory, and the usual starting place is with *The Theory of Games and Economic Behavior,* by John von Neumann and Oskar Morgenstern of Princeton, published in 1944, which said (among other precepts) that in a game situation, you had to calculate the risk accompanying the course to a particular reward, and to determine the "utility" of that course. In 1952 Harry Markowitz published a seminal article in the *Journal of Finance,* a version of his doctoral thesis at the University of Chicago. Markowitz showed that diversification could reduce risk, that you could measure the risk by measuring the variability in the rate of return, and that an efficient portfolio was one which provided the highest return for the amount of risk which the portfolio owner was willing to assume. (For this, Markowitz was called "the father of the beta." He now runs a small arbitrage fund that uses computer techniques but not much beta. At one beta seminar, Markowitz said that he was not the father of the beta but the grandfather, that William Sharp of Stanford was the father.

The beta enthusiasm had one mildly amusing sidelight. All this statistical work—and the implication that some formula, however sophisticated, can in some way replace the manager—is naturally threatening to the manager. At a seminar five years ago, the Markowitz model, as it is called, was discussed for a whole morning. It was roundly denounced. Markowitz had missed the whole point of diversification; one participant even suggested—and this remains in the mimeographed abstract—that "Markowitz's books be assembled and burned." But within five years, brokers—one of them represented at the seminar above—were offering beta studies to their clients as a merchandising come-on.

Beta theory is based on two simple ideas: one, that most stocks and groups of stocks bear a fairly close relationship to the market as a whole, and two, that to get higher rewards, you have to take greater risks. The portfolio's riskiness is determined by plotting its rate of return—capital gains plus dividends—against the rate of return on a convenient market index, say, Standard & Poor's 500. The beta coefficient is the measure of volatility, the sensitivity of that rate of return to the market. By definition, the market has a beta of 1.0. So a portfolio of 2.0 would be twice as volatile, on the average; it would go down or up as much as the market. (If you are wondering what happened to alpha, that is the residual influence not related to the market, the vertical axis against which the beta slope is plotted.)

Beta theory has provided a happy hunting ground for the type who love punching computer keyboards and desktop calculators, especially in Academia. When the *Financial Analysts Journal* did a bibliography on risk and return, it listed—and this in 1968—253 articles and 89 books. Those totals have now gone much higher.

The big push for beta came from the banks, and specifically from the Bank Administration Institute. In the late sixties the money was flowing out of bank trust departments and bank-managed assets and into performance funds and other forms of go-go. The people taking the money away were saying that the swingers were already up 50 and 100 percent, and that the bank-managed money hadn't moved in ten years. The banks wanted some form of statistic that would say, Sure, the gains are big, but look at the risks.

The Bank Administration Institute put out a report, *Measuring the Investment Performance of Pension Funds,* which had a considerable impact. Further reports came out of the University of Chicago's Business School, long a fortress of stock market statistical work, shortly to be renamed Beta U. And beta got a nod in the SEC's Institutional Investor Study.

All of this work was directed simply at refining comparisons, so that you didn't take Fund A and compare its record with Fund B without also taking into consideration the volatility—and hence the risks—in each. If the so-called beta revolution is real and not just another statistical fad, then all comparisons in the future will have to contain beta adjustments, mutual funds will disclose their beta assumptions, and incentive fees will be determined by incentive results adjusted by beta.

Just so you know what they look like, here are medium, high and low beta funds:

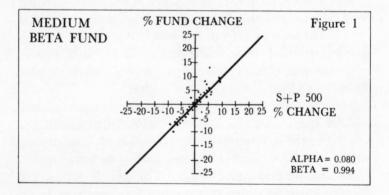

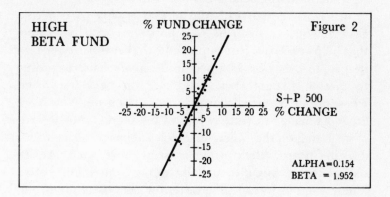

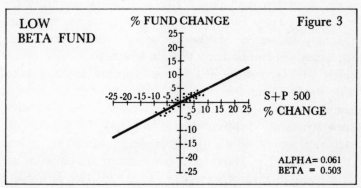

Source: Merrill Lynch, Pierce, Fenner and Smith, Inc.

Nice and easy, right out of the geometry books, $y = a + bx$.

There are, as you might have thought, still a lot of disagreements about beta. Does the variability of the rate of return really equal risk? Maybe that is only part of risk. Even if you can describe past portfolios with beta, does that help you build future portfolios? "Price behavior may be people behavior, but people do not behave according to thermodynamic laws," said a Penn beta researcher, whose paper reported that beta worked on the New York Stock Exchange in wide swings of the market, but seemed to be useless on the American Stock Exchange—back to the drawing board. (Beta proponents say, Sure, there are statistical biases, but they will be worked out imminently). There is no universal time series for beta. Beta might not work in portfolios with a short history. And could not some manager innocent of beta consider downswings as opportunity?

One of the beta theoreticians, after a lot of calculator time, suggested that maybe risk and the opportunity for gain didn't come out quite as congruent as the first runthroughs suggested. Maybe the opportunities for greatest gain came in emphasizing the moderate-risk course exclusively, and borrowing, if you could, to buy the moderate-risk stocks. That, he suggested, was the most aggressive course possible. Thus did the statisticians arrive at what superachieving children do instinctively, for this is the statistical curve of the ring-toss game charted by David McClelland, the Harvard psychology professor who has pioneered in measuring achievement. In *The Achieving Society,* McClelland noted that children with low-achievement drives tossed the ring randomly, from any distance, but the high-achievement children tossed from exactly that point that maximized not only their chances of success but their satisfaction from it.

It is a clean, dustless, fluorescently lit world, the beta world, full of the humming of computers. When the beta revolution arrives, you simply decide on the degree of risk you want, and dial that. If you accept the idea, you dial a beta of 1.8 for high risk, or 0.5 for low risk, and go home. So do all the security analysts. "The first step," said Professor James Lorie of the University of Chicago, "is to give up conventional security analysis. Its occasional triumphs are offset by its occasional disasters and on the average nothing valuable is produced."

The beta proponents are, by and large, those who believe the stock market is a random walk—touched on in *The Money Game,* the freshman course, and earlier here. The random walkers believed that charts were a lot of nonsense because, in my own postulate, *prices have no memory and yesterday has nothing to do with tomorrow.* Yet so far, the triumph of beta has been to correlate all the yesterdays. And, according to Chris Welles, author of a notable beta article:

> Unlike chemical formulas, investment formulas, if they become widely accepted, tend to self destruct by distorting the very environment from which they are derived . . . Underpinning the asserted need for and utility of such a system is the asserted futility of trying to outperform the market which is itself based on the asserted "efficiency" of the securities market. The market is presumed to be efficient in the sense that, in general, the price of any security at any given time accurately reflects the best available information on that security . . .
>
> Such a degree of efficiency, however, would seem to presuppose a large number of very industrious security analysts. If all security analysts were sent off to school to become metalworkers . . . the efficiency of the stock market would very swiftly decline.

Then there would be a lot of information that wasn't being used, and the few remaining portfolio managers who signed up for beta could outclass the computers with their specific information.

A couple of years ago there was a flurry in the computer world about relative strength as a technique. All you had to do, by definition, was to stay in the strongest stocks, on the grounds that *a stock is going up as long as it's going up.* One of these was George Chestnutt, who sold a service based on momentum, and whose American Investors Fund had risen 398.77 percent from 1959 to 1968. "The machine does all the work," George said, raising both hands—look, no hands. American Investors Fund went down 40 percent from December 1967 to June 1970. It had momentum, but it had too much beta, not enough alpha, and no soul.

Conscientious fellow that I am, I have been to a number of beta seminars. Here are my notes from one of them:

> Any one security can have a substantial positive or negative Alpha, and can have a fairly low Rho. (Rho is the correlation coefficient between the return on the stock and the return on the market.)

At this point I drew a ducky flying through the air.

> As we diversify, the portfolio's Rho tends toward 100% and Alpha tends toward zero.

A colleague of mine passed me a note. *Simulation does not prove that out,* said the note. I drew a little ship on the water.

> With Rho near 100% and Alpha near zero, the port-

folio's risk factors depend on its Beta and on the overall market's average return and standard deviation of returns.

I drew two more duckies, and wondered idly if I could get Teddy Kennedy to take the exam for me.

A questioner in the audience had a question.

> *Questioner:* What happens if in the estimating equation for the Beta, you have misspecified so that you have serial correlation in the residuals?
>
> *Moderator:* What?
>
> *Questioner:* What happens if in the estimating equation for the Beta, you have misspecified so that you have serial correlation in the residuals?
>
> *Panelist:* I think I can handle that. It is not a serious problem.
>
> *Questioner:* But what if you do?
>
> *Panelist:* I have written a very complex paper, which I am not sure I understand myself, and I can tell you it is not a serious problem.
>
> *Moderator:* Does that answer your question?
>
> *Questioner:* No.

I went up afterward to talk to our chief instructor. "Whaddya think of the market?" I said.

He looked at me like I was crazy. I had been reading a lot of the literature, so I may have looked a little addled. But I was longing for the good old simple days at Scarsdale Fats's luncheons, with Scarsdale saying, " What three stocks do you like best?" and the money managers all hustling each other. So I repeated the question. He saw I meant it.

"I have all my money in a savings account," he said.

Beta theory is going to be a useful tool. At least it is a handy way to describe some of the characteristics of a portfolio. Maybe it is going to be more than that; some people take it very seriously. Maybe all the security analysts and portfolio managers will indeed go off to become metal-workers. If not, beta will be integrated into the existing system, and you will get phone calls like this:

"This stock is selling at thirty-six, and we think it could earn three dollars easy. Keystone is looking at it very hard. The other stocks in the group all sell at multiples of twenty plus. And, oh, yes, it's got a beta of 1.6. That's pretty high, but this is a high beta market; everybody's looking to juice up their betas."

And before we know it, the accountants will get into the act, and decide that according to generally accepted accounting principles, the stock has either a beta of 0.3 or 1.9, depending on which way you want to look at it, and we will all be back on safe, familiar ground.

Even an elaborate quantification such as beta assumes that Monday will be pretty much like Friday, that the power will still be there for the computers and the stock exchange will be humming along, its thoughts of moving to Dubrovnik merely a passing nightmare. But as that great social philosopher Satchel Paige once said, *"Never look behind you, somethin' might be gainin' on you."* What could that be?

Well, Watchman, What of the Night? Arthur Burns's angst; Thirteen Ways of Looking at a Blackbird; Prince Valiant and the Protestant Ethic; Work and Its Discontents; Will General Motors Believe in Harmony? Will General Electric Believe in Beauty and Truth? Of the Greening and Blueing, and Cotton Mather and Vince Lombardi and the Growth of Magic; and What Is to Be Done on Monday Morning.

I think it was about five o'clock in the afternoon and the snow was getting worse and I began to ask myself what I was doing in the Pink Elephant Bar in Lordstown, Ohio. The Pink Elephant is on the highway, Route 45, and so is the Seven Mile Inn, and Rod's Tavern is just off the highway, and the highway is the one that goes by the new $250 million General Motors plant that makes Vegas on the world's most automated assembly line. My friend Bill and I go up, cold, to these various characters, some of them indeed with mustaches and long hair and sideburns, and there we are: boy social scientists, amateur pollsters. Can we talk to you? Can we buy you a beer? Rolling Rock or Genesee? Do you work in the Vega plant? Is that a good place to work? I mean, would you tell your brother or your son to get a job there? What do you do there? Does your wife work? Do you want another beer? When you get your paycheck, what do you spend it on? Do you spend it in stores, for things, or do you pay it to people—doctors, barbers, plumbers? What do you think of the kids in the plant? The old guys? The blacks? The foremen? The management? Do you want another beer? What do you want to do with your life?

At one point this character in a leather jacket comes up behind us who looks like an old pro football player gone a bit soft—not a tackle; a guard or a linebacker, maybe six-three, two forty-five—and he says, "I heard you talkin'."

We wait. Some tension in the air, momentarily.

"Air you fum West Vihginyuh?"

We are not from West Virginia. Bill is from Detroit and I am flown from the canyons of Gotham.

"I knew you wasn't fum here. You talk lahk you're fum another country."

Well, yes, I say, it is another country.

"Good, lemme buy you a beer, I lahk to talk to people fum other countries."

What do you make per hour? Would you rather have overtime or the time off? Is there a generation gap? Would you buy one of the cars you make? What does the union do for you? Why do you work there? What would you rather do? Do you think things are working properly in the country?

You can see all the contemporary social science bits going on: Attitude/Authority? Agree/Disagree Sick Society? Attitude/Work?

Our ambitions are very modest. Bill is doing a story. Maybe he can get another Pulitzer, why not have two? And as for me—why, I am just looking for clues, see, The Future of American Capitalism. I am going through the money-management macro bit in an untraditional way. The man running the money comes into his office, puts on his green eyeshade and his sleeve garters, and says: How goes the world today? And how will it go in six months? A year? But what does he know then? He reads reports and numbers, but what do they tell?

I have just told you about some events in our recent history, in which the system survived and some bright people failed. Are we really then back to normal, a big sigh of relief and business as usual? Or is there Something Else Going On? Maybe the system is changing, maybe our view of reality was distorted all the time. The very bright people were in charge of the government, and making the world safe for democracy, and not only is the world not safe for democracy, it is not even safe in Central Park and downtown Detroit and nobody wants to go out after dark. We put the money into public housing and it turns into disasters such as Pruitt-Igoe in St. Louis, and twenty-two downtowns look like Berlin in 1945. We did put men on the moon, but do we really know how to manage, and how to perform?

The estimable white-haired and pipe-smoking chairman

of the Fed, Arthur Burns, comes to report to the Joint Economic Committee of Congress. Clutched in his hand is the Fed's report for the year, and its promises for the future. The report is all about the Fed's business, which is money and credit, and the estimable white-haired and pipe-smoking chairman says that the Fed is going to do everything just right: it is not going to let the recovery falter for lack of credit, nor is it going to put out so much credit that we will have another inflationary spiral. But before Burns delivers the report, he has to make some remarks that are not in the report. Maybe "old-fashioned remedies"—that is, those available to Arthur Burns: the levers of credit—can't do the job. Businessmen aren't responding in the usual ways. Consumers aren't responding in the usual ways. "Something has happened to our system of responses. Troubled times have left a psychological mark on people. Americans are living in a troubled world, and they themselves are disturbed."

What can the matter be? Well, "a long and most unhappy war," and busing, and the youth vote, and campus disorders, and urban race riots, and the fact that "women also are marching in the streets." Oh my God, women are marching in the streets.

"If only life would quiet down for a while," said the chairman of the Fed. The classic economic policies would have a better chance of working *if only life would quiet down for a while.*

So said the chairman of the Fed, hardly one of your bomb-throwing radicals.

Something has happened to our system of responses. If only life would quiet down for a while.

Poor Arthur Burns, you press the levers and the right things don't happen, and the problem is life itself. But maybe that is life; maybe that is the way things are going to be from now on. Good God, women marching in the streets, nobody responding in the usual ways. Mind-boggling.

So that is one of the reasons I am getting a bit bloated on Rolling Rock beer in the Pink Elephant Bar on Route 45 in Lordstown, Ohio. The economists have made their usual cheery predictions—ah, for the days when Keynes hoped that someday economists would be accorded the status of good dentists—and the analysts are off chasing the new nubile lovelies in a new game of *après nous le déluge*. But I do not have to show performance weekly or even quarterly, so I can take the time to worry these metaphysical questions that all the money folk will worry about some other time, that have Arthur Burns fingering his Gelusil.

If you simply read the financial pages, you would find no hint of anything different. The type face is the same, the language is the same, and the reports are all of prices: bonds are up, the dollar is down, retail sales are up—sheer minutiae. So everything is back to normal, we had a bad turn there at the end of the sixties, we had to hold our breath a little, but now we can go back to the old stand, Eisenhower is on the throne, the pound is worth a pound and the bells ring out over the land on the Fourth of July. From *Time* magazine on the Fourth of July, 1955:

> From Franconia Notch, New Hampshire, to San Francisco, California, this week, there was clear and convincing evidence of patience, determination, optimism and faith among the people of the U.S. In the 29 months since Dwight D. Eisenhower moved into the White House, a remarkable change had come over the nation . . . The national blood pressure and temperature had gone down, the nerve endings had healed . . . In and around the cities, bulldozers and pneumatic drills and rivet guns

played an unending symphony of progress . . . at the
office coffee breaks, talk was easy and calm, not about the
coming war or the coming depression.

Has the symphony of progress come back? Or does Arthur
Burns really have something to worry about?

They say, for example, that the good old Protestant
Ethic has died away. Whatever happened to work? Doesn't
anybody want to? And growth: the whole system is geared
to growth, that is its justification, it *works* better. What is
all this about no-growth, zero population growth, zero
economic growth? There is only so much stuff in and on
the planet, and at the rate we are using it up in x years
there will be no planet. Apocalyptic literature arrives not
only on the ecological side but on the cultural side. "The
revolution of the twentieth century will take place in the
United States," writes a French critic, Jean-François
Revel, "and it has already begun." "There is a revolution coming," writes Charles Reich. "It will not be like
revolutions of the past. It will originate with the individual
and with culture, and it will change the political structure
only as its final act . . . this is the revolution of the new
generation."

If *any* of this is true, we cannot simply go back to where
we were. Radical change is very hard for most people to
contemplate, and money managers are no different. Their
attitude is: Sure, changes, we sell something and we buy
something else to fit the changes. You say work is going out
of style? We'll buy play. Here are my six Leisure Time
stocks, and let me tell you how long I've owned Disney.
Money managers operate on the theory of displacement:
the framework will be the same, but inside you move
things around. My favorite is a gentleman I ran into after
I got back from the Vega plant. I told him that one problem among others in certain localities was dope addiction,

I

and at one plant—though the number sounded very high to me—the rate was reported to be 14 percent.

"Well," he said, "I haven't owned an auto stock for years. But fourteen percent! Geez, *who makes the needles?*"

> The Chairman was pleased to report sharply higher profits for the year, due to increased sales of the entire line of hospital supply equipment. The reasons for the record profitability, said the Chairman, were Medicare, Medicaid, and the sharply increased use of the company's new handy throw-away needle by the burgeoning heroin addiction market.

Now it may be that displacement is all we have to consider. Ah, *things* are out, quality of life is in, back to the countryside; there is a waiting list for ten-speed bicycles, who makes the ten-speed bicycles? Ah, the ecologists are gaining strength, where is our list of water-pollution companies?

That is probably good thinking on the tactical level, but there is also a strategic level, and the strategic level has to consider what the more profound changes are, and in fact it ought to even without the rather parochial justification of buying and selling.

So this is why I am in Lordstown, just as one stop, looking for the sources of Arthur Burns's angst: Will life quiet down?

In the automobile industry, to consider the parochial side for a moment, rewards and punishments are very tangible, and since the automobile industry is such a fantastic part of America, that would affect us all. General Motors—my God, nobody can comprehend the *size* of General Motors; it makes one out of every seven manufacturing dollars in the country; its sales are bigger than the budget of any of the fifty states, and of any *country* in the world except the United States and the Soviet Union. But even General Motors has problems. As Henry Ford II said, *the Japanese are waiting in the wings.* Someday, he said, they might build all the cars in America. The problem, or one of them, is that imports keep rising, in spite of the theology of Detroit, which always maintained: little cars, fah! Americans won't buy them; Americans want power, a sex symbol, racing stripes, air scoops for nonexistent air, portholes for nonexistent water; they want to leave two big black tire marks going away from the stoplight, rubber on the road. And the names went with the technology: Firebirds and Thunderbirds, Cougars and Barracudas and Impalas, *growrrrr,* nothing about driving a handy little car there—so the handy little cars sold were foreign.

Eventually enough handy little cars were sold that the balance of payments continued in its sickening ways and even Washington began to lean on Detroit, and Detroit figured Okay, we'll build a handy little car. General Motors was not about to have any more of the problems of urban Detroit; it put its $250 million Vega plant in the middle of an Ohio cornfield. And then this work force showed up, the youngest work force around, and *look* at them—hair down to the shoulder blades, mustaches, bell-bottoms, the whole bit; it looks like Berkeley or Harvard Square.

It was a Ford official who wrote the following paragraph, but the same thing applies not only everywhere in the automobile industry but probably in much of factory work. The memo is from an industrial relations man to his superiors, and he is talking about the present and the future. This gentleman is nobody's fool, and his memo should be in the sociology texts, not in the filing cabinets. (The memo was xeroxed, and a friend of mine got a xerox and xeroxed it again, so I have one, and I guess the UAW has one, because its vice-president Ken Bannon used some of the same phrases word for word in an interview. Communication by *samizdat*: think what Xerox will do in Russia when it gets going.) The rate of disciplinary cases was going up; turnover was up two and a half times; absenteeism was alarming on Mondays and Fridays. (Hence the useless advice never to buy a car built on a Monday or a Friday. But your dealer will tell you *his* cars are built only on Tuesdays and Thursdays.) Furthermore, the workers weren't listening to the foremen and the supervisors. And why?

> For many, the traditional motivations of job security, money rewards, and opportunity for personal advancement are proving insufficient. Large numbers of those we hire find factory life so distasteful they quit after only brief exposure to it. The general increase in real wage levels in our economy has afforded more alternatives for satisfying economic needs. Because they are unfamiliar with the harsh economic facts of earlier years, [new workers] have little regard for the consequences if they take a day or two off . . . the traditional work ethic—the concept that hard work is a virtue and a duty—will undergo additional erosion.

General Motors was going to outflank that stuff with the newest, most automated plant; machines would take over a lot of the repetitive jobs; the plant would be in that cornfield in Ohio, near Youngstown, away from all those problems of the, uh, you know, core city. Everything at Lordstown would be made in America, no imported parts, the apogee of American industrialism. The head of Chevrolet buzzed in for a Knute Rockne pep talk. *America* was going to make the small car, by golly, and that was the end of the elves in the Black Forest and the industrious Yellow Peril in Toyota City, who thought they had been in the small-car business. Planeloads of newsmen were flown in. The line is going to do a hundred cars an hour, lots of it without any people; *kachunk* goes the machine that pops the wheel rim into the tire, *pffft* goes the machine that blows up the tire.

So what is all this about trouble in Lordstown? The line is not going at a hundred cars an hour—at least not much of the time—and there are all these characters, all good UAW Local 1112, average age twenty-five, the youngest work force practically anywhere, peace medals, bell-bottoms, and hair like Prince Valiant, and the union president is twenty-nine and has a Fu Manchu mustache like the one Joe Namath shaved off, and GM is going up the wall. Where is the *productivity?* Curtis Cox, the supervisor of standards and methods, is getting apoplectic. "I see *foreign cars* in the parking lot," he says. "The owners say they are cheaper. How is this country going to compete?" The GM people practically weep when they think about Japan: all those nice, industrious workers, *singing* the alma mater in the morning ("Hail to Thee, O Mitsubishi"); whistling on their way to work like the Seven Dwarfs, for God's sake—never a strike, never a cross word; playing on the company teams; asking the foreman if it is okay to get engaged to this very nice girl as soon as the foreman meets her.

So I ask General Motors quite routinely if I can go see this apogee of American industrialism, say, Tuesday, and General Motors says *no,* never.

I admit to being a bit stunned. Do they not fly plane-loads of people there all the time? Did they not fly alleged same planeloads at the end of the GM strike, together with appropriate refreshment, to watch the first Vega come off the line, with a handout about the Vega was going to

Mrs. Sadie Applepie, library assistant of Huckleberry Finn, Illinois, with a quote all ready from Mrs. Applepie: "Oh, I have been waiting so long for my Vega, I can't believe it's finally here, I'm so excited," did they not? What do they mean, No, not that guy? Who the hell do they think I am, Ralph Nader? I begin thumbing my other notebook that has the number of the pay phone in the hallway of Nader's boarding house, and it's off to Lordstown. Because even with plant guards, General Motors is not Russia, and anybody who has graduated from the good ol' U.S. Army knows how to deal with the lower levels of great bureaucracies. (Where you going with that rake? What rake, sir? *That* rake. Oh, *this* rake, the captain, sir, he said take it over there. *What* captain? The other captain. What other captain? Beats me, lieutenant, they just told me take the rake.)

So we are walking around the plant at Lordstown, all $250 million of it very visible, like an iron-and-steel tropical rain forest with the electric drills screaming like parakeets and the Unimate robot welders bending over the Vegas like big mother birds and the Prince Valiants of Local 1112 zanking away with their new expensive electrical equipment. Vegas grow before your eyes. Beautiful. I recommend it, next time you are taking the Howard Johnson tour across the land of the free.

But what are these cars waiting for repair, marked *no high beam signal, dome lite inoperative, no brakes . . .* no brakes? *no brakes.* But what is this on the bulletin board?

Management has experienced serious losses of production due to poor quality workmanship, deliberate restriction of output, failure or refusal to perform job assignments and sabotage.

Efforts to discourage such actions through the normal

application of corrective discipline have not been successful. Accordingly, any further misconduct of this type will
be considered cause for severe disciplinary measures, including dismissal.

"Corrective discipline"? My God, you can get *court-
martialed* in this place. They should have an industrial
psychologist read the language on the bulletin board. I can
hear the Glee Club louder, "Hail to Thee, O Fair Toyota."

Hi there.

Hi.

What is that?

That's the window trim.

Is this a good place to work?

Well, it will be, as soon as we get it shaped up.

Would you buy one of these cars?

Sure, if it wasn't so expensive; it's a well-engineered
little car.

Wouldn't you rather be out on your own, say, a garage?

Naw, a garage don't have no benefits.

Say, I don't want to bother you, two of those Vegas just
went by without window trim.

Well, they all go by without somethin', this line is
moving too fast.

That's productivity, man.

Oh, is that what they call it?

I can give you a few notes of our brilliantly unscientific
survey of Lordstown, but they are just that. Our people
would rather have had the time off than the overtime.
But their wives worked because they needed the extra
income. They would tell their brothers to get a job there,
and in fact some of them did. Supervisors bugged everybody. Sabotage? Beer cans welded to the inside of a fender?
Well, there might be a few hotheads, but that's silly, man,
the Vega is our bread and butter—the more Vegas they

sell, the better for us. If the foremen bugged our people too much, they would get another job somewhere else; they took for granted there would be such a job.

We asked the older types if the young bucks were any different. They said, "Yes. They're smarter. They don't put up with what we did."

Our favorite Prince Valiant haircut said: "I am not going to bust my ass for anybody. I don't even bust my ass for myself, you know, working around the house."

But beware. One has to be an epistemological agnostic considering any such report, whether done by journalists or social scientists. How do we know people who talked to us are representative of a work force of ten thousand? Further: journalists and social scientists are verbal, conceptual people. They would probably score very low in electrical repairs around the house; unconsciously they feel: How do they stand it? I wouldn't like to work here. They did not sleep through senior year in high school with Sister Maria Theresa droning on about Wordsworth and look at the plant as a relief from that. My companion Bill once did a piece about labor for *The New York Times Magazine*, and some paragraphs were picked up by a social scientist writing a paper. When he subsequently went to do research for a book, properly in awe of all the academic sources, he found the sources quoting *him*: a second social scientist quoted the first, with appropriate footnotes, and a third quoted the second, with footnotes and notes, and so on—the old beagle pack in cry. This doesn't mean the job can't be done, but it takes a large, thorough, well-funded effort, with the appropriate discipline of statistics and all the modes and variants in place.

So all right, it makes sense to have a demurrer for the statistical discipline, but the *feeling* is there, Something Else Is Going On: the world is not necessarily going to settle back to the Fourth of July, Eisenhower Regency, with life all quieted down. The key phrases are from the xerox of the xerox of the xerox of the confidential memo at Ford; the next key phrases are from the banks of the Charles River. Lordstown is the biggest and bestest example from industrial America, and the Harvard Business School is the West Point of capitalism, or at least so its denizens tell each other, and certainly the place has provided one of the great Old Boy networks of modern times. Let a Business-School-type foul up out there in the world and he need not fear: another Business-School-type will come to his rescue and they will call it merger, or recapitalization, or synergy, or something. I have two straws in the wind to submit from the West Point of capitalism.

Admittedly, these come from an unusual time. Two years before, the greedy little bastids in Investment Management could hardly wait to get going on their first five million, as I said before. Now there is a new crop of greedy little bastids; naturally, the course is still wildly popular, but outside, the Cambodian invasion has been timed neatly with my spring visit. The feeling that all is not well in the world has even penetrated the clouds of greed in my three sections. Around Harvard Square the graffiti was getting political; nobody had written *Heloise Loves Abelard* in quite a while; instead this flowed in large letters for a third of a block: JOHN HANCOCK WAS A REVOLUTIONARY, NOT AN OBSCENE LIFE INSURANCE SALESMAN But that, of course, was on the College side of the Charles River, where the life style is different—beards and mustaches and poor-boy clothes, almost as much a uniform as the gray flannel jackets and khaki pants of a generation before. But across the river at the Business School, the budding *apparatchiks* are coming to class in Brooks Brothers suits and button-down white shirts, looking like sub-assistant secretaries in the Nixon Administration.

There is no revolutionary chatter in the course catalog at the B School. You find one of the major preoccupations of the catalog is control: "The field of Control deals with the collection, processing, analysis, and use of quantitative information in a business." In a previous year, when an SDS faction took over University Hall in the College and there was a big bust, the College as an institution seemed very confused, but the Business School had a Contingency Plan in a fat binder with colored index tabs. I had the classes at that time, too, and one B-School faculty member, fearing some Dickensian carmagnole in the streets, Paris, 1789, said of the dissenters: "They'll never make it to this side of the river. We'll blow the bridges first."

So: this is not the Last Bastion, it is not Bob Jones University or even Utah State; it is where they grow the *apparatchiks,* the technicians who sop up the top spots a generation hence, and if Something Else Is Going On, these types will either lead it or fight it or try to take it over after it gets going.

First straw. *Notes from A Class.*

The Guest Lecturer has posed a Case. You are running a portfolio of a hundred million dollars. (Baby Stuff.) You are in a competition not unlike the one the Chase Manhattan runs among competing money managers. The worst-performing portfolio managers at the end of a certain time get fired. The best get more money to run, and presumably appropriate rewards.

Company A is a notorious polluter, but its profits are unimpaired. Company B is buying antipollution equipment that will depress its profits for years. Other things being equal, which do you buy, A or B? The Case was not too far from reality. Ralph Nader's Project on Corporate Responsibility was trying to put some people on the General Motors board, and Harvard owns 305,000 shares of General Motors. Harvard's treasurer reportedly said he was going to vote for management "because they are our kind of people," after which both faculty and students generated a furious debate. The Case is not only limited to pollution; the same principles of the social purpose of investment can be applied to defense contractors, the makers of napalm, companies with investments or branches in South Africa, and so on.

All right, you want to achieve performance in your portfolio, and this performance is being measured competitively. It may affect your career. Do you buy Company A, the profitable polluter, or Company B, the unprofitable antipolluter?

> *Student One:* I would try to evaluate the long-term effect . . . because in the long run Company B is going to have a better image.
> *Student Two:* But in the long run you would have lost the account. I think you have to know the wishes of the constituency. If it's a fund, how do the fundholders feel? What do they want?
> > *(Scattered boos. The class begins to chant, "A or B, A or B")*

Several other students offer comments, all trying to hedge, to keep both the profit and the social purpose.

> *Student Three:* I buy the polluter. *(Cheers, then scattered boos)* It isn't the business of a fund manager to make a social decision, or to discriminate between companies on his own ideas of some social purpose. That could be dangerous. If we want to combat pollution, let society vote for it, and have a consensus. I doubt that consumers really want to pay the price. You can't ask profit-making organizations to subsidize society.

The Radical Student (The Radical Student is only radical by standards of this side of the river, which is to say that he is neatly shaven but is wearing a colored shirt and a tie that is a bit wider than the 1955 width.) Maybe that's the problem. Everything in this school is geared to the purpose of the corporation, and that purpose is maximized profit.

We ask the Radical Student: "What are the goals of a corporation, if not to maximize profit?"
Silence in the classroom, a rustling of papers. The idea is very confusing.
What are the goals of a corporation, if not to maximize profit?
Not a hand goes up. It is just too hairy a question. We ask it once more. More shuffling, an occasional left wrist shoots out from the cuff with the wrist watch exposed.

The Radical Student: You know the trouble? It's the way we look at it. We're concerned with property rights.
At the Law School, say, they talk about civil rights. We're objective, but maybe objectivity has been overdone. Is our one purpose to measure *things*?

My second straw is the Resolution. This was, as I said, an emotional time. The Business School voted and passed this, then bought an ad in *The Wall Street Journal* to publicize it. The Resolution called for American withdrawal from Southeast Asia, not startling for a student resolution at that time. But this was the Business School, normally heavily Republican, heavily Republican in 1968, and it was the *language* juxtaposed to the source that was startling:

We condemn the administration of President Nixon for

its view of mankind [*its view of mankind*?] and the American community which:

1. Perceives the anxiety and turmoil in our midst as the work of "bums" and "effete snobs";

2. Fails to acknowledge that legitimate doubt exists about the ability of black Americans and other depressed groups to obtain justice;

3. Is unwilling to move for a transformation of American society in accordance with the goals of maximum fulfillment for each human being and harmony between mankind and nature.

Harmony between mankind and nature?

I asked the former dean of admissions what was this about harmony between mankind and nature; when had that crept into the Business School?

"I don't know," he said. "I guess it means they're not going to work for Procter and Gamble and make those dishwasher soaps that don't dissolve and smother the lakes. They don't want to work for big companies anyway, or so they say; I'd like to see what they say a couple of years out. The big companies treat them as objects, they say. In the fifties, the guys here all wanted to get to the top of Procter & Gamble. In the sixties it was finance."

"Last year," I said, "my classes all wanted to go right to work for a hedge fund. You couldn't even offer them twenty thousand a year, because they were going to run five million into ten in a year and take twenty percent of the gain. I used to say, 'Good morning, greedy little bastards.' "

"The guys in the fifties," said the ex-dean, "wanted to run the Big Company, and the guys in the sixties wanted to be Danny Lufkin, make a big bundle by the time you're forty and run for something."

"And now?"

"And now, they're just confused. I've never seen such malaise. I don't think the big companies have gotten the message yet, and maybe the *Fortune 500* can run without the Harvard Business School, but I have the feeling something will give on one side or the other."

More recently, I talked to the same ex-dean, who now teaches a popular course, and asked him what changes there had been. Popular journalism had said that things were "back to normal," whatever that was. Nader's Raders had been swamped with applicants in the emotional summers, and now the young law students were scuffling in the line when the man from Sullivan and Cromwell came to interview. It was said *pro bono* was over. The law students didn't even want the social courses any more; they wanted Taxation and Trusts and Corporations. Were the current B-School classes still holding out on the big corporations? Were the big corporations bending at all?

"They're bending to the extent that they don't come and interview the wives and tell them they have to fit to corporate life, and move fourteen times in fifteen years," he said. "But other than that, all you can say is that they're conscious of some change. As for my students, I think they have an acceptance of corporate life and they're looking for something inner. I hear a lot about life styles, how they want a non-anxious working life. They don't want to have what one of them called a dumbbell life, which is to say a blob of work at one end, a blob of home life at the other, and a conduit between, a railroad or a freeway. There's a lot of stuff about walking on the beach, that the worthy cause is themselves, and that work should fit life, not the other way around, and they talk a lot about intimate relationships, wives, children, and so on.

"So if I had to divide the decades again, I would still say that the fifties produced the corporate man who would rise to the top and die seventeen months after retirement, leaving a beautiful estate; the sixties students wanted a piece of the action; and currently the fantasy is a balanced life—just *enough* success to include it all; they want to run things but not at any cost; they still want power but now they want love, too."

Maximum fulfillment for each human being? Harmony between man and nature? That's not the *old* Business School. How do you put those things into a balance sheet? Can we operate a corporate society without objectivity, or at least what has passed for objectivity?

I wrote in my notes: *Will General Motors believe in the harmony between man and nature? Will General Electric believe in beauty and truth?*

It is not, of course, a revolutionary idea in the limited history of capitalism in this country to make something for less than a maximum profit. First of all, profit was not necessarily something that could be controlled; it came like the rain on the crops, between the costs and the market. Moreover, when the bulk of business was family-owned, its purpose was to take care of the family—sons, nephews and so on—and of the product's reputation, if it had a reputation of value. So a wagonmaker could simply make a good wagon, and a book publisher could publish an author simply because he wanted to. What we have come to call social purpose was a matter of individual integrity, randomly and haphazardly applied.

But these businesses sold out to bigger ones, and those in turn to bigger ones. Supercurrency! That New York Stock Exchange listing, that broad market with the stock selling at a fancy multiple, the sons of the Founders with Caribbean estates, and the grandsons in their pads all secure to blow their minds with 3K electronic guitar apparatus and not worry about work because the Supercurrency has been salted and peppered into hundreds of trusts so the tax man cannot get it. Only the Supercurrency has to stay Super, the profits have to keep growing, the multiple has to up, and the accountants can't do it all.

Multimillion-dollar businesses can't be run by intuition or seat-of-the-pants engineering. There has to be objectivity, whatever that is, and the continuous quantification of results; we have to have what the course catalog at the school calls "a rigorous and systematic approach," that is, the collection, processing, analysis, reporting and use of quantitative information. But there is competition, maybe, and the judgment of those crazy crapshooters up in New York; if the earnings go down they will bomb the stock, and then what will our report card as a manager look like?

For our man in the green eyeshade asking how goes the world, how will it go, the harmony between man and nature becomes an important question, and not just a spiritual one.

Nobody is against such harmony. When ecology first crept into the scene, industry seized it as an advertising opportunity; not a filter was bought that the buyer didn't take an ad about cleaning up the rivers and waters. In fact, at one point someone figured out that more was spent drumbeating about cleanup than on the equipment. Industry began to sense that the public belief that more was better was beginning to fall away. Union Carbide dropped its slogan, *There's a Little Bit of Union Carbide in Everybody's Home.* They wanted you to think of the plastics and the sandwich bags, and instead a Little Bit of Union Carbide meant: the wind's shifted, here it comes again, shut the doors, close the windows, you know what it cost to have the curtains cleaned last time. President Nixon gave an Ecology Speech, and somebody slipped him a real good quote from T. S. Eliot. "Clean the air! clean the sky! wash the wind!"—that's what we were going to do, said the President, not realizing that the very same quote went on, "Take stone from stone and wash them . . . Wash the stone, wash the bone, wash the brain, wash the soul, wash them, wash them!" Not ecology at all, but the blood of murder in the cathedral.

But while everybody agrees that mankind and nature should live in harmony, few agree on what that means, or how the cost shall be borne. They have not changed the consciousness of the way they think. To paraphrase University of Colorado economist Kenneth Boulding, man has lived through history in a "cowboy economy" with "illimitable plains" and "reckless, exploitative, romantic, and violent behavior." Consumption was "linear"—that is, materials were extracted from supposed infinite resources, and waste was tossed into infinite dumps. But we are shifting to a "spaceman economy." The earth is becoming finite, like a closed spaceship; consumption must become "circular"—that is, to conserve what we have, resources must be continuously recycled through the system. Air and water have always been free, and few realize that we are approaching the point in our cowboy ways where we will wrench the earth's ecology out of shape. In *The Closing Circle,* biologist–ecologist Barry Commoner writes that we have to reconsider the true value of the conventional capital accumulated by the operation of the economic system: we have not considered the true cost.

> The effect of the operation of the system on the value of its *biological* capital needs to be taken into account in order to obtain a true estimate of the overall wealth-producing capability of the system. The course of environmental deterioration shows that as conventional capital has accumulated, for example in the United States since 1946, the value of the biological capital has *declined.* Indeed, if the process continues, the biological capital may eventually be driven to the point of total destruction. Since the usefulness of conventional capital in turn de-

pends on the existence of the biological capital—the eco-
system—when the latter is destroyed, the usefulness of the
former is also destroyed. Thus despite its apparent prosperity, in reality the system is being driven into bankruptcy. Environmental degradation represents a crucial,
potentially fatal, *hidden* factor in the operation of the
economic system.

So we do not even have a true picture of how well we
have done. This parallels the arguments of the British
economist Ezra Mishan. If a wage earner dies sooner
because of exposure to mercury, radiation and DDT, but
doesn't have extra medical bills, is there not still the cost
of the lost earnings from the extra years? They have to be
assigned a value, even if the human anguish of the missing
years is ignored.

According to Commoner, intense environmental pollution in the United States has come with the technological
transformation of the productive system since World War
II. Production based on the new technologies has been
more profitable than the older technologies they replaced;
that is, the newer, more polluting techniques yield higher
profits. We could, of course, survive with new technologies,
new systems to return sewage and garbage to the soil, retire
land from cultivation, replace synthetic pesticides with biological ones, recycle usable materials, and cut down the uses
of power. That would cost about six hundred billion, or a
quarter of our current capital plant.

Placed in the kind of terms used in the analysts' societies,
this debt-to-nature means there is suddenly a liability on
the balance sheet we didn't know was there. It must have
been in the footnotes, in fine print. We have been very
profitable, but the plant is falling down. We can build a
new plant, but we are going to have to amortize the charges
against earnings for a long time.

Ah, but then we have a spanking new plant. Isn't that good? Not in the terms, necessarily, that we have been used to considering as good. Of course, if we survive, that's good. And perhaps even prevent life from getting more noxious, that's good. But we have been measuring good as profitable. New capital expenditures are—at some point —supposed to increase the profits. That is why the class is so confused when asked what the purpose of the corporation is. Good is profitable; profitable is new technology; new technology has been pollutive, and profitable. Killing whales is very profitable until the day when there are no more whales, because we have only been amortizing the ships and the radar and the depth charges and harpoons. We haven't amortized the whales, and anyway, how do you replace whales?

But the debt to nature, paid, does not increase either productivity or profitability. Thus, probably the corporation is not going to pay up unless the society compels it, induces it, inveigles it or brings it about in some other way. The vision of good is simply too far removed from the vision of what has been perfectly good in the hundreds of years of cowboy economics.

This is going to be true not just for the United States and not just for capitalism. The Cellulose, Paper and Carton Administration of the Ministry of Timber, Paper, and Woodworking in the U.S.S.R. is going to have its problems, too. It has its quotas, and the boys at the Ministry get their satisfactions from churning out the stuff, and ecology freaks are everywhere. This is from Professor Marshall Goldman's account of the pollution of Lake Baikal, the world's oldest lake and largest body of fresh water by volume. The manager of the plant at Bratsk is asked why a new waste filter has not been installed. Says he: "It's expensive. The Ministry of Timber, Paper and Woodworking is trying to invest as few funds as possible in the construction of paper and timber enterprises in order to make possible the attainment of good indices per ruble of capital investment. These indices are being achieved by the refusal to build purification installations."

The finite-earth argument leads almost inexorably to a call for an end to growth, both in population and industrial output. Growth in industrial output is one of the justifications for both capitalism and socialism, each to each. When Khrushchev talked about burying us, he was bragging about increases in industrial production. Increases in our Gross National Product have been hailed as the triumph of our system. (Leave aside for a moment what GNP measures. It does measure only quantity; so if everybody goes and buys triple locks for their doors because crime has increased so much, the GNP goes up, though the quality of life may have gone down. There are those who believe we should attempt to measure such quality.)

The most dramatic assault on growth came from a group at MIT headed by Dennis Meadows, which built a mathematical model of the world system with the interrelationships of population, food supply, natural resources, pollution and industrial production. The Meadows group produced a doomsday equation: the world is out of business in less than a century, unless the "will" is generated to begin "a controlled, orderly transition from growth to global equilibrium." Even new technologies, such as nuclear power sources, said the group, wouldn't help much. The team doubled the resources and assumed that recycling cut the demand to one-fourth; even optimistic estimates didn't put the day of doom off longer than 2100. We are going to stop growing one way or the other, said the group, the other being the collapse of the industrial base through depleted resources, and then lack of food and medical services.

[262]

This report did not lack for critics. One economist said it was "Malthus, with lights and a computer"; others said the base was too skimpy for the assumptions, and that future science and future technology were unknown. If you had assumed our population growth in 1880 without the automobile, you could have assumed asphyxiation by horse manure. If materials were going to become visibly scarce, would not the prices begin to anticipate scarcity? And would not new materials and new power sources be developed? The representatives of less developed countries who considered the report at a Smithsonian symposium were particularly alarmed, because freezing growth without some sort of worldly distribution of income would keep them at their current levels. The poorer nations, said the Indian ambassador, would "slide down to starvation." At another international conference, the Malaysians said: "Some of us would rather see smoke coming out of a factory and men employed than no factory," and "We are not concerned with pollution but with existence."

At the laissez-faire end of the spectrum, economists like the University of Chicago's Milton Friedman think that in arguments over social issues "there is a strong tendency for people to substitute their own values for the values of others." The current pollution concern is "an upper-income demand—the high-income people want to get the low-income people to pay for something that the high-income people value . . . people move from the clear, clean countryside to the polluted cities—not the other way around—because the advantages of the city outweigh the disadvantages." Left alone, "people are more likely to act in their own interests, to evaluate the costs and benefits of their own activities."

It is, of course, hard to legislate changes in consciousness. But most economists are unwilling to give up growth as a goal. World population is certain to grow for many years to come, an extra billion between 1960 and 1975, three more billion in the next quarter-century. Even if that rate of increase is slowed, you need growth just to keep pace. In a world of no growth but more people, you only accomplish one person's well-being, or one nation's, at the expense of another. That is the kind of redistribution of wealth we had before there was any surplus wealth to compound, when people in skins hit each other over the head with mastodon thighbones to accomplish the redistribution. Presumably we have only recently outgrown such activity, and the record of social maturity is not a record anybody would trust to the application of economic problems. So the doomsday equations have at least the virtue of getting people to think about the problems of a finite earth; it will take long enough to do something about it anyway.

It is from the increments that poverty is alleviated and the goals of the society met. If there are social problems—such as pollution—that can't be met by the market mechanism, they can be met by a pricing system: penalizing the polluter, let us say, or giving a tax incentive to achieve the desired end. This is not a net gain to growth in the traditional ways we have measured growth, because the stimulus from investments in pollution control is outweighed by the price rise in the end product, hence a damper on total demand. A study prepared for the Council on Environmental Quality, a government office, indicated this could be done for a small percentage of annual GNP, less than 1 percent, for air and water.

What is the impact of all of this on the man in the green eyeshade considering how goes the world? In the short run—and the short run is all that is considered by many of the men in green eyeshades—he can continue to play the game of displacement: who makes the needles. (If the Meadows model were to be true, and we were to be

closer to doomsday, and the pricing mechanism were left
alone, the man in the green eyeshade could make incredible killings by buying up commodities on the eve of their
disappearance.) But in the longer run, the demand for
social purposes, whether in pollution control or health,
education and welfare, is going to come out of the savings
flow. (*Institutional Investor* magazine polled forty-one of
the nation's leading academic, governmental and business
economists, and two-thirds of them believed that (a) growth
should continue, with a change in priorities, and (b) that
additional "income-wealth redistribution is required.") If
the government borrows in the capital markets to deliver,
it tips the balance we discussed in an earlier chapter. If it
raises taxes to deliver, that comes at least partially out of
profits. And if it, in effect, prints the money to deliver,
then inflation also will cut into profits. As is often said in
this sort of discussion, there ain't no such thing as a free
lunch.

There are some items to be balanced against this. One
is the value of the compound in a trillion-dollar economy.
One is the growing role of services in the economy; by 1980
the Department of Labor says more will be employed in
services than in manufacturing. Services are nonpollutive,
but the productivity curve also begins to flatten because
there are no economies of scale from doctors, teachers,
barbers and string quartets.

The man in the green eyeshade is a capitalist and a
manager: "The capitalist and managerial classes may see,"
writes Robert Heilbroner in *Between Capitalism and
Socialism*, "the nature and nearness of the ecological crisis
. . . and may come to accept a smaller share of the national
surplus simply because they recognize that there is no
alternative."

Some conclusions are inescapable. Even if the ecological
crisis is overstated and far away, even if social problems

can be solved with the existing mechanism—both of those points arguable—the consensus is moving away from the market as decision-maker and from the business society. As soon as you get all the articulation of "goals" and "priorities," you are moving from decision-making by market to decision-making by political philosophy. (This is an idea developed by Daniel Bell both in *The End of Ideology* and in *The Post-Industrial State,* and by others.) "What's good for General Motors is good for the country," said Charley Wilson, one of Eisenhower's businessmen Cabinet members. It would be interesting to see, year by year, what percentage of the people agree with that, and to watch the change.

So the money manager in the metaphorical green eye-shade will no longer be operating in a world where the market determines totally what is produced (and induced), nor in a society run by business decisions. Capital is scarcer and profits are thinner. He is still looking for three stocks that will double, but the range of his options is less. He has always looked not just at profits, E, but at the rate of change in estimated profits, $E + \triangle E$, and in the long run —the broad run, the macro scene, whatever—*his expectations are diminished.*

Open-ended expectations are an integral part of the markets we have grown up to know. Without them, the calculators can calculate the rates of return, and everybody can be on their way home at 10:05 A.M. to work on their Leisure Time, or more likely, to attend some committee meeting that will be devised to take up the remaining hours. The expectations are what Keynes called "animal spirits":

> A large proportion of our positive activities depend on spontaneous optimism rather than on a mathematical expectation, whether moral or hedonistic or economic. Most,

probably, of our decisions to do something positive, the full consequences of which will be drawn out over many days to come, can only be taken as a result of animal spirits—of a spontaneous urge to action rather than inaction, and not as the outcome of a weighted average of quantitative benefits multipled by quantitative probabilities . . . thus if the animal spirits are dimmed and the spontaneous optimism falters, leaving us to depend on nothing but a mathematical expectation, enterprise will fade and die—though fears of loss may have a basis no more reasonable than hopes of profit had before . . . individual initiative will only be adequate when reasonable calculation is supplemented and supported by animal spirits, so that the thought of ultimate loss which often overtakes pioneers, as experience undoubtedly tells us and them, is put aside as a healthy man puts aside the expectation of death.

None of this will happen tomorrow, and it was also Keynes who said that "in the long run we are all dead" and that the conventions by which we operated were a succession of short terms—those looking at the long run did so at their own peril. We have a marketplace in which it is possible to float all the services as well as the manufactures, and so probably many happy hours of playing with the displacements await our men. But if we are to give up the "illimitable plains" of the "cowboy economy," the new and smaller horizon is going to affect our ability to believe that we can compound and extrapolate with impunity, that the three hot ones we heard about at lunch today can go from 5 to 100. We have already lost our gunslingers, a phrase I once applied to some of our citizens, and if our Big Sky goes we will have to give up some of our fantasies. But they always were fantasies anyway, and maybe there are other energies to make our wheels spin.

Having thus dispatched the spirit of capitalism, let us see what we can do with the Protestant Ethic. That phrase describes a devotion to thrift and industry, postponed pleasure and hard work, the hustle as approved by the Lord. It accompanied the Puritan temper, a rather forbidding and pleasure-shy view of life, and is aptly described in the confidential Ford memo together with the complaint that it is disappearing: "the traditional work ethic—the concept that hard work is a virtue and a duty—will undergo additional erosion." (You have already seen the seeds of conflict, because if Prince Valiant at the Pink Elephant says, "I am not going to bust my ass for anybody, I don't even bust my ass for myself," it is safe to say he does not believe that "hard work is a virtue and a duty.")

We may keep using the phrase Protestant Ethic—everybody does—but for the record we should now split Protestant from Ethic. We call it that because Max Weber called it that in one of the classic works of political economics, and the sociologists and political economists are still sending students to the paperback stores for Max Weber, and not just for the *Protestant Ethic and the Spirit of Capitalism*. The textile families of northern France—Catholics all—sent letters to their sons, and to each other, that could have gone right into *Die protestantische Ethik*. Weber did not say, of course, that Protestantism was the sole cause of capitalism. In his commentary on Weber, Julien Freund says that the *Protestant Ethic* was at least in part a reaction against Marx's solely economic motive. Embryo capitalism had existed in other societies—Babylonian, Indian, Chinese and Roman—but the "spirit" of capitalism only developed with the mystery-less, magic-free character of Protestantism, with its rationality and rationalization. (This will come up again in a moment in the counter-culture's objections.) The accompanying asceticism of Protestantism said that you worked hard in your calling to succeed—a sign of election by God—but did not spend the wealth created, because only sobriety pleased God. "Thus the Puritan came to accumulate capital without cease." Even Keynes's assumptions in *Essays in Persuasion* seem to be based on a kind of Protestant society, where wealth increases because the margin between production and consumption increases.

Talk about industry, thrift and the way to salvation, the Protestant Ethic has found its happiest current home in a very non-Protestant country—at least in name—Japan. A while back, on a visit, I would ask people in Japan: How much vacation do you take a year? And the answers would come back: two days, one day, three days. Why so little? Well, if you work on your vacation you get paid more, and the beaches are too crowded anyway. And I remember sitting with the translator of my own book, himself a distinguished director of the Bank of Japan, everybody cross-legged, a sliver of raw fish poised between his chopsticks, a garden scene framed perfectly by the door.

"In the 1960's," said the honorable director, "our total output passed Italy, France, Germany and England; at this rate we will pass the U.S.S.R. in 1979. How? Our people save twenty percent of their wages. No other country saves so much. In the U.S. it is closer to six percent."

It is indeed, and when sour years come and the people clutch a little and the savings rate goes up to 8 percent, the President gathers his economic advisers to Camp David and wants to know what the hell is wrong with the Consumer, how do we get him to loosen up?

"Of course," said the director's research assistant, "we will not pass the United States until . . ." and everybody stopped talking because that was not courteous.

"Sometime in the 1990's," said the director, "and many things could happen by then: we have social overhead building up."

"But we have done this without resources, without oil, without surplus food," said the assistant, "with industry and thrift, industry and thrift."

(The voices in Osaka rise to haunt the finite-earth model builders, in the morning alma mater:

"For the building of a new Japan
Let's put our strength and minds together
Doing our best to promote production
Sending our goods to the people of the world,
Endlessly and continuously,
Like water gushing from a fountain.
Grow, industry, grow, grow, grow!
Harmony and Sincerity!
Matsushita Electric! Matsushita Electric!")

Industry and thrift, dedication and devotion; you could imagine the United States without them, but not without the mythology and ethic behind them. What is at stake is the happiness of Arthur Burns, whether we will always have a cost-push inflation, whether we stay Nation Number One like President Nixon wanted, and what happened to our dreams of becoming rich. Nothing unambitious about that, either.

Once again, the Ford memo:

For many, the traditional motivations of job security, money reward, and opportunity for personal advancement are proving insufficient.

Insufficient! Security, money, and personal advancement? Do you know what we have to throw off to get to this point?

I give you the honorable Cotton Mather:

There are *Two Callings* to be minded by *All Christians.*

Every Christian hath a GENERAL CALLING which is to
Serve the Lord Jesus Christ and Save his own Soul . . .
and every Christian hath also a PERSONAL CALLING
or a certain *Particular Employment* by which his *Usefulness* in his Neighborhood is Distinguished . . . a Christian
at his *Two Callings* is a man in a Boat, Rowing for Heaven; if he mind but one of his *Callings,* be it which it
will, he pulls the *Oar* but on *one side* of the Boat, and
will make but a poor dispatch to the Shoar of Eternal
Blessedness . . . every Christian should have some *Special
Business* . . . so he may Glorify God, by doing *Good* for
others, and *getting* of *Good* for *himself* . . . to be without
a *Calling,* as tis against the *Fourth Commandment,* so
tis against the Eighth, which bids men seek for themselves
a comfortable Subsistence . . . [if he follow no calling] . . .
a man is *Impious* toward God, *Unrighteous* toward his
family, toward his *Neighborhood,* toward the *Commonwealth* . . . it is not enough that a Christian *have* an
Occupation; but he must *mind* it, and give a *Good Account,* with *Diligence* . . .

and so on to *Poor Richard's Almanac*: A sleeping fox
catches no poultry; one day is worth two tomorrows; diligence is the mother of good luck; early to bed and early
to rise provides a man with job security, money reward
and opportunity for personal advancement.

The extension of this ethic into industrial America was
a real triumph. The Ford vice-president has a distinct problem: it is very hard to think of working on the line as a
Calling. Cotton Mather's listeners did not take this lightly,
nor did he: "Man and his Posterity will Gain but little, by
a Calling whereto God hath not Called him"; a Calling
was to be *Agreeable* as well as *Allowable*. It does make
work seem softer and more important to have been prayed
for:

It is a wonderful Inconvenience for a man to have a *Calling* that won't *Agree* with him. See to it, *O Parents*, that when you chuse *Callings* for your *Children,* you wisely consult their *Capacities* and their *Inclinations;* lest you Ruine them. And, Oh! cry mightily to God, by *Prayer,* yea with *Fasting* and *Prayer,* for His Direction when you are to resolve upon a matter of such considerable consequence. But, O *Children,* you should also be *Thoughtful* and *Prayerful,* when you are going to fix upon your *Callings;* and above all propose deliberately *Right Ends* unto your selves in what you do.

It is a bit hard to imagine, then: "Ma, I have fasted and prayed and sought the wisdom of God. I know my Calling, and I am going to work on the line at Ford, $4.57 an hour, as an assembler."

It seems almost simplistic to suggest, but you are more likely to bust your ass when everybody has been fasting and praying for you and what you are doing and your oar of the boat on the way to the Shoar of Eternal Blessedness than if none of those things are true, and if you are Ford, you have an extra problem if that spirit has departed.

Not that it has departed everywhere. It is still in the literature. Ralph Waldo Emerson's "Self-Reliance" and "Wealth" are in a direct line from Cotton Mather and Poor Richard; be not only industrious, be clever, absorb and invest. Bishop Lawrence, doyen of the Episcopal Church at the turn of the century, really did say, "In the long run, it is only to the man of morality that wealth comes. Godliness is in league with riches." Some of our major corporations have institutional advertising even today that could have been written by the Social Darwinists, and Dale Carnegie courses run on principles that were devised by Benjamin Franklin. The Man Who Gets Ahead in Business Reads *The Wall Street Journal* Every Business

Day. (Did you ever see the television commercial about
The Man Who Gets Ahead in Business? Business is a field
event, pole-vaulting, and the bar is set at about a hundred
feet, and the poor bastard is there in his business suit and
his Knox hat and his briefcase, and he looks up nervously
at this bar a hundred feet high and fingers the pole uncer-
tainly. After knocking the bar off the first time, he makes
it the second, presumably because he has read *The Wall
Street Journal*. *The Wall-Street Journal* may be one of the
best papers in the country, but I suggest that anyone who
sees his job as a hundred-foot pole vault with no track
shoes is in the wrong Calling and should pray for guid-
ance.)

While the literature of the Protestant Ethic has been
exhorting everybody for three hundred years in this country to be industrious and thrifty, sober and wise—to "post-
pone gratification," in the words of the scholars—another
literature has sprung up. It is literature really only in the
McLuhanesque sense, but it is with us every day, and that
is advertising. The purpose of the advertising is not to get
you to produce and save but to spend, to buy the goods,
and this has been the case since at least fifty years ago,
when mass marketing and mass advertising really got
going. Now we have commercials in living color, and the
populace spends far more time with them than the old
populace did with Cotton Mather. What do we see? First
of all, we never see anybody *working* except when they are
candidates for medication: aspirin, pain relievers, tranquilizers, cold remedies. At least not office or factory work;
the White Tornado and the Man From Glad will come and
help with the housework. The rest of the time, people are
at play: is is possible to sell soft drinks without running
into the surf? You only go around once in life, says the
beer commercial, so you have to grab everything you can;
that character is hanging precariously onto the rigging of

his boat because one hand is clutching a beer can. And the airlines—well, there is the bell tolling the end of the Protestant Ethic: Fly now, pay later, Pan Am will take you to an island in the sun where you can be a beachcomber (not a Calling approved by Cotton Mather) and Eastern wants to fly you and Bob and Carol and Ted and Alice *all* to your own little love-nest in Jamaica.

The message of capitalism has been schizophrenic: at work, be hard-nosed, industrious, single-minded, frugal and thrifty, and once you leave work, *whoopee,* have you seen Carol *and* Alice in their bikinis? It may be that some doers can step into a telephone booth and emerge as Clark Kent, but I doubt if it works for a whole society.

The second literature of exhortation, advertising, sometimes recognizes this, and tries to say that the deferred gratification of the Protestant Ethic is a matter of hours, not lifetimes and generations. "You've worked hard, you deserve this," says the clever ad, whether it is a beer, the reward for a day, or a vacation, the reward for a season, or whatever: buy, try, fly.

The less intensive attitude toward work also applies to play. In the winter of 1972 Columbia barely managed to field a basketball team for its Ivy League opener; it could send only six men to Providence to play Brown. "Four members," *The New York Times* reported (January 6) "had resigned, making it a particularly dramatic example of student unhappiness with organized extracurricular pursuits . . . Several other college teams have suffered similar player shortages in the last month." Said the team's second-highest scorer as he departed: "My father thinks I'm just a degenerate hippie now, because when I left high school I had all these fantastic ambitions for wealth and fame—and I wanted to be the greatest lawyer in North Carolina. Now I just don't have that."

Oppose this to that paragon of the extreme ethic, Vince

Lombardi. You could say, of course, that this is not quite fair: soldiers and professional football players are supposed to win. But the example is not frivolous. When Lombardi died, his death was a major front-page story in all—including the most serious—of newspapers, and personally grieved the President of the United States. Lombardi's hold on the country and the President was that for ten years the teams he had coached had either won championships or come in second. The ethic according to Lombardi, all from *Lombardi* and *Run to Daylight:*

> Winning is not everything. It is the only thing.
>
> The will to excel and the will to win, they endure. They are more important than any event that occasions them.
>
> To play this game, you must have that fire in you, and there is nothing that stokes fire like hate.

And from Lombardi's players:

> He had us all feeling that we weren't going to win for the Green Bay Packers, but to preserve our manhood . . . and we went out and whipped them good and preserved our manhood.
>
> Vinny believes in the Spartan life, the total self-sacrifice, and to succeed and reach the pinnacle he has, you've got to be that way. The hours you put in on a job can't even be considered.
>
> He treated us all equally—like dogs. I don't think I'd want to be like Lombardi. It takes too much out of you. You drive like that, you've got to give up a lot of time with your family, and you lose a lot physically . . . Still, now that I'm in business, I'm applying Lombardi's principles. I sent my secretary home crying my first three days

on the job. One gal retired on me. I was putting them
through training camp. I walked in and the first thing I
said was, "Your job is on the line. If you don't make it,
you're through." I said to the secretary, "What the heck
you been doing all day? I don't see anything you've done."
And if she gave me a letter and there was one mistake in
it, I'd make a big X all the way across it and say, "Type
it again." It worked out pretty well. They're organized
now . . . I'm strict. A lot of him has rubbed off on me.

And the players on the changes:

If you were told to beat your head against the wall, you
did it . . . I think we're entering a different period now.
I think we now have to give youngsters a good reason
to get them to beat their heads against a wall.

Kids today don't fight like we did. They can play football
and basketball like hell, but they're very gentle, very kind.
They're out playing for fun, and it's not going to interfere
with their demonstration for the week or with the things
they consider important . . . Those kids don't look at it
like the whole world is going to fall apart if you don't
beat the Bears.

The examples are so eloquent they need no comment.
Someday we may have such technology and science-and-
compound-interest that whether people work hard or not
would be marginal, but meanwhile there has been a lot of
talk about alienation and unhappiness and The Blue-
Collar Blues and, for that matter, The White-Collar Blues.
Industry notices this because of absenteeism, turnover and
the lack of candidates for foreman, but at bottom nobody
really *knows*.

Five years ago [from 1970] the National Commission on Technology, Automation, and Economic Progress tried to survey existing knowledge on job satisfaction and dissatisfaction under modern industrial conditions. There was pitifully little. With all the talk about alienation, dehumanization, and the loss of satisfaction from work, you would think that many researchers would be trying to find out the facts, by asking questions and by devising more direct measurements, by trying to figure out what aspects of particular routines are most destructive of satisfaction, and what loss of production would result from changing the routines. But apparently not so. (Robert Solow in *Capitalism Today*)

I suspect, pending the reconvening of the National Commission to fill in the gaps, that two things are true in this country. One is that there are certainly a lot of jobs in this country that are boring, not built to the human spirit or the human body, or not fulfilling in some other way, and that most of American industry is only beginning to pay attention to this. The second is that people like to work, as opposed to not working or hanging around the house. They like to work, or at least they like to go to the place where work is, because they see their friends, they have a beer afterward or a coffee break during, and it gets them into motion, and anyway we have not developed the tradition of playing the lute and counting that as a good afternoon. Given any degree of pleasantness, encouragement and satisfaction, they would go to work even without the exhortations of the Ethic and the prospect of the Shoar of Eternal Blessedness.

It is almost axiomatic in the literature of work that part of the problem comes of bending the men to the machines. But computers are machines too; the pay may be less than that around nonelectronic machinery; yet the blues are not so much heard from this sector, and among the differences may be style, atmosphere and air conditioning.

How hard, or with what care, people work is something else. William H. Whyte, Jr., and the other observers of the fifties told us of the crossover: the executives were working the seventy-hour week and taking work home while the blue-collar hours were going down.

The difference is that both the executive and the blue-collar worker are now conscious of *options* that heretofore they did not think they had. Conscious only, for relatively few have acted on the alternative; behavior and attitude do not necessarily go immediately together. Most of the attention has been paid to the younger generation; at least the future executives were thinking about a balanced life, and the corporations were getting a bit shyer about telling them how demanding corporate life was going to be. Whatever the terrors that haunted the Man in the Gray Flannel Suit—not Making It, not having the House in the Suburb —the terrors do not have quite the same intensity that they used to. The terrors are also less for the industrial workers. For one thing, if you have a house and a car, another house and another car become much less urgent, however pleasant or convenient. (There is a lake within cruising range of the Vega plant in industrial Ohio which is, to put it baldly, a blue-collar lake, which is to say most of the boats belong to union workers from the plants. If they put five more boats on that lake you will not be able to see the water for the boats; thus if you are an industrial worker and don't have a boat to take the kids in, the chances are you have a friend who does, or maybe your old man will lend you his.)

A lack of *things,* unless those things are food, clothing and shelter, does not provide terror except for a Man in a Gray Flannel Suit who has bought a distortion of the old ethic, its tangible evidences without its spirituality. Back to the Ford memo:

> Because they are unfamiliar with the harsh economic facts of earlier years, [new workers] have little regard for the consequences if they take a day or two off.

That's about as succinct as one can be. The harsh economic facts of earlier years were an unpleasant but effective motivator. You do not even have to have gone through a Great Depression yourself, if you heard enough talk about it while you were growing up. Now it has been more than thirty years since the end of the Great Depression, and not only do the Prince Valiants in the plant not know about it, they have not even heard that much about it because granddad does not live with them. I had a series of chats with Daniel Yankelovich, social scientist and the head of the leading marketing research and social science research firm that bears his name, a firm that polls continuously in this area for corporate clients. Only in the last five years has this change in attitude taken place so strikingly. The changing of work goals from salary to interpersonal relationships to content of work has also been documented by Professor Ray Katzell, chairman of the Psychology Department of New York University, and others. It took that long—almost two generations—for the motivation by economic fear to fade.

Granted, all the moonlighting to make ends meet at the current levels; granted, all the places and pockets that have been missed, and some of the unemployment which persists. Mass employment is not a political possibility—almost everyone would agree to that—and the economic whiff of grapeshot (what this country needs to shape up these deadheads is a good depression) has gone out of the lexicon of bargaining. What Yankelovich calls the "sacrifice consensus" is breaking down.. The sacrifice part of that phrase means that deferrals for something else are not as popular or necessary: I am doing this for my family, I am working so that my son has a better life than I do. And the consensus, obviously, is that there was agreement that this was a right and proper way of life. The breakdown of this sacrifice consensus does not mean that it is replaced right away with something else, only that now there are many elements present—some sacrificers, some not, but no agreed-upon consensus.

("If women's lib breaks the equation between masculinity and being a good provider, what does that do to motivation? And, say, to insurance?" Yankelovich asked at one point, which started something that made us both late for dinner.)

So: our productivity curve begins to flatten not only because we are becoming a service economy, but because some of the motivations—the spirit and the fear—have gone out of the producers. And maybe our inflation is persistent. If you want the dank side of the extrapolation, some of the workers retire right there on the job and wait for their pension, some take Fridays off. The servicing of all our *things* (and indeed even the services themselves) become so erratic and sloppy that the manufacturers have to work to make them service-free, no checkup for ten thousand miles, and the consumers get so irritated they transfer that irritation into political channels and gladly accept more government regulation of business.

So: it is affluence itself that has taken the edge off our edge. But the President need not exhort us to get out and return to the honesty of a day's work for a day's pay, which he has done on several occasions. Nation Number One will not be unique, because these elements don't stop at the water's edge; at different times, but for the same reasons, they will take place in all the Western industrial countries. The exhortations of Chairman Mao may be to a different end than the Shoar of Blessedness, but the tone is the same. In the capitalist industrial countries, it is the first generation off the farm that provides the longest hours and the most uncomplaining workers. Somebody who has spent sixteen hours a day looking at the wrong end of an ox for sub-subsistence on a patch in Poland may not complain at all when he emigrates with a paper suitcase to a steel mill on the south side of Chicago, but his grandson may not think it is that good a deal. We are the furthest off the farm. Japan had a generation that made its industrial reputation; those glee-club singers in the Matsushita plant think Matsushita is about the most dazzling thing that ever happened, but meanwhile the Germans are using Turks and Spaniards—again, fresher from the farm—to fill out the ranks in the Volkswagen plants. All of which does not solve our problem, but gives us company.

Perhaps that just gives us a challenge. Adolph Berle, among his other activities, was coauthor with Gardiner Means of the granddaddy classic in all this line of thinking, *The Modern Corporation and Private Property*. In one of his later books, *The American Economic Republic*, Berle suggested that we had a flexibility of response which he called the Transcendental Margin, those qualities that accounted for the prosperity of Israel but not Iraq, of the Netherlands but not Bulgaria—a certain creative energy. It propelled our system not toward profits but toward— are you ready?—beauty and truth. In a younger and more optimistic America that did not seem so strange. If we still have it, or something like it, it should be possible to make of work something fulfilling that does not need either the spiritual exhortation or economic fear to motivate it. That is a tall order and a big challenge, but the luckier of our citizens who have experienced something like it know

that under those propitious circumstances it can be fun
to bust your ass.

We ignore revolutions at our peril. Current evidences
may or may not lead to profound changes, but we know
that even when changes seem to happen quickly the ideas
behind them have been hanging in the air for a long time.
Our man at the desk considering how goes the world, had
he been in the City of London in 1913, would have been
one of the merchant princes of the world: to him for capital came the Moscow Power and Light Company, the brew-
eries of Bohemia, the trolley lines of Shanghai, the apples
of Tasmania, the oil of Mexico, the ranches of Texas and
Arizona, the tin mines of Malaya, the hemp of Tanganyika,
and the railroads of absolutely everywhere. Half a century
later our man was still at his desk and still at work, a bit
shabbier, but his role and the world had changed.

At this point the metaphor is going to break down,
because revolutions do not come neatly across a desk; if the
change is profound enough, the frame through which we
have looked at this scene will go away, and the desk and the
chair will still be there but nobody will be sitting at them.

But once again, a degree of skepticism is in order. In
going through an inordinate amount of the literature, for
example, I found one phrase a number of times: "Our
youth is in revolt." The writer is a verbal, conceptual person, usually an academic, and what he *means* is "*My graduate students are in revolt*"; or, "My students have just
worked their way through some Marcuse and they have
had it with the System." The Faculty of Engineering is not
so prompt to report that the students are in revolt.

This is not at all to write off small numbers of people.
They may have a symbolic value to everybody else articu-
lating what larger numbers feel. But I think it is important
to distinguish the flavor of what has been done: green-

house people have reported on greenhouse people, which is to say that academics and book writers have talked about students, who may not end up being greenhouse people, protected from the storms and freezes of life, but who are in a stage of life—being at school—where they are protected from what shapes everybody else. Just the simple *numbers* have gotten so much bigger. Twenty-five students here and there do not make the impact that a "counterculture" of a million makes, but that million counterculture is possible because of a trillion-dollar economy and, among other things, a student population of eight million. When everybody has to spend sixteen hours a day behind an ox, there is no counter-culture.

Obviously I would not have taken this time and space if I thought we were still at July 4, 1955, in the Eisenhower Regency. Obviously, in spite of the looseness of the ways in which we have learned, Something Else Is Going On. I belong to a Club housed in a magnificent old building in New York which is supposed to be made up of Distinguished Intellectuals, because, I suppose, somebody had written *The Wealth of Nations* as an achievement by my name. The Club has been infiltrated by foundation executives and downtown lawyers, and the average age of the members is 94.3, because foundation executives and downtown lawyers are very long-lived. Anyway, following the precepts of intellectual inquiry, we had a debate one night on Charles Reich's *The Greening of America*. This is the most talked-about of the revolutionary tracts. Corporate America—an idea, incidentally, from the old Berle and Means classic—has taken over the country, to the mindless end of its own perpetuity. "This apparatus of power has become a mindless juggernaut, destroying the environment, obliterating human values, and assuming domination over the mind and lives of its subjects." We are not only an incredibly rich country, but a desperately poor one, because we have disorder, corruption, hypocrisy, war, distorted priorities, an artificiality of work and culture, powerlessness, absence of community, and a loss of self. (Apologies for the abruptness of the summary.) But out of biological necessity, a new consciousness "has emerged out of the wasteland of the Corporate State, like flowers pushing up through the concrete pavement." The revolution is individual and cultural, and only changes the political structure as its final act.

I did my homework quite properly and intensively, because there was much that was not only naïve but diffusely derivative, some of it funny: seven times Mr. Reich stated that there was no more chunky peanut butter; the Corporate State had the power to deliver only homogenized peanut butter. The Corporate State gave us snowmobiles "instead of snowshoes, so that the winter forests screech with mechanical noise," yet four times the author celebrated light motorcycles "to restore a sense of free motion," and he obviously never tried to read or think near a quiet road patrolled by a kid with a new Honda. Moby Grape was celebrated for the positive feelings of "It's a beautiful day today," which did seem to me to ignore "Oh, what a beautiful mornin'" (Consciousness I) and Peggy Lee's "Now it's a good day" (Consciousness II). That was fun and games; my real barbs came for the greenhouse thinking.

Yet, five minutes after the discussion started, I threw my notes away, because there wasn't any debate. My distinguished seniors had read the book and they were so furious they weren't even *listening,* their faces were becoming purple over their white wing collars. What in the world could be so *threatening?* On the spot I had to switch sides and become the public defender, because the argument from the other side was: *It does not exist.* And the point I have been making is that however imperfectly assessed, Something Else Is Going On.

Jean-François Revel's tract, largely a pamphlet to needle his fellow Frenchmen, says that only in America can the true revolution take place: "It is *the* revolution of our time . . . it is the only revolution that . . . joins culture, economic and technological power, and a total affirmation of liberty for all in place of archaic prohibitions." (It is nice of somebody to say we are still trying.) And he mentions some of the political activities that have taken place: sit-ins, civil-rights marches, student strikes and so on.

But it is important to separate out, for this discussion, the *political* aspects. Martha Mitchell may have looked out the window and seen the milling students as the 1917 St. Petersburg mobs, but few others did. And it becomes important to separate out what is *style*. Long hair may or may not represent something profound, but if you compare yearbook pictures of the class of 1872 and 1972 the beards and the sideburns look much the same; the only difference is that in 1872 Daddy had a beard or muttonchops too. If we leave out politics and style, that brings us back to behavior; within that, loosely, there *is* a revolutionary idea. And that is: Where did all those bright people get us, anyway? Weren't McGeorge Bundy and Robert McNamara two of the smartest people walking around? "Consciousness II," wrote Reich, "rests on the fiction of logic and machinery; what it considers unreal is nature and subjective man . . . Consciousness III is deeply suspicious of logic, rationality, analysis, and of principles."

We don't have to look very far for a prime example of the causes of a suspicion of logic, rationality and objectivity. If we do not stop the Communists in Vietnam, they will think we are chicken, they will take over Asia, and so on. We analyze the problem. We will send x numbers of men, we will drop y numbers of millions of tons of bombs. Every day our television screens will carry the body-count report: *Them, 5357, Us, 422*; *Villages pacified today,*

324. The next day the score is the same, and the next. They see the score and we see the score. Therefore we win the war and achieve our principles, and the Communists will learn the lesson. It is all there, measured, in what Yankelovich called the McNamara fallacy:

> The first step is to measure whatever can be easily measured. This is okay as far as it goes. The second step is to disregard that which can't be measured or give it an arbitrary quantitative value. This is artificial and misleading. The third step is to presume that what can't be measured easily really isn't very important. This is blindness. The fourth step is to say that what can't be easily measured really doesn't exist. This is suicide.

Thus the use of feeling, emotions, ritual and magic by the unconscious revolutionaries as a rebellion. "The marked tendency," says Theodore Roszak in *The Making Of a Counter-Culture* (a literary essay which isn't really about that at all) "has been to consign whatever is not fully and articulately available in the waking consciousness for empirical or mathematical manipulation to a purely negative catch-all category (in effect, the cultural garbage can) called the 'unconscious' or the 'irrational' or the 'mystical' or the 'purely subjective.'"

Reich:

> Accepted patterns of thought must be broken; what is considered "rational thought" must be opposed by "non-rational thought"—drug-thought, mysticism, impulses. Of course the latter kinds of thought are not really "non-rational" at all; they merely introduce new elements into the sterile, rigid, outworn "rationality" that prevails today.

That is the *real* end of the Protestant Ethic—not only

everybody *stoned,* man, but the end of the *rationality* that led to the burgeoning of capitalism.

"It is as if," Yankelovich wrote, "the great victories in succeeding centuries won by Protestantism, individualism, rationalism, science and industrialization all were gained at a terrible cost—the sacrifice of community." And to define *community* he quoted from still another sociologist, Robert Nisbet:

> Community encompasses all forms of relationships which are characterized by a high degree of personal intimacy, emotional depth, moral commitment, social cohesion, and continuity in time. Community is founded on man conceived in his wholeness rather than in one or another of the roles, taken separately, that he may hold in a social order.

Max Weber, one of the founders of sociology whose phrase gave us the melody for this sonata, and who was the masterful historian of rationalism, wondered whether all the secularization and rationalism would not strip life of its mystery, charm and meaning.

But obviously—and "obviously" is admittedly a rational adverb—the complex technological society is not going to go away. Some small numbers of people may try to go away from it, to manage on communes with *The Last Whole Earth Catalog* as a textbook. (I wouldn't knock that, and I found myself inordinately tickled to have a book of mine included in the catalog among the kerosene lamps and potter's wheels.) The rest of us are left to cope, to try to reintegrate what is missing into what we have. We can use a seeming-rational approach to try to assess, for our own rational and managerial ends, what the changes in ethic and spirit mean, but totally to accept a nonrational world is to say goodbye to our role.

. . .

Anyway, irrationality and mystery and magic are no strangers to us in the money markets. That was one of the points of *The Money Game,* to show that while the language of the game was built on rationality and precision, the Game itself was played by behavior, and with all sorts of totems and taboos that would do credit to any tribe in New Guinea with an anthropologist in residence.

Changes do not occur overnight. The moral code which accompanied the accumulation of capital for the past several hundred years has encouraged us to applaud and honor purposiveness. In his remarkable and extraordinary essay "The Economic Possibilities for Our Grandchildren," Keynes wrote:

> Purposiveness means that we are more concerned with the remote future results of our actions than with their own quality or their immediate effects on our own environment. The "purposive" man is always trying to secure a spurious and delusive immortality for his acts by pushing his interest in them forward into time. He does not love his cat, but his cat's kittens, nor, in truth, the kittens, but only the kittens' kittens, and so on forward for ever to the end of cat-dom. For him jam is not jam unless it is a case of jam tomorrow and never jam today. Thus by pushing his jam always forward into the future, he strives to secure for his act of boiling it an immortality.

It may be that the era of purposiveness, with its inherent dictum of sacrifice is winding down, however slowly. That does not mean another era of something else is immediately at hand. The counter-culture may not be a proper guide to the future because it is defined by its opposition; it is easier to describe what it is against than what it is for. But it may serve to stimulate some sort of synthesis, to make us broaden the idea of what is "rational," to help crack the consensus. Long before the term "counter-culture" came to be bandied, Keynes had delineated the lopsidedness of the accumulative society. "We have been trained too long to strive," he said, "and not to enjoy." Perhaps in a hundred years, he wrote—a hundred years from 1931, that is—the chief problem of mankind would be to live agreeably and wisely and well.

What would bring us to that point? Science and compound interest, incremental technology and accruing wealth. Some of the members of our affluent and post-affluent society are already into that spirit, as we have seen.

But alas, our views of both science and compound interest are changing. Science is no longer the unmitigated good the late Victorians saw, the radio added to Pasteur added to the electric light added to the steam engine. There is even some doubt about how incremental scientific growth is: in *The Structure of Scientific Revolutions,* Thomas Kuhn argues that each generation of scientists rewrites its textbooks to make everything a continuous flow. And as for compound interest—well, Keynes did say, in a phrase usually overlooked, "assuming no important wars and no important increase in population." Compound interest does not solve our economic problems if population compounds faster, because *per capita* is our divisor.

Unexpected turns in the road do have a way of materializing; it was only a generation ago that some of our industrial societies were worried about how to get the birth rate *up*. If we could indeed count on the cushion of science and compound interest, then indeed we could look forward to the day when (Keynes again) "there will be great changes in the code of morals . . . All kinds of social customs and economic practices, affecting the distribution of wealth and of economic reward and penalties, which we now maintain at all costs, however distasteful and unjust they may be in themselves, because they are tremendously useful in promoting the accumulation of capital, we shall then be free, at last, to discard."

But what do we do on Monday morning?

All of these exercises come under the perilous heading of long-term expectations, and we know that the long-term investor must seem—Keynes again—"eccentric, unconventional and rash in the eyes of average opinion." If the long-term investor succeeds, that confirms the belief in his rashness, and if he does not, "he will not receive very much mercy. Worldly wisdom teaches that it is better for reputation to fail conventionally than to succeed unconventionally." Meanwhile:

> Avarice and usury and precaution must be our gods for a little longer still. For only they can lead us out of the tunnel of economic necessity into daylight.

If we are left with capital and not community, we still have to do our best to make our garden grow. Even the Enlightened One said that some hours must be spent in chopping wood and carrying water. But it would be folly not to be *aware*, even for parochial purposes, of the changes going on around us, and that awareness is not a traditional sensitivity in the rational preciseness of a game played with numbers.

Meanwhile the mechanism and the structure of the markets in which our game is played have survived. The currency and the Supercurrency are still there. Maybe some of the players have gotten a little heavier. All of us have to make choices on the uses of our energies; some things are as they are and not as they ought to be, but this is the way the world is. If you are still for the Game, why, may you prosper; I wish you the joys of it.